Key Chart for The Great Work
Self-Knowledge & Healing Through the Wheel of the Year

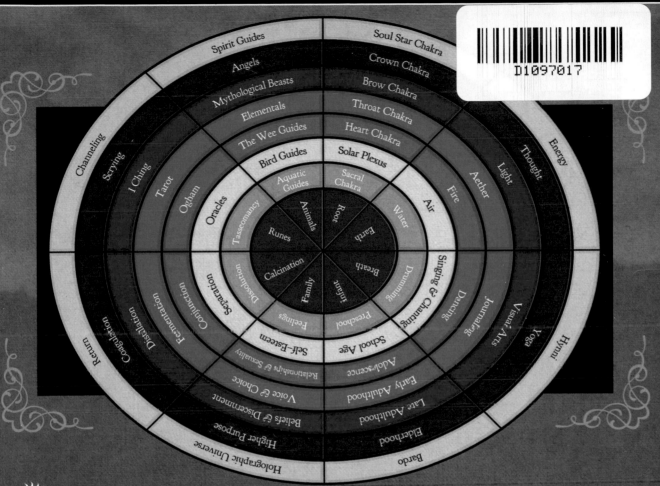

 The Eight Cycles

Roots & Foundations	Dec 21 – Jan 31
Gifts from the Inner Child	Feb 1 – Mar 14
Nurturing Empowerment	Mar 22 – May 2
Union & Partnerships	May 3 – June 13
Shining Truth & Creativity	June 21 – Aug 1
Visioning Self	Aug 2 – Sept 12
Effects of Gratitude	Sept 20 – Oct 31
Healing from Loss	Nov 1 – Dec 12

The Four Phases

Innocence & Openings	Mar 15 – 21
Fullness & Fruition	June 14 – 20
Experience & Community	Sept 13 – 19
Rest & Respite	Dec 13 – 19

Pause & Integration	Dec 20

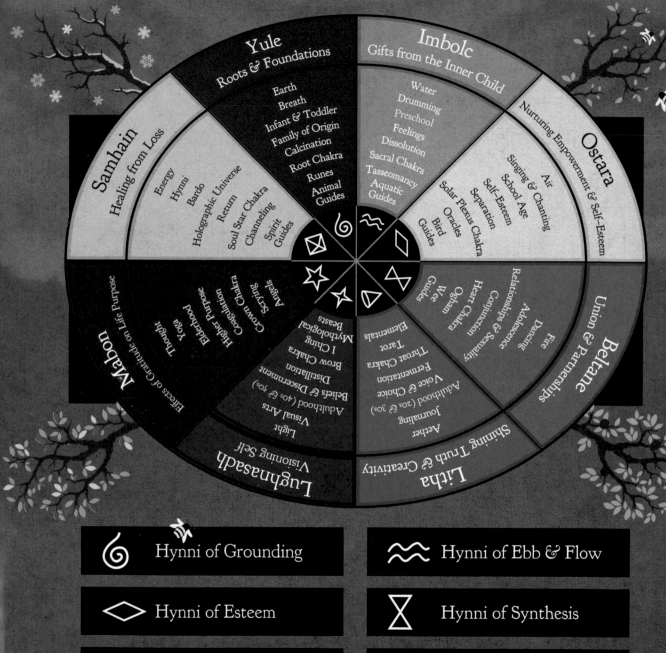

The Wheel of the Year
Integration of Cycles

Yule — Roots & Foundations
Earth, Breath, Infant & Toddler, Family of Origin, Calcination, Root Chakra, Runes, Animal Guides

Imbolc — Gifts from the Inner Child
Water, Drumming, Preschool, Feelings, Dissolution, Sacral Chakra, Tasseomancy, Aquatic Guides

Samhain — Healing from Loss
Energy, Hynni, Bardo, Holographic Universe, Return, Soul Star Chakra, Channeling, Spirit Guides

Ostara — Nurturing Empowerment & Self-Esteem
Air, Singing & Chanting, School Age, Self-Esteem, Separation, Solar Plexus Chakra, Oracles, Bird Guides

Mabon — Effects of Gratitude on Life Purpose
Thought, Yoga, Elderhood, Higher Purpose, Coagulation, Crown Chakra, Scrying, Angels

Beltane — Union & Partnerships
Fire, Dancing, Adolescence, Relationships & Sexuality, Conjunction, Heart Chakra, Oracles, Wee Guides

Lughnasadh — Visioning Self
Light, Visual Arts, Adulthood (40s & 50s), Beliefs & Discernment, Distillation, Brow Chakra, I Ching, Mythological Beasts

Litha — Shining Truth & Creativity
Aether, Journaling, Adulthood (20s & 30s), Voice & Choice, Fermentation, Throat Chakra, Tarot, Elementals

Hynni of Grounding

Hynni of Ebb & Flow

Hynni of Esteem

Hynni of Synthesis

Hynni of Expression

Hynni of Vision

Hynni of Karma

Hynni of Unity

the
GREAT WORK

....

© CCMurphy Photography

About the Author

Tiffany is a Spiritual Psychotherapist with over sixteen years experience in Transpersonal Psychology. She completed training in Spiritual Psychotherapy at the Transformational Arts College of Spiritual and Holistic Training in Toronto where she also taught in the college's Discovering the Total Self Program, Spiritual Psychotherapy Training Program, Spiritual Directorship Program, and Esoteric Studies Program. She served as a staff psychotherapist and case supervisor. She continues to teach at the college as a guest facilitator.

An international presenter and keynote speaker, Tiffany has conducted workshops for many conferences and organizations, including the 2013 Energy Psychology Conference. She was one of the co-creators and co-organizers of Kitchener's SPARKS Symposium (2010–2012).

Tiffany is the owner of the Hive and Grove Centre for Holistic Wellness, with a private therapy practice offering individual, couples, and group therapy. She has developed two self-development programs, Patterns of Conscious Living Program and the Spiritual Language of the Divine Program, as well as a creative workshop, The Art of the Divine. As a satellite school of the Transformational Arts College, she also teaches the college's ten-course Discovering the Total Self Program.

To Write to the Author

If you wish to contact the author or would like more information about this book, please write to the author in care of Llewellyn Worldwide. We cannot guarantee that every letter written to the author can be answered, but all will be forwarded. Please write to:

Tiffany Lazic
℅ Llewellyn Worldwide
2143 Wooddale Drive
Woodbury, MN 55125-2989

Please enclose a self-addressed stamped envelope for reply, or $1.00 to cover costs.
If outside the USA, enclose an international postal reply coupon.

TIFFANY LAZIC

the
GREAT WORK

Self-Knowledge and Healing Through the Wheel of the Year

Llewellyn Publications
Woodbury, Minnesota

First Edition
Third Printing, 2018

The meditative approaches in this book are not a substitute for psychotherapy or counseling nor are they a substitute for medical treatment. They are intended to provide clients with information about their inner workings that can add another helpful dimension to treatment with a trained medical or mental health professional, as their circumstances may warrant.

Book design by Bob Gaul
Cover design by Ellen Lawson
Cover illustration by Wen Hsu
Editing by Jennifer Ackman
Additional cover image: iStockphoto.com/38539476/©aleksandarvelasevic
Interior art: *Classic Tarot* by Barbara Moore and Eugene Smith © Llewellyn Publications
        Charts, Dingbats, Icons, Illustrations, and Tables © Llewellyn Art Department
        Wheel of the Year and Key Chart Color Insert © Cameron Lacey

Llewellyn Publications is a registered trademark of Llewellyn Worldwide Ltd.
Lazic, Tiffany, 1966–
  The great work: self-knowledge and healing through the wheel of the year/
by Tiffany Lazic.—First Edition.
    pages cm
  Includes bibliographical references.
  ISBN 978-0-7387-4442-1
1. Hermetism. 2. Occultism. 3. Spiritual life. 4. Religious calendars—Neopaganism. 5. Psychology—Miscellanea. I. Title.
  BF1999.L324 2015
  158—dc23

                      2015000475

Llewellyn Publications
A Division of Llewellyn Worldwide Ltd.
2143 Wooddale Drive
Woodbury, MN 55125-2989
www.llewellyn.com

Printed in the United States of America

Other Writings by Tiffany Lazic

....

Llewellyn's 2016 Herbal Almanac (contributor)
Llewellyn's 2016 Witches' Companion (contributor)
Naming the Goddess (Moon Books, 2014)

Contents

Acknowledgments   *xv*

*Introduction: Self-Knowledge and Healing Through
    the Wheel of the Year*   *1*

**PART ONE: Cycle One (December 21–January 31):
Roots and Foundations**

ONE: Mythological Reflection on the Birth of the
    Wonder Child   23

Two: Elemental Reflection on Earth and Active Reflection
    on Breathing   27

THREE: Psychological Reflection on Family of Origin and
    Developmental Reflection on Birth to Three Years of Age   31

FOUR: Alchemical Reflection on Calcination   39

FIVE: Energetic Reflection on the Root Chakra   43

SIX: Guidance Reflection on Animal Guides and Intuitive
    Reflection on Runes   47

PART TWO: Cycle Two (February 1–March 14):
Gifts from the Inner Child

SEVEN: Mythological Reflection on Purification Through Light   59

EIGHT: Elemental Reflection on Water and Active Reflection
on Drumming   63

NINE: Developmental Reflection on Preschool Age and
Psychological Reflection on Feelings   67

TEN: Alchemical Reflection on Dissolution   79

ELEVEN: Energetic Reflection on the Sacral Chakra   87

TWELVE: Guidance Reflection on Aquatic Guides and
Intuitive Reflection on Tasseomancy   91

PART THREE: Process Phase One (March 15–21):
Waxing Moon

THIRTEEN: Waxing Phase of Innocence and Openings   101

PART FOUR: Cycle Three (March 22–May 2):
Nurturing Empowerment and Self-Esteem

FOURTEEN: Mythological Reflection on the Celebration
of Life   109

FIFTEEN: Elemental Reflection on Air and Active
Reflection on Singing and Chanting   113

SIXTEEN: Developmental Reflection on School
Age and Psychological Reflection on
Empowerment and Self-Esteem   119

SEVENTEEN: Alchemical Reflection on Separation   127

EIGHTEEN: Energetic Reflection on the Solar Plexus Chakra   133

NINETEEN: Guidance Reflection on Bird Guides
and Intuitive Reflection on Oracles   137

PART FIVE: Cycle Four (May 3–June 13):
Union and Partnerships

TWENTY: Mythological Reflection on the Synthesis of Spirit
and Matter   149

TWENTY-ONE: Elemental Reflection on Fire and Active
Reflection on Dancing   153

TWENTY-TWO: Developmental Reflection on Adolescence and
Psychological Reflection on Relationships   159

TWENTY-THREE: Alchemical Reflection on Conjunction   169

TWENTY-FOUR: Energetic Reflection on the Heart Chakra   173

TWENTY-FIVE: Guidance Reflection on the Wee Guides
and Intuitive Reflection on the Ogham   177

PART SIX: Process Phase Two (June 14–20): Full Moon

TWENTY-SIX: Full Moon Phase of Fullness and Fruition   189

PART SEVEN: Cycle Five (June 21–August 1):
Shining Our Truth and Creativity

TWENTY-SEVEN: Mythological Reflection on Celebration
of Effort   195

Twenty-Eight: Elemental Reflection on Aether and Active Reflection on Journaling 199

Twenty-Nine: Developmental Reflection on Early Adulthood and Psychological Reflection on Voice and Choice 205

Thirty: Alchemical Reflection on Fermentation 209

Thirty-One: Energetic Reflection on the Throat Chakra 213

Thirty-Two: Guidance Reflection on Elementals and Intuitive Reflection on Tarot 217

Part Eight: Cycle Six (August 2–September 12): Visioning Self

Thirty-Three: Mythological Reflection on Reaping First Harvests 239

Thirty-Four: Energetic Reflection on Light and Active Reflection on Visual Arts 243

Thirty-Five: Developmental Reflection on Adulthood and Psychological Reflection on Beliefs and Discernment 249

Thirty-Six: Alchemical Reflection on Distillation 255

Thirty-Seven: Energetic Reflection on the Brow Chakra 259

Thirty-Eight: Guidance Reflection on Mythological Beasts and Intuitive Reflection on I Ching 263

Part Nine: Process Phase Three (September 13–19): Waning Moon

Thirty-Nine: Waning Phase of Experience and Community 275

PART TEN: Cycle Seven (September 20–October 31):
Effects of Gratitude on Life Purpose

FORTY: Mythological Reflection on Thanksgivings   281

FORTY-ONE: Energetic Reflection on Thought and Active
Reflection on Yoga   285

FORTY-TWO: Developmental Reflection on Elderhood
and Psychological Reflection on Higher Purpose   291

FORTY-THREE: Alchemical Reflection on Coagulation   301

FORTY-FOUR: Energetic Reflection on the Crown Chakra   307

FORTY-FIVE: Guidance Reflection on Angels and Intuitive
Reflection on Scrying   311

PART ELEVEN: Cycle Eight (November 1–December 12):
Healing from Loss

FORTY-SIX: Mythological Reflection on Entering the Mystery   321

FORTY-SEVEN: Elemental Reflection on Energy and Active
Reflection on Hynni   325

FORTY-EIGHT: Developmental Reflection on Bardo and
Psychological Reflection on the Holographic Universe   331

FORTY-NINE: Alchemical Reflection on Return   341

FIFTY: Energetic Reflection on the Soul Star Chakra   345

FIFTY-ONE: Guidance Reflection on Spirit Guides and
Intuitive Reflection on Channeling   349

PART TWELVE: Process Phase Four (December 13–19): Dark Moon

FIFTY-TWO: Dark Moon Phase of Rest and Respite   359

PART THIRTEEN: (December 20): Pause and Integration

FIFTY-THREE: The Self-Actualization Survey   367

Appendix A: List of Emotional and Psychological Issues and Their Prescriptions   373

Appendix B: List of Physical Issues and Their Prescriptions   379

Appendix C: Cycles and Phases by Month   381

Selected Bibliography   395

Acknowledgments

There is a strong circle of support and encouragement that has been a constant presence through the visioning and writing of this book. My deepest thanks go to Jhenah Telyndru, Vyviane Armstrong, and Nicole Ferrill. Without them this all would have unfolded so much differently. There is nothing more valuable in life than to have those who see the best in you in ways you may not see yourself and who offer the enticing invitation to soar. I have been blessed to work with my editors extraordinares, Elysia Gallo, who brought a dream to life, guiding with her exquisite eye to detail and commitment to excellence, and Jennifer Ackman, who ensured the highest of standards with both patience and humor. Their enthusiasm and dedication is a gift to any author, most especially to one new to the publishing experience. A heartfelt thanks to the team at Llewellyn for welcoming me into the family, a warm and wonderful place to be.

This book would never have come to be without my first teachers: Kathy Ryndak and Gord Riddell, founders of the Transformational Arts College of Spiritual and Holistic Training, who provided a solid bedrock for my work on so many levels. They continue to inspire me in countless ways. Over twenty years later, I still vividly remember the classes of Linda Kuschnir and Ken Sullivan, who instilled a passion for the work which has never waned. What a gift that is!

I am ever grateful to my tribe of sisters, those of the womb and of the heart. Thanks to Lisa Theodore and Stacey Springall for bringing keen eyes to a manuscript still tottering on wobbly legs and helping to steady it with a kind but ruthless red pen. To Sue King for being so excited that she read the manuscript in one sitting and to Linda Buchanan for being the very first to dedicate herself to the daily journey through all the Cycles. To Barbara Ann Cowie for her mother-love that filled my cup. To Sara Nagy, Karen Andrews, Alexa Stewart, Lasairfhiona O'Callaghan, Kathleen Roussell, Rose Makirvirta, and Dorothy Quesnal for holding the vision month by month. They are extraordinary women all and have filled my heart, both with their support of this book and far, far beyond.

I have been so aware that I stand in the center of enormous support. I see around me circle upon circle of those whose encouragement has been significant and tangible. (And another thanks to Jhenah for providing that imagery!) But there is one who stood, not in the circles, nor in the center, but wherever was needed. I hold gratitude beyond words for George Lazic for his love and support, both through this process and all the other times I have said "Hey, I have an idea." He has sacrificed for me, cheered beside me, smiled with those around me and, countless times, prowled the edges to confront those winged nasties of doubt trying to get in. He knew the times to gently say "Let's go for a walk" and overlooked the after-effects of those absent-minded author moments like finding a banana peel in the dishwasher. There could be no greater Champion for this book nor Companion through this adventure.

They say the birthing of the book is akin to the birthing of a child. In bringing the words of the book from the author's head to your hands, continuing the analogy, I say it takes a village. I have been wellblessed in my village.

I dedicate this book to my beloved parents,
Howard and Yvonne Lacey.

To my Dad—whose lifelong commitment to
the written page was with me in every word.

And to my Mum—whose vision of life as an adventure
to be experienced gave shape to the words.

Now as always, they guide me in how to bring Spirit
to life and they are missed beyond measure.

Introduction:

Self-Knowledge and Healing Through the Wheel of the Year

· ·

We are living in changing times. This is a truism held for many centuries and through many ages, but it is an undeniable fact that our world is changing now almost faster than we can keep up. In the past twenty years especially, the explosion of technology has made the world almost unrecognizable to previous generations. The arena of health and wellness has also seen a transformation. In the mid-twentieth century very few would have heard much of (or paid much attention to) the teachings of the East. Now meditation, yoga, and Reiki are practically household words. There is much wisdom in these teachings from the East, but there is also a rich Western tradition that offers a different perspective. Eastern traditions tend to teach *transcendence*. This approach encourages us to rise above the ego, to practice mindfulness, and to enter the expansive experience of the All. Western traditions tend to focus on *transformation*. This approach urges us to enter into the dark and mucky inner spaces. It drops us into ego, so that we may transform our dark and shadow into light. Ultimately, they both take us to the same place, but the experience of the journey is very different.

It seems that now, perhaps more than ever before in history, people are interested in self-development. The earlier drive to explore uncharted lands and outer space seems to have changed direction toward the wondrous frontiers of our inner psyches. One of the most significant concepts in the work of transformation is that of Essence. Essence is described as that divine spark we each carry inside. It is our own light and our truth. It is all we know to be special and unique about us—our gifts, our strengths, and our passions. We come into this human life as pure Essence, but life experiences can create the impulse to push it to the farthest reaches of inner space. Childhood trauma, hurts, and rejection cause us to unconsciously push this precious part of ourselves far out of view. We relegate our Essence to the dark of the shadow. As will be illustrated throughout this book, there are many elements that can contribute to disconnecting us from our Essence. This feels protective, but it comes at a high cost. It is the underlying root of many of our issues, which from a holistic perspective range from chronic physical illness to debilitating depression, and causes us to live in a way that feels inauthentic.

The human journey is never an easy one. There are thorns along the path and dragons around the bend. We often feel that we are grown up in our bodies, but it is a scared child who is trying to negotiate this challenging path. We may look like adults, but we don't feel like adults. We feel anxious, powerless, and helpless. Doing inner work gives us the tools necessary for walking the path as an empowered, autonomous, and self-actualized adult. The healing path of transformation is one that allows us to explore what caused our disconnection from essence, and what can support us in bringing this light back from the dark.

The intent of *The Great Work* is to provide a map of the inner frontier that facilitates rescuing Essence from the dark. In the following pages you will find the markers and signposts to your inner landscape and inner cycles, along with the tools necessary to clear the way in order that you may step into the adventure of a life in full bloom. The culmination of the journey is a rich, abundant garden nourished by self-acceptance, healthy supportive relationships, balanced responses to life circumstances, and a sure connection to the flow of the Divine in your life. In these rapidly changing times, and for many, uncertain times, the best thing we can do for ourselves is create a solid foundation that will support us through any circumstance. It brings us back to balance in all aspects of ourselves, promoting physical health, emotional balance, mental clarity, and the ability to imbue meaning into our lives with spirit. When we are armed with the knowledge of the strengths we have at our disposal, and the wisdom that comes from looking at what was gained through all our experiences, the human journey is truly a rewarding and fulfilling one. When we have plumbed our own depths to excavate the truth of our hearts and souls, there is nothing on this earth that can shake us. Doing this work is arguably the most important work we can do. This is *The Great Work*.

This book grew out of a passion for psychotherapy, alternative healing practices, and ancient Western spirituality based on the rhythms of nature. It is a passion that has carried me almost as long as I can remember. Some of the first books I remember reading while teetering on the cusp of adolescence were *Transactional Analysis for Teens* by Alvyn M. Freed and Regina Paul-Janse, and *Dibs: In Search of Self* by Virginia M. Axline. Encountering the concept of codependency blew my mind, even while not recognizing those same patterns in myself at the time. I once retrieved a rejected copy of *Bradshaw: On the Family* that was gifted to my mom from the wastebasket—"one person's trash is another's treasure" in action. We subsequently had many wonderful conversations on the subject. My early twenties expanded this interest in two significant directions. I completed a degree in film studies, which opened me to the world of comparative mythology and the impact of story to illuminate the human experience. And in the process of filming a student documentary on the topic of non-mainstream spirituality, I found my feet on a spiritual path rooted in the rhythms of nature. The film itself was never completed because the topic proved far too huge for a five-minute student film. But for me, it served a far greater purpose. I had been introduced to a whole new world, and began to experience how myth could be entered into through a connection with nature and the power of story to transform.

Through my twenties I worked in many different, fascinating areas of the independent film industry, dove into exploring my personal spiritual path, and for fun, read the innumerable self-help books that were available in the early 1990s. Then, one bright spring day as I was lost in thought walking down the street, a pamphlet fluttered to my feet. Something—an unexplained nudge—prompted me to pick it up. It was the course calendar for a school in Toronto called Transformational Arts Centre (now the Transformational Arts College of Spiritual and Holistic Training), which offered a program in spiritual psychotherapy. Spiritual psychotherapy? I had never heard of it. How intriguing!

As I discovered, spiritual psychotherapy builds on the firm foundation of traditional psychotherapy that addresses issues in family systems, relationship dynamics, and addictions. But, stemming from transpersonal psychology, it allows for inclusion of information from all aspects of our selves. It addresses cognitive issues, but its holistic perspective expands the range of exploration to include the body-mind connection, emotional healing, and the power of experiences derived through energy work, intuition, and meditation. It was a revelation for me. I particularly loved the approach of transformation. It appealed to my belief that there is wisdom in the dark. It may be painful and awful at times, but there is so much beauty to be found in the muckiness of human experience as well. After completing my training I began to work professionally as a spiritual psychotherapist and teacher, and personally continued to explore the path of nature-based spirituality. It was all wonderfully compartmentalized until 2003. I soon learned that when one embraces a holistic approach, life can never be compartmentalized.

Around October and November of that year, as I went along my normal course of professional work, I began to notice how many of my clients were accessing their grief. Many were dealing with old grief that was resurfacing after a long time. It struck me that though the particulars were unique to the individuals, the main theme was exactly the same. I pondered the question "Why grief now?" And the response that blasted into my head was "because it is the time of death, decay, and loss." The compartment that contained all the wonderful knowledge I had acquired around mythology and the ancient festivals celebrating the seasonal cycles crashed into the compartment of my professional training. What resulted was like a mytho-psychological Reese's Peanut Butter Cup.

I began to pay closer attention to the themes that were presented at different times of the year, and came to see that more often than could be attributed to coincidence, these recognizable patterns would show up in session. I began to sense that as human beings, we carry a deeply unconscious connection to the rhythms of nature. We respond whether we are aware or not. We become introspective in winter and we feel ourselves come alive in spring. When we work with these inner impulses, instead of pushing them aside or fighting against them, we are truly in our natural flow.

Shakespeare said that art is a mirror held up to nature.
And that's what it is. The nature is your nature, and all
of these wonderful poetic images of mythology are referring
to something in you. When your mind is trapped by the image
out there so that you never make the reference to yourself,
you have misread the image.

—Joseph Campbell, *The Power of Myth*

Looking to history and mythology, I began to see the wealth of information that could provide information on how to work with these inner, natural impulses through a systematic approach. Though positioned very differently, the ancient stories of the gods and goddesses teach so much about how to embrace both the dark and the light for the purpose of transformation. I saw the potential for the integration of nature, mythology, and Spiritual Psychotherapy.

Our Mythological Inheritance

Focusing on the common themes that appear in ancient Western cultures, I was inspired by eight key ancient seasonal festivals as the skeleton upon which to build *The Great Work*. Though there is evidence of many different celebrations throughout the ancient world, these eight in particular, which focus on the Celtic and Norse traditions, became adopted into the fairly contemporary system known as the Wheel of the Year. The themes presented in eight festivals (or spokes of the wheel) have danced through history for centuries and are consistent from the most western tip of Ireland to the warm breezes at the eastern edge of the Mediterranean. The names of the mythological players connected to the festivals may change from place to place, but the core themes have an integrity that speaks to a higher truth. The correlations to psychology and healing were evident. I saw the pattern of fusing the relationship we have with our natural environment and the common mythological themes for the purpose of supporting inner growth and change.

In *The Great Work* it is these mythological themes of the eight festivals found on the Wheel of the Year that are highlighted. It starts from the premise that there is truth inherent in the traditions from the past, that the myths and stories from centuries ago represent energies that are still relevant today, and that, though the externals of our world have changed, as human beings we are still intimately connected with nature, and respond to shifts in our environment and in the seasons on a subtle, unconscious level. This book presents a system for applying the mythological themes that arose from the human-ecological dynamic of ancient agricultural cultures to the modern individual quest into personal inquiry for the purpose of self-transformation.

The Structure of *The Great Work*

The intent of *The Great Work* is to offer a map for self-understanding on all levels of self, using the festivals found on the Wheel of the Year to provide the key themes for each particular time of the year. The festivals are presented as eight separate cycles that each offer an additional eight reflections, which reflect the theme in the context of physical, emotional, mental, and energetic health.

Mythological Reflection

Ancient peoples had an intimate relationship with the earth. Survival depended on knowledge of the attributes of each season, and dedication to working in alignment with those conditions. The ability to thrive depended upon paying attention to the external environment. Clearly, survival would not be successful if one planted crops in winter. In modern times we have distanced ourselves from a direct relationship with nature. For the most part, we have become dependent on those others who maintain that relationship (i.e., farmers), but our psyches have not changed. Many of the traditions we celebrate in modern times have their roots in the practices of those ancient peoples. Originally, these traditions were developed to create alignment for agricultural success and abundance, but the themes of these traditions also hold psychological merit that is applicable in today's world. We may not recognize that relationship overtly, but we do respond to it symbolically.

The Mythological Reflection section introduces the eco-mythic energies or themes of the ancient seasonal festival. This provides the anchor for subsequent reflections of the cycle.

Elemental Reflection

The concept of the elements as being the basic building blocks of life is rooted in ancient teachings. Since the Golden Age of the Greek philosophers, humans have been trying to determine what is the "stuff" that makes up the universe. There has long been disagreement around which element was *the* key building block, but it has been always accepted that it is "something." In the ancient Greek view, Thales said it was water, Anaximenes said it was air, Xenophanes said it was earth, Heraclitus said it was fire, and Empedocles stated that all these elements were present together. Then Plato put a wrench in the works by stating that they were all present, but each element itself consisted of atoms that were an even more basic building block. The Celts saw the key elements as land, sea, and sky. The ancient alchemists added the fifth element of aether. The holistic perspective afforded by the transformational approach acknowledges our higher vibrational being, and thus introduces non-traditional elements such as thought, light, and energy. It allows for a full range of self-exploration from the solid physicality of earth to the highest vibration of energy and the significance of each to achieving overall balance.

Active Reflection

The ability to experience and learn through our bodies and our physical selves takes us out of a purely intellectual approach to self-understanding. We can know something in our mind, but that may not make a whit of difference if we have not pulled that knowledge into our experience. There is a wonderful saying that "awareness plus acceptance plus action equals change." We may have all the awareness in the world, but if we do not translate that into action, it is not going to result in change—or as Carl Jung said in one of my most favorite quotes ever, "Concepts butter no parsnips." This means that thinking about buttering your parsnips is not the same thing as buttering your parsnips. If you want buttery-tasting parsnips, you need to actually apply the butter.

Each Active Reflection section illustrates an activity such as dancing, journaling, or even as basic as breathing. These activities allow for deeper understanding in a way that is experiential, and often, very fun. You may not resonate with each and every activity, but trying them out can reveal valuable information about your sense of self and your own resistances. It is the translation from theory to practice that activates change in our experience of the world, in our relationships, and within ourselves.

Developmental Reflection

Traditional psychology (particularly in the areas of family systems and addictions) shows that as we move through childhood, there are particular needs and areas of growth that may or may not have been fulfilled. Becoming aware of where we may have experienced hurt or trauma allows us to address these areas in adulthood, resolving past emotional and psychological wounds, and moving us toward healing and wholeness.

Erik Erikson developed a theory of psychosocial stages of development that indicates the main inner tasks that one must accomplish at each stage in order to become fully integrated individuals. He positioned these tasks as oppositional qualities, shedding light on what blocks may occur if one does not resolve the task of each particular stage. Successfully navigating the task of each stage of development results in anchoring the ego strength for that stage. Ego strength is defined as the quality that contributes to the positive sense of self that underpins mental and emotional health. Ego strength contributes to healthy self-esteem and efficacy in implementing life choices.

This is the first of two reflections that focus on emotional and mental health. The Developmental Reflection sections expand on Erickson's model to offer a map of the human journey from birth through to death and beyond. It presents signposts for what is most helpful for us to be aware of at each stage, such as infancy or adolescence, and provides the opportunity to revisit past stages in order to heal what may still be causing difficulty and challenge in our lives.

Psychological Reflection

As the second of two reflections that focus on emotional and mental health, the Psychological Reflection builds upon the tasks presented in the Developmental Reflection in order to highlight the key emotional issues that impede our ability to live empowered lives. This reflection presents many of the common ways that we unconsciously keep our Essence hidden. It offers tools and techniques for reclaiming our Essence, allowing it to shine in all areas of our lives without fear of being hurt or wounded anymore. It is often these two reflections that require the most attention.

Alchemical Reflection

Alchemy is the ancient process of transformation. It is a cornerstone of Western esoteric tradition, though its teachings can be found across cultures in Eastern tradition as well. It has the reputation of being about the quest to turn lead into gold—a pursuit of material gain. However, its roots are far more altruistic, and certainly contemporarily it is common to perceive alchemy as the spiritual pursuit to transmute our leaden human selves into the golden light of Essence—our own inner Philosopher's Stone.

At the center of alchemical teachings is *The Emerald Tablet*—a short document of seven paragraphs (or rubrics) said to hold the key to all understanding. Though the tablet itself has been lost, the words have been handed down through history. Alchemy stepped into the modern ages with the work of Carl Jung who saw in alchemy the perfect template through which to make sense of the images and symbols presented from the unconscious. Jung had gathered much material on the contents of the unconscious, but felt he needed to find a historical parallel. With the discovery of alchemy he felt he had found a process that showed the ego's relationship with the unconscious, and the means through which metamorphosis and transformation could occur.

With its seven clear stages and depth of imagery and symbolism, alchemy offers the potential to gain great clarity upon internal shifts and experiences. The interconnection of alchemy and psychology is a key component of the approach in *The Great Work*. The Alchemical Reflection is the first of two reflections that illustrate the relevance of a profound ancient wisdom system through modern application.

Energetic Reflection

Based in teachings dating back thousands of years, chakras are energy centers in the body that act as mediators between the human body and universal energy. The word chakra means wheel, or turning, in Sanskrit, which gives a good sense of what they look like on the energetic level. They are like little vortexes that pull energy in and send energy out, connecting us to the pulse and vibrancy of all of life around us.

Though there are different levels of chakras, it is the seven major chakras located along a central energetic column in our bodies that are the focal point of the body-mind-spirit connection. These chakras have associations with our physical health and vitality, our emotional balance and sense of self, and our energetic flow and spiritual connection. There is an eighth chakra, located outside of our physical bodies and presenting a slightly different focus, which has begun to gain more recognition in recent years.

When chakras are open and healthy, the energy flow is strong and unhindered. When we experience hurts, wounds, or bumps and bruises, these centers can become blocked. To work with releasing the blocks in our chakras is to release heaviness and negativity, so that our Essence can shine through each of these little powerhouses. The Energetic Reflection is the second of two reflections that illustrate the relevance of a profound, ancient wisdom system through modern application.

Guidance Reflection

The Guidance Reflection is the first of two reflections that open us to a Higher Self perspective. The Guidance Reflection presents the different ways that guides, totems, and messengers can appear to us, offering insights on our process, the gifts of our experiences, and our particular strengths that we can draw upon.

Intuitive Reflection

The last reflection, and the second of the two that offer a higher perspective, presents methods of divination or intuitive tools that open us to insight and inspiration. Some of these methods are fairly straightforward, requiring little more than trust in the message received, and some methods are incredibly complex systems that have developed and evolved over centuries, deserving of entire volumes devoted just to them. The presentation of these approaches in the Intuitive Reflection is intended to be the mere taste of an introduction. The basic structure of each method is outlined, along with some very basic steps for practice. Different people respond to different intuitive tools. You may find yourself drawn to one rather than another. In order to achieve wholeness and self-actualization, one does not need to become adept at each intuitive tool. It can be interesting to engage in an initial exploration to see where your preferences lie. If you find yourself excited by a particular tool, there is a lot of wonderful information available to deepen your exploration.

The Process Phases

After every two cycles there is a different opportunity for exploration afforded in the Process Phases. As the cycles are inspired by the sun's annual cycle, the Process Phases are inspired by the moon's far shorter phases. Whereas the cycles give insight into how we operate in the world and with others, the Process Phases allow for a pause in which to explore the movement from "trial to triumph." Aligned with the sun cycle the cycles and their reflections represent our growth from the perspective of consciousness, action, and awareness. But the ancients were also keenly aware of the power of the moon, which represents the unconscious and the energies of receptivity and intuition. These four Process Phases bring different levels of awareness of the movement from dark to light. They allow us to step outside the activity of growth and change to observe how we are engaging in the process itself. The Process Phases invite you to take stock of your journey and fully experience the power of each stage of transformation.

How to Approach *The Great Work*

Each cycle and Process Phase offers a slightly different perspective, and a different opportunity for learning. As a complete system, *The Great Work* illuminates the places in our lives where we may be experiencing discordance. It offers the information and tools to help move into a place of personal and internal harmony. The book itself is intended to be interactive. Each part presents a different cycle or phase, and each cycle is structured with an introduction to the main themes through the Mythological Reflection, and with the different reflections through which to explore those themes. There are three ways to approach the cycles.

Follow the Cycles

The Great Work can be read from start to finish. Beginning at the Winter Solstice each of the eight cycles is presented in a six-week structure. Each of the weeks invites you to excavate aspects of self through a different reflection, which may require attention, understanding, and/or healing. After every two cycles a Process Phase allows a week to access how you are responding to the journey of discovery and self-awareness.

Follow Your Own Cycle

The beautiful thing about a cyclic approach is that it is ever-beginning and ever-ending. Winter cycles around to winter once again, even if we start to pay attention during the height of summer. Regardless of when you start to work through the cycles in this book, you will come back to the front pages eventually. You may even arrive there with deeper insights as you move into the exploration of your roots.

Flip to the Appropriate Cycle

Depending on life circumstances you can flip to the cycle that most interests you or feels most necessary at any time. The Prescriptions at the beginning of each part indicate which situations, behaviors, or energies may be alleviated by the work of that cycle. There is also a list of presenting issues in appendix A that can direct you to the appropriate cycle to address the issue.

Activities in *The Great Work*

The Great Work introduces an integrative approach that is both practical and magical, awakening the imagination with tangible applications and practices that encourage active participation for lasting transformation. It is an invitation for play and a welcoming hand to embark on an adventure. As has been said many a time, it behooves no one for us to remain small. The greatest depth of learning and the greatest potential for change occurs when we filter new information through the personal experience. The interactive elements for each cycle encourage the exploration of the themes as applied to your own life's experience. Several of these activities incorporate meditation, one of the simplest and yet most powerful tools we have at our disposal for facilitating physical health and personal insight. A basic familiarity with meditation techniques before starting these activities is helpful.

There are many different forms of meditation. It can be as easy as finding a quiet place, closing your eyes, and breathing deeply into your belly, releasing stress and tension. The approach in *The Great Work* is that of guided visualization, popularized by Shakti Gawain. To get the most out of these meditations, there are two options. You can read the guided visualization before closing your eyes and starting the meditation. This will give you a sense of the overall flow and allow you to follow the guided visualization at your own pace. Alternately, you may choose to record the guided visualization. With this method you can allow yourself to sink deeply into the experience itself, without concerning yourself about what happens next. Let your own voice be your guide. If you do this, remember to allow pauses (generally of at least a couple of minutes), so it doesn't feel like you are being raced through the meditation.

Meditation

Meditation is one of the ways we can experience an altered state of consciousness. It is always important to take some time to readjust yourself to your normal state of consciousness after meditating. If after taking a couple of deep breaths with your eyes open you find yourself feeling a bit spacey, it can help to touch your feet, drink some water, or eat something like crackers or nuts. Each of these techniques helps us feel grounded, centering us back in the physicality of our bodies and the normal course of our day-to-day lives.

Personal Reflections

Following the exposition of each reflection there is a section of daily reflections and questions that offer an opportunity to see how the information is reflected in you. If you are following the book consecutively from Cycle 1, these Personal Reflections start on December 21, beginning the self-inquiry with our first moments in this lifetime. As you follow all the cycles and phases through to December 20, the Personal Reflections sections guide your inner process, ending with a Self-Actualization Survey that provides feedback on where you are balanced in your life and where you may want to focus further attention if you choose. Even if you are not following the book in order, you can do the Personal Reflection any day the spirit moves you just by turning to the question for that day.

Intuitive Workings

Each Intuitive Reflection contains a basic outline for how to work with the divination tool presented in that particular reflection. As conveyed above, some of these tools are fairly straightforward in terms of procedure, whereas others are incredibly complex systems that have developed over centuries. The basic outline is not intended to be comprehensive, but to offer the barest bones of a structure upon which you can develop a deeper practice, if you choose. Trying out each different system can be a fun way of exploring some of the many options available for connecting with the Divine, and can open you up to working in a way you may not have previously contemplated.

The Hynnis

In the same vein, as many current energy healing modalities, *Hynni* is a system for facilitating healing through achieving holistic balance. It developed as a natural extension of the creation of the cycles and phases system, and is specific to the material in *The Great Work*. The more the system of fusing seasons, psychology, and intuition came together, the more evident it became that there needed to be a practical application on the energetic level as well. It felt important to me that this be an energy healing modality that fully embraced and acknowledged all the reflections, including the ones that focus on emotional healing.

The name hynni comes from Welsh, one of the oldest Celtic languages that almost disappeared, but is thankfully once again thriving. Welsh gives us the word hynni for energy: a reflection of the Divine consciousness that connects us all. Pronounced "honey," this word also implies that the purpose of our quest for self-knowledge and wholeness is to attain the gift of sweetness in life and all it has to offer.

Hynni is a healing modality that incorporates all the material presented in *The Great Work*. It offers a path to self-insight, illuminating the patterns of conscious living. It intertwines work on all levels of energetic vibration, from the densest physical levels to the highest vibration of our spiritual selves, highlighting our own mythic dimensions. Most significantly, it incorporates our emotional and mental levels to facilitate consciousness, awareness, and change on all levels. Hynni as a practice helps one to achieve inner and outer balance through the work of shifting limiting self-perspectives and illuminating Essence. It helps reveal the places in your life where there may be cacophony, offering guidelines for moving into personal harmony in order to align your unique and wonderful song to that of the Universal Symphony.

The end of each cycle includes a multi-layered meditation that incorporates the many reflections associated with that cycle. These complex meditations activate the energetic resonance of the cycle represented by the Hynni symbol included in the meditation, and facilitate the integration of all aspects of body, mind, and spirit within.

Further Exploration

It is my intention for this book to offer nuggets that inspire further exploration. By no means is it comprehensive on any singular topic. To be such would require a tome of such breadth (and weight) as to be completely unwieldy. Where there are resources that focus on the specific topic for a particular reflection, they have been listed after the reflection's description. These resources can help to deepen your understanding of the information presented in the reflection.

Start Your Own Journal

To fully engage in the interactive aspects of the book, it would be a great idea to pick up a journal to jot down your discoveries and experiences. The Personal Reflections sections, in particular, benefit from making note of your responses. As you continually shift and grow, *The Great Work* is a book you can return to again and again. Keeping track of your journey through the book, in the pages of your own journal, makes a wonderful reference that highlights where you have changed over time.

Additionally, writing what comes up for you in the Elemental Reflection meditations, the messages that come to you through the Guidance Reflections, the insights you receive through working with the Intuitive Reflection tools, and your hynni experiences will help to clarify your own inner emotional and symbolic language. It becomes a very valuable resource for future insight.

You Are *The Great Work!*

It has been my passion and my pleasure to craft the system that is presented in *The Great Work*. It is the culmination of years of study and practice, both personally and professionally. But, ultimately what unfolds in the pages to follow is merely a network of beakers and test tubes awaiting the animating alchemist to light the fire that can reveal the essence through the culmination of the work. The work of alchemy is referred to as the *Magnum Opus*, which literally translates from Latin as "The Great Work." To enter into a dynamic with nature that would allow the alchemist to access the highest truths and workings, enabling him or her to transmute a lower substance to its highest form as the Philosopher's Stone, was considered sacred work. One of the greatest teachings that comes to us from alchemy is that, as you work to create the Philosopher's Stone, you cannot separate yourself from the process. The alchemist, the work of alchemy, and the result of the alchemical process are all inextricably linked.

If there are two quotes from the ancient world that, for me, continue to echo through the ages ringing with the purity of truth, they are:

Gnothi Seauton (*γνῶθι σεαυτόν*): *Know Thyself*
   —The greatest adventure is that of exploring our inner worlds.
Carpe Diem: Pluck the Day
   —Each dawn is an opportunity for us to step into the full potential of ourselves.

We are both of the earth and of the stars. Each one of us is a wonder of spirit, cloaked in human form. Each reflection in the pages that follow echoes that vision back to you. Each reflection offers the opportunity for you to understand and shift your inner world in alignment with the natural world, to acknowledge and befriend your emotions and thoughts, and to see your life as a mythic journey. It is my hope that all who journey through these pages will discover the hynni that reveals the sweet essence of their own song, and know the Divine applauds.

As you engage in your own Magnum Opus, know that you are *The Great Work*.

Our birth is but a sleep and a forgetting:
The Soul that rises with us, our life's Star,
Hath had elsewhere its setting,
And cometh from afar:
Not in entire forgetfulness,
And not in utter nakedness,
But trailing clouds of glory do we come.
—*William Wordsworth*
(from Ode on Imitations of Immortality
from Recollections of Early Childhood)

In these pages, may you remember…

Part One

Cycle One
December 21–January 31

Roots and Foundations
"Be Excellent to Yourself"

PRESCRIPTIONS

Go through this section if you are experiencing any of the following:

- A sudden, unexpected loss or change of life circumstance
- Feeling isolated or disconnected from the world or other people
- Fear around new directions in life
- A persistent sense of being ungrounded
- Being triggered by spending time with your family

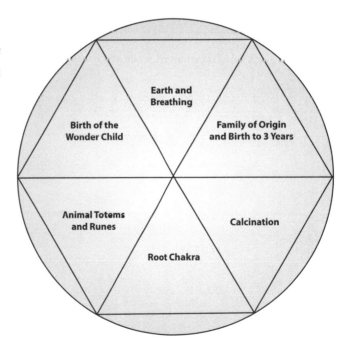

One

....

Mythological Reflection on the Birth of the Wonder Child

In the Northern Hemisphere this is a time of the deepest darkness. For ancient peoples, it was a time of scarcity and uncertainty. What had been sown and harvested was carefully stored and preserved, as this was all the tribe had to last through these dark times. They had to hope that they had planned well. Not enough stores would threaten survival, generally of the very young and very old. Self-sufficiency was key. In ancient times tribes were cut off from each other, as travel was difficult and dangerous during these cold days. As such, it was a time to pull within—recognizing a dependency upon each other to get through these treacherous days. But also, there was celebration of the community. It was a time of gathering around a hearth fire to hear a tale, and to be transported out of the cold, dark barrenness one saw all around.

The Winter Solstice itself is a time of great importance. As the shortest day and longest night of the year, it marks the moment after the sun begins to grow in strength once more. This is the rebirth of the light. At its heart, it is a celebration of order over the forces of chaos, of light over dark. In many traditions this is symbolized as the birth of the sun god, the Divine Child of Light, who brings joy, hope, and the promise of new life. It is this theme that most imprints upon this annual phase. This is the moment that we absolutely know that the light will return once more, and we have survived yet another period of chaos and uncertainty.

Ancient celebrations focused on revelry. The ancient Egyptians held the festival of "Amun-in-the-festival-of raising-heaven," lasting several days, which culminated in filling in the sacred eye of the sun god. The ancient Babylonians celebrated the birth of Tammuz, and the ancient Persians lit massive bonfires in celebration of the light's defeat of the forces of darkness. One of the best-known ancient festivals is that of the Roman Saturnalia. This much-beloved festival celebrated the triumph of Jupiter (order) over Cronos (chaos), over seven days of unrestrained festivity and unbridled feasting, when the masters served the slaves, who could do as they wished.

For *The Great Work*, the celebration of the Winter Solstice marks the birth of the Wonder Child. In each of us, there is such a child. We come into this world emanating our essence, untouched as of yet, by the perceptions and constraints we later experience. The process of self-knowledge is achieved, through the excavation of limiting perceptions. Each layer we uncover and release helps to reveal the light that shines beneath. It is this journey of excavation and revelation that we undertake throughout the year to come. This is the process of reclaiming the Wonder Child. The Winter Solstice marks the promise of the future, and the start of our journey toward self-actualization.

Main Themes for Cycle 1:
Place within tribe
Victory of order over chaos
Rebirth of the Light

Ancient Cultural Archetypes of the Child of Light

Marduk *(Babylonian)* battled the monsters of chaos to bring order, beauty, and peace to the world.

Mithra *(Persian)* was particularly beloved by Roman soldier,s who referred to him as "Sol Invictus" (Resurrection of the sun). His name (*Mithra*) means "facilitator of contracts."

Horus *(Egyptian)* is the son of Isis and Osiris who was born as a result of Osiris's resurrection. He is pictured as the falcon-headed sun god who offered protection.

Dionysus *(Greek)* or **Bacchus** *(Roman)* is the youngest son of Zeus. Known as the god of grapes and wine, he represented joy and revelry.

Baldur *(Norse)* is the son of Odin and Frigg. Loved by all, he was the champion of goodness and forgiveness.

Personal Mythological Reflections

December 21: Reflect on a time in your life when you experienced chaos.

December 22: How do you feel when everything around you seems dark?

December 23: Have you ever had a moment of losing control?

December 24: What symbols speak to you of optimism and hope?

December 25: What aspects and traits about yourself do you feel are unique and special?

December 26: What difference would you like to make in the world or in the lives of others?

December 27: In what ways do you celebrate you?

Two

....

Elemental Reflection on Earth and Active Reflection on Breathing

Earth: The Ground Beneath Our Feet

For those who seek to experience spirit in their lives, it is abundantly clear that we have this other aspect of self to be acknowledged, and with that we must work and integrate. That is, the aspect of our physical selves. We are, in part at least, made of matter and experience a good portion of our lives in the material world. In seeking to bring spirit into our lives, the acceptance of our physical selves is absolutely necessary. Our bodies are our connection to earth, and as much as we are "made of stars," we are also "of the earth." It is part of what makes a human experience both complex and wondrous.

It can be an enticing draw to focus on the higher vibrations of spirit in which we feel expansive and inspired. But it is through the earth that spirit becomes manifested. There is a saying that "the One created diversity in order that It could know Itself." Pure spirit, which is boundary-less, created delineation and definition (matter) in order to experience itself. The element of earth represents the realm of matter—the heaviest and densest expression. Thus, when we don't take care of earth, we limit spirit's potential for expression.

Earth is the solid foundation beneath our feet. Connecting with earth helps us to know our place in the world—where we stand. When we are comfortable with earth, we are able to put down roots knowing it is safe to do so. We are grounded and stable. From this place we are able to explore how to reach up and expand, but we need to have the firm foundation beneath us in order to be able to do so.

We acknowledge earth when we pay attention to our physical needs, and when we nourish our bodies with healthy food and get enough sleep. We also acknowledge earth when we create an environment for ourselves that feels safe, secure, and supporting. This includes our physical earth, which sustains all life. Our survival as human beings depends on the health and abundance of the earth. Paying attention to what supports and sustains us personally, communally, and globally is a key aspect of honoring the element of earth.

Earth helps us to accept our human nature. It opens us to understand limits, and to embrace our limitations. It informs us when we are out of balance, or not paying attention to our physical needs.

Messages that help to connect us to the element of earth are:
I am safe and secure.
I honor and meet the needs of my physical body.
I know how to take care of myself.
I create a solid foundation upon which to build.
I am grounded.

Breathing

Breath is the most basic process that gives life. We can go weeks without food, and days without water, and still function on a physical level. But we can only go minutes without breath. Breathing is an automatic function that delineates our movement from the realm of spirit to that of matter. An infant reacts and responds in the womb, but it is the first breath upon entry into the world that prompts the cry "I have arrived." The brain may still exhibit activity after the last breath is exhaled, but we stand by our loved ones watching for the "last breath" as the marker that our loved one has crossed over. Breath is so basic that we often take it for granted. We don't think about it. We rarely pay attention to how we breathe. And we don't often truly allow ourselves the full experience of breath moving in and out of our bodies.

The Latin word for the verb "to breathe" is *spire*. It is from this root that the English word respiration comes from, but the Latin spire has other meanings. Not just defining the function of physical breath, it also reverberates with a sense of "the breath of life," and spirit. From this, we actually get the words spirit, aspire, inspire, and all the numerous variations of those roots. To breathe is not merely about keeping our physical bodies on this earthly plane. To breathe is to take in the very essence of spirit, and move it into all the areas of our lives that uplift us and fill our lives with meaning. It is another means that spirit finds expression in matter.

However, odd as this may sound, most of us have forgotten how to breathe. That infant who takes its first breath has it down pat. With no self-consciousness around body image, and no stress or tension held in the body, the infant breathes deep down into its belly, expanding the diaphragm and filling his or her lungs. Watch a baby breathe. Those little bellies rise up like balloons. As adults, we are loath to experience our bellies as expanding balloons! Thus, we constrict and control our breath. By the time we reach adulthood, most of us breathe in short, shallow, tension-ridden patterns that keep our breath high up in our chests, rather than full, slow breaths that move through our torsos.

Breathing is healing. Technically, when we breathe we are pulling needed oxygen into our systems on the inhale, and releasing carbon dioxide on the exhale. This process of exchange is called respiration, and the mode of transport is breath. Taking a moment in between the inhale and exhale allows for fuller exchange more oxygen in the system and more carbon dioxide out. When we allow for this full exchange, it helps slow the heart rate, lowers blood pressure, promotes blood flow, boosts the immune system, and contributes to feeling more relaxed, aware, and energized.

One of the greatest challenges we experience in current times is the seriously negative impact of stress upon our physical health and well-being. Stress is a blanket term that denotes a negative response to a situation and/or environment that can contribute to a wide range of ailments on all levels of being—physiological, emotional, and psychological. Practices that have been recommended to address the presence of stress in one's life include meditation and yoga, which both use breath as their foundational component. Belly-breathing is the key to a successful meditative practice, and pranayama is the technique of breath control used in yoga. Exercise is another great way to reduce stress, which also serves to shift our breathing patterns, allowing for more oxygen to be taken into our bodies. One of the best things we can do for ourselves is to learn how to truly breathe as we did when we first came into this world. It enlivens us both in our physical bodies and in our very spirits.

Personal Elemental and Active Reflections

December 28: In what circumstances do you feel safe and supported?

December 29: Reflect on how stable you feel in your work and home life.

December 30: What aspects about your body do you like, and which do you dislike?

December 31: In what ways do you take care of your body and your physical needs?

January 1: Reflect on what commitment you can make to your own sense of security.

January 2: Reflect on how you naturally take in and expel breath from your body.

January 3: In what ways does slowing your breath shift tension that may be held in your body?

Three

Psychological Reflection on Family of Origin and Developmental Reflection on Birth to Three Years of Age

Family of Origin

None of us are born in isolation. We come into this world dependent on others. This is absolutely necessary in order for us to survive the tender, early years of our lives, and is true across the animal kingdom, although the structure differs across species. The young of all are vulnerable and in need of others to ensure survival. As humans, what that looks like also differs widely from individual to individual. Some are born into large, bustling families, and others have that familial foundation shattered at an early age.

Family of origin is a term used to describe the system or environment in which we experienced our influential developmental years. It is the system that provides a framework that much of our adulthood is based on, either in repetition or reaction. Having an understanding of what constitutes a healthy, supportive system is integral to creating a healthy foundation in adulthood, either for one's own self or for one's own family of choice. Knowing what a healthy family looks like allows one to comprehend what may have been awry in childhood, acknowledge and release any pain from those early years, and reclaim the birthright of support, safety, and acceptance that a healthy family system provides.

In a healthy family system, each individual within the system is accepted and appreciated for his or her own unique contribution. There is an inherent, underlying message of respect. It is understood that each individual has their own particular perspective. Mom may disagree with Dad, but still appreciate that Dad's perspective is valid to him. Yet even within the context of that understanding, there is a dedication and commitment to the family as a whole. Mom and Dad may disagree on perspectives, and still be able to coordinate agreement on approach through communication and collaboration. Each member of the family is precious, but that does not mean chaos reigns. The parents act as the captains of the ship, so to speak, but everyone on that ship is important and necessary in order for movement to occur.

In a healthy family system there are rules and guidelines. There needs to be a structure that is recognized by each member for each to feel secure. These are clear guidelines. They can be open to discussion, they can be open to change, and most certainly, each member of the family has the right to express feelings. But each member of the family understands, even if only on an unconscious level, what the "rules of engagement" within the family are.

As the family shifts and grows, so do the guidelines. Nothing can remain static. To do so results in stagnation and decay. Homes change. Jobs change. Children grow up. Different times call for different needs. A healthy family is able to be flexible, and adapts to life's changes as required.

Unhealthy family systems operate from a place of fear and control, as opposed to respect and encouragement. Parents who have not looked at their own deeply held feelings of inadequacy cannot help but foster an environment that reverberates with a message of shame. The more profound or unconscious the shame, the more unhealthy the family system will be, often manifesting in issues of substance abuse, and other forms of addiction.

As with any form of imbalance, an unhealthy family system can be present in either of two polarized extremes.

The *Controlling System* operates from fixed, rigid rules that are set in stone. There is little or no acknowledgment of differing needs for differing members in the family. There is certainly no forum for expression or discussion. There is usually one absolute authority who wields power in the family through instilling shame and fear.

The *Chaotic System* presents unclear or inconsistent rules. The winds can change depending on a parental mood, or more devastatingly, the engaging of an addiction. "Dad is withdrawn and absent when sober, but raging and authoritarian when drunk." This establishes a rat's nest of mixed messages, resulting in a need for family members to be hyper-vigilant about how exactly the wind is blowing. This can also lead to role reversal, where a child unconsciously steps into parental behavior, because the parent is incapable when caught up in the addiction.

In unhealthy families, there is a denial that anything is wrong. With a lack of communication, and little or no support for individuals' feelings, it sometimes becomes necessary to ignore the "bizarre," and develop defenses and coping mechanisms to try to protect one's self.

Every person has needs, but the unhealthy family system does not have a foundation to recognize and meet family members' needs. As such, unconscious roles are assumed in an attempt to meet those needs. Studies by Alfred Adler show that children develop certain roles depending on where they fall in order of birth. This is highlighted in unhealthy families. The more unhealthy the system is, the more marked the role will be.

First Born or The Hero Child: This can also manifest in roles known as the perfectionist, the pillar-of-strength, and the over-achiever. The Hero Child compensates for an inner feeling of inadequacy by being "The Good One," always striving for positive attention. There can be many benefits to seeking perfection. The positive accolades can temporarily alleviate the feeling of inadequacy. However, the costs are very high indeed. The sense of being accepted and acceptable is based solely on external presentation and performance. And regardless of what levels of achievement have been attained, the underlying message of shame and inadequacy cuts down any joy that may be experienced from perceived success.

Second Born or The Scapegoat: This role can also be known as the black sheep or the rebel. The Scapegoat Child accepts the badge of "The Bad One," unconsciously believing that negative attention is preferable to zero attention. This sadly confirms the erroneous inner message of not being good enough. The Scapegoat is often identified as "the problem" in the family, when in fact, The Scapegoat is expressing the problems that are inherent in the family system itself. It is often the second born who is voicing the truth that, as written by Shakespeare, there is "something rotten in the state of Denmark." In adulthood, The Scapegoat may try to escape inner pain and turmoil by engaging in compulsive or addictive behaviors.

Third Born or Lost Child: With little expectation for attention, "The Lost Child" (also known as "The Invisible One") is often met with relief by the parents in an unhealthy family system. The Hero Child pulls the positive attention and The Scapegoat pulls the negative attention. Feeling like an outcast in the family, The Lost Child withdraws and isolates, creating an illusion of independence that masks the pain of not being seen nor heard. The benefit of being The Lost Child is self-reliance, but it comes with the cost of never feeling part of a community. There is a loneliness within The Lost Child that carries into an adult belief that one never really belongs anywhere. It is this lack of connection with others that needs to be healed.

The Last Born or The Mascot: This role can also be known as "The Clown" or "The Under-achiever." This child tries to diffuse the underlying family tension through levity and humor. The Mascot tends to be the perennial baby, fostering an attitude of dependence that inhibits taking self-responsibility. This is another role that tends to be received with relief by the parents in the unhealthy family system, although it can be met with frustration by other children in the family. Outwardly, The Mascot brings a sense of fun and playfulness, but the outer smile hides inner pain. In adulthood, The Mascot often attracts a Hero Child partner, compensating their own under-responsibility with their partner's over-responsibility.

It is of great benefit to think back to the environment that one was raised in in order to gain a sense of what the overriding energies were that laid the foundation for the adult life one has created. Self-actualization is the process that we become conscious, aware, and autonomous. If we are still reacting to our childhood experiences and environment, we have not created an adult environment of choice.

The truth is that all families are unhealthy to a greater or lesser degree. The epidemic of shame that permeates our culture simply does not allow for the climate of truly healthy family environments. That being said, there is a wide range of scenarios that one may have experienced. Knowing the dynamics that existed in your own family of origin, and what may have contributed to those dynamics, is a huge step forward in being able to have the choice to create healthier dynamics in your own family of choice.

Further Exploration on Family of Origin

Bradshaw On: The Family: A New Way of Creating Solid Self-Esteem by John Bradshaw. Health Communications, Inc., 1990.

Family Secrets: The Path to Self-Acceptance and Reunion by John Bradshaw. Bantam, 1996.

Family Ties That Bind: A Self-Help Guide to Change Through Family of Origin Therapy by Dr. Ronald W. Richardson. Self Counsel Press, Inc., 2011.

The Birth Order Book: Why You Are the Way You Are by Dr. Kevin Leman. Revell, 2009.

The First Born Advantage: Making Your Birth Order Work for You by Dr. Kevin Leman. Revell, 2008.

Birth to Three Years of Age

There is a lot of growth going on in these first few years of life—so much so that there are literally three different stages encompassed in the first three years.

The Infant Stage refers to the first nine months exutero. This is a highly dependent stage. Upon the birth of my son, I was told by my midwife, "Nine months in the womb, nine months on the womb," meaning that the child's needs in these months are as all-encompassing as when the child was being completely supported and nourished by Mom's physical body. In utero the child's every need was met. For the first several months exutero the need is no different. What becomes an understandable challenge is the parents' ability to meet every need. Given that we are human beings with limited resources (at times more limited than others), we are guaranteed to fail. And this is okay. We get tired, or we have other things that pull our attention, or are trying to juggle several different things at once. Being 100 percent successful is not the important thing. Understanding the significance of trust-building is.

At this stage, as the child is welcomed into his or her tribe (family of origin), the most significant message that needs to be experienced is that his or her needs will be met. It is impossible for that child to meet his or her own needs. This is the stage in which we develop trust: knowing that our needs will be met, that we are safe, we are loved, and accepted.

These months are a new little being's first moments on this earth. Coming from a place of spirit requires adjustment. Imagine taking the expansiveness of "All That Is" and squeezing it into a teeny, fragile form. It takes some getting used to. Mirroring helps an infant learn how to act and respond in this new realm. New information will be filtered through observing how others respond, particularly Mom. Enmeshment (the fusing of one's personality into the experience of another's personality "I am you") at this stage is absolutely okay, and in fact, necessary. It is how the infant is learning how to acclimate. No need to worry that you are creating a dependent child. Time for differentiation will come.

The Toddler Stage, which lasts from nine months to three years of age, involves two distinct elements—opposition and exploration. This is the first great movement in the very, very long process of growth toward autonomy. What is the momentous event that propels this movement? It literally is mobility. Once a child learns to navigate this world on his or her own, a whole new ballgame starts—a ballgame that will be played out in many different forms over the next years and decades. Once a child becomes mobile, he or she introduces the massively impactful element of option and choice. "I can go here or I can go there." Very early on in our time on this earth we begin to carve out a unique personality and present a self-determined sense of self. This becomes quickly evident with the appearance of the infamous "NO!" Frustrating as it can sometimes be for parents, when a child says no, what is actually being said is, "I get how you want me to see the world, but I actually experience it very differently from you and so I reject your perspective." Fair enough, and in truth, this is a message to be celebrated. However, it is not a message toward which one should bow when encountered at this tender age. A two-year-old has not yet experienced enough of the world to know if his or her perspective is one that is safe and life-enhancing, or one that will cause no end of troubles. Therefore, it is the adult's job to establish some boundaries and ensure there is safety around new experiences. A toddler will exercise his or her own willpower. That is an important element of their development. If a parent is able to recognize that acting out from a place of will is the first, tentative foray into self-knowledge and not see it as a power struggle, it will be far easier to establish appropriate boundaries in a loving but firm manner. We need to express our feelings and desires. We need to be encouraged to explore. But we also need to be informed as to what is appropriate and what is safe.

As adults, how we experienced and how we were supported and guided in these early years has a huge impact on our inner relationship and our approach to life. Adults who as children experienced disruption and/or trauma in these early years of life may find themselves unable to trust themselves, their choices, or other people. Not realizing that they have internalized a message of mistrust from very early experiences of neglected needs, mistrustful adults see proof of their perspective in the environment around them. Fear of abandonment (and its cagey counterpart, the fear of engulfment) stem from this time. For some adults, the prospect of a relationship ending can elicit panicked emotions more akin to a threat to survival. This harkens to the experience of neglected needs in infancy and toddlerhood—a time it truly did feel as though being abandoned was the end of the world. If anyone has ever encountered the hysteria of a lost toddler, you know this internal perception is the case. Not knowing where Mom is leads to complete terror. On a deep core, instinctive level we fear for our very survival.

By the age of three children who are nurtured in a stable, healthy environment will have developed a positive sense of self as separate from Mom. They will have started to exhibit unique personality traits and will have established a curious approach to the world with a willingness to explore without fear, but with balance and care. By this age, from an ideal perspective, the firm foundation of trust and autonomy will have been created.

 Personal Psychological and Developmental Reflections
January 4: How trusting do you feel yourself to be?

January 5: What role may you have played in your family of origin?

January 6: How comfortable are you in taking risks?

January 7: How encouraged were you to explore new things in childhood?

January 8: How comfortable are you with saying no?

January 9: In what ways do you experience yourself as perfect?

January 10: Who or what constitutes your tribe?

Four

Alchemical Reflection on Calcination

"Its father is the sun."

FROM *THE EMERALD TABLET*

CALCINATION ASSOCIATIONS [1] "THE BLACK PHASE"

Element: Fire • **Metal:** Lead • **Planet:** Saturn
Symbols: King, Sol, Wolf, Red Lion, Phoenix, "Starry Salamander," Crow
Dream Imagery: Skulls, funeral pyres, dragons, deserts,
fevers, earthquakes, avalanches, forest fires

Calcination is the first stage in the alchemical process of transformation. Chemically, it involves the intense heating of the material being worked on in order to drive off any water and impurities so that all that is left is a fine, dry powder. The term has its roots in the Latin word *calx*, meaning "lime" (a reference to the remaining white, fine powder). Literally, it is the reduction of earth to ash through the application of fire.

....

1 Calcination associations adapted from *The Emerald Tablet: Alchemy for Personal Transformation*, Dennis William Hauck (New York: Penguin/Arkana, 1999).

Psychologically, we experience calcination during those times in our lives when we feel that everything has fallen apart. Extreme change causes us to question those elements in our lives that we had thought to be solid. Loss in the form of sudden unemployment, divorce, or death can precipitate the experience of calcination. It is a time of upheaval and confusion, often accompanied by emotions of anger and fear.

In the journey from attachment to the material world, to embracing a life that acknowledges the input and influence of spirit, calcination is imperative, uncomfortable though it may be. Technically, it is during these times that we literally burn off the heaviness of adapted personality in order to reveal the soul. If we have gone through much of our lives gaining a sense of self from elements that are external, losing those elements causes a crisis of identity. For example, if my sense of who I am and my importance comes from my job, who am I if I lose my job?

From a psychological perspective, calcination addresses the attachment to the unhealthy ego, or the revelation of the illusion of the persona or false self we may have become accustomed to presenting to the world. We create these false selves as a way of protecting ourselves from judgment, from rejection, and from shame. These are the same as the roles created out of an unhealthy family of origin environment. But, created from a place of fear and uncertainty, these are not reflections of the best or the truth of us. They are shame-based, and thus, soul-limiting.

Calcination can be experienced as a "dark night of the soul"—lonely, frightening times when we feel we have lost our way and do not know where to turn. From a human perspective we do everything we can to avoid the circumstances presented in calcination. We hold on to jobs that feel soul-crushing. We hang on to relationships that feel empty, or worse, abusive. We neglect our bodies, feeling, and yet ignoring, the physical effects. We resist change, even if it is toward the positive, because that change can set off a series of questions that will cause us to have to look at some uncomfortable places. If not this, then what? But, as has oft been said, the Divine does work in mysterious ways, and it is our purpose in this life to step into our full potential and our truth. Spirit does not intend for us to remain small, uncertain, and afraid. Calcination, though far from comfortable, is the Divine's faith in us. It is the reminder that we are both human and spirit. It is the call for us to remember our Essence. Thus, from the perspective of spiritual growth, this is a significant moment. It is the moment when we become open to the possibility that there is far more to life than is offered in the material world. It is a moment when we are faced with the limitations of an unhealthy ego and the potential of soul-full life. There is a rich, vibrant, nourishing inner world waiting to be discovered; one that aligns us with authenticity and self. The next stage—*dissolution*—starts us truly on the way.

Personal Alchemical Reflections

January 11: Have you had times of feeling you don't know who you are?

January 12: Reflect upon a time in your life when you felt lost and uncertain.

January 13: What do you consider the most important elements or aspects in your life?

January 14: If you have experienced depression, what has helped to lift the heaviness?

January 15: What qualities do you most dislike or reject within yourself?

January 16: What gives you comfort in troubled times?

January 17: What do you consider your greatest strength?

Five

Energetic Reflection on the Root Chakra

Root Chakra[2] Associations

Name: Muladhara • **Location:** Base of spine • **Color:** Red • **Tone:** Low C
Gland: Suprarenal or Adrenal • **Body:** Solid parts (spine, bones, teeth),
Elimination (rectum, colon), Blood and cells • **Yoga Path:** Hatha or Kundalini
Symbol: Four-petalled lotus • **Stones:** Garnet, Obsidian, Apache Tear, Smoky Quartz,
Agate, Bloodstone, Ruby, Red Coral, Fire Opal, Hematite, Lodestone

The root chakra is located at the base of the spine. It faces downward, connecting our energy with that of the earth. It supports the structural elements in our bodies upon which everything else is hinged. Our spine and our bones, including teeth, are the domain of the root chakra. A dream about losing teeth, for example, may be an indication of a blocked root chakra. The cells that are the building blocks of every single element of our bodies, and the blood that flows through us to nourish those cells, are also supported by the root chakra. When our bodies are in good physical health, it indicates that the root chakra is healthy and open. Nourishing our bodies is accomplished through our digestive system, and that too is supported by the root chakra, especially the ability to eliminate (bladder

2 Root chakra associations adapted from *The Chakra Handbook: From Basic Understanding to Practical Application*, Shalila Sharamon and Bodo J. Baginski (Wilmot, WI: Lotus Light Publications, 1991).

and colon). The root chakra grounds us in our physicality, helping us to maintain what makes us strong and vital, and releasing what weakens us or causes disease.

Physically, a blocked root chakra can manifest as low blood pressure, poor circulation, bladder infections, and abdominal, colon, or digestive issues. Do you often feel fatigued? Do you find yourself in a cycle of illness, continually fighting off colds or the flu? It could be an indication of a blocked root chakra. With its connection to our digestive system, an eating disorder can also indicate an imbalance in this chakra.

Psychologically, if we are balanced in our root chakras we will be centered, grounded, and flexible. We have a sense of our place in the world and are secure in that understanding. We are able to embrace change knowing that, even if the ground shifts beneath us, we will land on our feet in the end. In reflection of early childhood developmental needs, the root chakra indicates our relationship with trust. Trust is the foundation on which all relationships are built. If there is no trust, there is a very shaky foundation indeed, and it is near impossible to create a dynamic of substance and support. We trust that our jobs will be there for us when we show up to work. We trust that our friends will be understanding and compassionate. We trust that our families will strive to see the best in us. We trust that we are able to care for ourselves. If we do not experience trust in these more human areas of our lives, it is unlikely that we will experience trust in the Divine.

A blocked root chakra is indicated in those who have a fear of commitment, and are unable to root themselves with any degree of certainty in jobs or relationships. Fear of engulfment—the fear of being swallowed up by another—can contribute to an inability to commit. With fear of engulfment, there is an unconscious belief that we will be trapped and suffocated. It can feel as intense as the fear of being buried alive. On the other hand, fear of abandonment also indicates a blocked root chakra. This fear is prompted by the unconscious message that we will not survive if we are left (abandoned). It triggers unresolved Infant Stage issues of trust, security, and safety.

If we are blocked in our root chakras, we will be needy, fearful, and self-destructive or stubborn, rigid, and domineering. We will feel physically depleted and often exhausted. We may find ourselves in unstable relationships. We may have chronic money issues. We may find that we never feel we belong anywhere. We need to have an open, healthy root chakra that connects us to the vitality of earth energy, and the belief that all areas of our lives are built upon a firm, grounded foundation. This not only provides stability it our lives; it also provides healthy energetic flow to the other chakras.

Messages that help to balance the root chakra are:
I am safe in the world and with others.
I am comfortable with change.
My body is strong and healthy.

 Personal Energetic Reflections

January 18: The color red makes me feel …

January 19: How do you respond to being alone?

January 20: Reflect on how many home or job changes you have experienced in your life.

January 21: What has been the cause of relationships ending for you?

January 22: What situations would prompt a feeling of fear in you?

January 23: In what ways do you exercise your body and encourage its strength?

January 24: Reflect on whether your eating and sleeping habits feel healthy and balanced.

Six

....

Guidance Reflection on Animal Guides and Intuitive Reflection on Runes

Animal Guides

Humans have always had a special relationship with the animal world. From the cave paintings in Lascaux, France, to the animal-headed gods of the Egyptians, to shamanistic garb, we see evidence of how we have acknowledged our interconnection with the beasts that walk on the same earth that we do. For earliest humankind, the recognition of interconnection rested upon the need for survival. It is thought that the cave paintings were a kind of "sympathetic magic." Invoke the spirit of the beast and there will be success in the hunt that would ensure survival of the tribe. Through the centuries that dynamic shifted. The Egyptians did not identify their gods with animals to ensure survival. They imbued certain traits they identified in certain animals with Divine significance. The Egyptian gods and goddesses were often pictured with animal heads: the jackal-headed Anubis, the falcon-headed Horus, and the cat-headed Bast, to name a few. This shifted the dynamic from that of the actual animal found in the physical world, to the essence of the animal found in the archetypal realm—the realm of spirit.

Ancient cultures also saw certain gods and goddesses as having special relationships with animals. The deities would often be pictured with these beasts by their side, rather than taking on the animal's physical characteristics. There are countless examples of this. Artemis's deer and hound, Ceridwen's sow, or Epona's horse. These animals were considered sacred to the Divine, and offered a means through which the individual could connect with the Divine.

The concept of totem animals is found in many indigenous cultures. A totem denotes a special relationship, or kinship, that the tribe or family has with a certain animal or animals. The totem poles of the First Nations peoples of the Pacific Northwest, including the Haida, have long fascinated. The animals or beings depicted on the totem poles indicated the guiding energies of the family or tribe. They also indicated relationships between families that had the same guiding energies. The Twisted Hairs tradition of the Americas presents that we are all born with a totem animal, depending on our sitting place, similar to an astrological assignment. That animal will guide us through our entire walk upon the earth.

Contemporarily, many people approach a totem animal as being one with whom a deep and close connection is felt. It does not necessarily stem from a tribal or family connection, but there is something in the traits and characteristics of the animal that resonates with our sense of self. Using totem animals in this way can help us to learn about ourselves and offer us insights into situations. Rather than using the animal as an entrance way for Divine connection, the animal becomes a teacher for us to gain self-understanding. In this way the animal becomes a guide for us—helping to lead the way for us to become aligned with our highest and true self. Some animal guides stay with us for years, reflecting our core issues that we cycle through many times in order to grow. Or they stay with us to remind us of our Essence and our truth, acting as a beacon to light our way. Other animal guides will pop into our lives for a brief time in relation to a particular situation that their energy would be the most helpful.

Often, in working with the animal world we find we resonate with those we find around us in our environment. For example, a North American may resonate to the strength of bear rather than the strength of lion. There is a particular nuance to the teachings of each animal that is intimately connected to the land upon which they walk. The strength needed for the woods is different than the strength needed for the plains, and on a deeply unconscious level, we respond to the connections that tie us as well to our environment.

There are several ways through which to determine your animal guide. For many First Nations peoples, including the Lakota Sioux and the Ojibwa, a vision quest is a way to discern and connect with your lifelong animal totem. One of the aims of a vision quest is to purify yourself and release any fears in order that your totem may present itself. A vision quest may not be possible in a contemporary, urban setting, but the key feature of any vision quest is that the animal chooses you!

You can determine your animal guide in a way similar to a vision quest through meditation. It is important to enter the meditation free from tensions, stress, or fears. Taking some time to ready and purify yourself is important. Have a bath, releasing the dirt and grime of both body and soul. Prepare a space free from interruption. Rest solely in the space of the movement of your breath until it feels like you are completely grounded in your own center. Then ask to call in your animal guide. A true guide will present three times, in three different ways, to let you know for certain that it has chosen you.

Animal guides may also present themselves to us in the physical world. Is there a certain animal that you see over and over again? Or that seems to show up at significant times in your life? Or that you encounter in unusual circumstances? This could be an indication of an animal guide.

Once you have determined your animal guide, spend some time becoming familiar with its habitat, behavior, method, and manner of communication. This is about developing a relationship, no different than a human relationship. The more you understand the particular attributes of your animal guide, the clearer the message behind that guide's choice of you will become. Meditating with the energy of the animal or collecting statues and pictures will also facilitate a strong connection. Working with these animal guides connects us both to ourselves and to the earth.

Some Common Examples of Animal Guides

Armadillo How to use defenses	**Badger** Keeper of stories	**Bat** Initiation, Rebirth, Changes	**Bear** Strength, Caution, Earth power	**Boar** Leadership, Spiritual strength
Cat Magic, Independence	**Cow** Community, Contentment	**Deer** Gentle, Alert, Ability to listen	**Dog** Loyalty, Friendship, Protection	**Donkey** Patience, Humility
Elephant Family, Memory	**Fox** Cunning, Ingenuity, Patience	**Goat** Agility, Independence	**Gorilla** Gentle strength, Nobility	**Groundhog** Tenacity, Boundaries
Hedgehog Protection, Lightness, Wonder	**Horse** Travel, Power, Stamina	**Jaguar** Tenacity, Psychic vision	**Leopard** Inner instincts, Overcoming past	**Lion** Leadership, Nobility, Power
Mole Grounding, Introspection	**Monkey** Trickster, Integrating dark	**Moose** Appropriate revelation, The sacred	**Mouse** Stealth, Attention to detail	**Opossum** Knowing when to fight or rest
Panther Ferocity, Valor	**Pig** Resourcefulness, Fearlessness	**Polar Bear** Endurance, Solitude	**Porcupine** Innocence, Wonder, Trust	**Prairie Dog** Community, Caretaker
Rabbit Movement, Fertility	**Raccoon** Disguise, Protection, Dexterity	**Ram** Agility, Strength, Safety	**Rat** Social, Survival	**Sheep** Confidence, Peace, Community
Skunk Respect, Steadiness, Peace	**Squirrel** Activity, Preparedness	**Tiger** Power, Tact, Adventure	**Weasel** Sly, Stealthy, Instincts	**Wolf** Steadfast, Social, Adaptability

Further Exploration on Animal Guides

Animal-Speak: The Spiritual & Magical Power of Creatures Great & Small by Ted Andrews. Llewellyn Publications, 2002.

Animal Spirit Guides: An Easy-to-Use Handbook for Identifying and Understanding Your Power Animals and Animal Spirit Helpers by Steven D. Farmer. Hay House, 2006.

Animal-Wise: Understanding the Language of Animal Messengers and Companions by Ted Andrews. Dragonhawk Publishing, 2010.

Song of the Deer: The Great Sun Dance Journey of the Soul with Other by Thunder Strikes with Jan Orsi. Treasure Chest Books, 1999.

Runes

Based in northern European tradition, runes consist of a set of letter symbols that constitute both a language and a symbolic system. The system itself, known as *futhark*, is named for the first six letters that appear: fehu (f), uruz (u), thurisaz (th), ansuz (a), raidho (r), and kenaz (c or k). This differs from traditional alphabets that are named for the first two letters: alpha (a) and beta (b). There are several variations of the futhark, but the most common that is familiar to us is known as the Ancient or Elder Futhark. It is the Elder Futhark that is commonly used for divination. The term runes refers to the individual symbols (or letters) that make up the futhark. In the Elder Futhark there are twenty-four runes. Contemporary rune sets often include a twenty-fifth "blank rune," which was not part of the original system.

It is said that the Norse god, Odin, gave the runes to humankind. In order to gain this great wisdom Odin sacrificed his left eye and hung upside down on an ash tree. On the ninth day he was bestowed with the knowledge of the runes, which he gifted to the world. Evidence of runes can be found carved in stone in northern Europe dating back to 250 CE, but it was not until the 1700s that it came into common use for written communication. There has long been a veil of mystery surrounding the runes. In fact, one possible root for the word rune may be from *ru*, meaning "mysterious thing." The runes were an integral part of the Norse culture.

For omens and the casting of lots, they have the highest regard. Their procedure is always the same. They cut off a branch of a nut-bearing tree and slice it into strips; these they mark with different signs and throw them completely at random onto a white cloth. Then the priest of the state, if the consultation is a public one, or the father of the family if it is private, offers a prayer to the gods, and looking up to the sky picks up three strips, one at a time and reads their meaning from the signs previously scored on them.

—Tacitus, *De origine et situ Germanorum*

As the Norse culture expanded through Viking raids, the runes filtered west from northern Europe. They can be found in Germanic and Anglo-Saxon tradition. The symbols themselves remain fairly consistent, although there can be significant difference in the spelling of each rune name.

The twenty-four runic symbols are divided into three lines of eight runes each. This grouping of eight runes is called the *aett* (pronounced eight) in Norse. The three lines refer to the three levels of consciousness and are associated with the deities of those realms. The *first aett* are ruled by the god Frey and the goddess Freya. These runes illuminate qualities and experiences of the Middle World, or the earthly realm. The *second aett* are ruled by the god Heimdall and the giantess Mordgud. The runes in this aett guide us in recognizing obstacles and successes as we embrace evolution. It tends to be connected with the unconscious or Underworld. The *third aett* are ruled by the god Tiwaz and the goddess Zisa. The higher realms are explored in this aett: guidance around justice, relationships, and how to move into fulfillment. In a modern set the blank rune is included to indicate the mysterious hand of the Divine. Its message is one of trust and wonder, encouraging an attitude of conscious awareness in the nature of co-creation with the Divine. The Divine will provide the opportunity to enter the mystery with complete trust in order to experience the magic of transformation.

Although some modern rune sets can be found carved in wood or pictured on cards, the most commonly available are as stone or crystal sets. Working with the runic symbols in this way connects us to the messages of the Divine and the flow of living a human life through the grounded medium of stones.

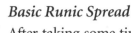

Basic Runic Spread

After taking some time to center yourself, hold an intention that you will be guided to receive the message that you most need to hear in this moment. Reach into the bag that holds your rune set and pull out three runes. Place the first rune in the position to the far left. Place the second rune in the center position. Then place the third rune in the position to the far right.

First position: This position represents the past. It is the energy that lays the foundation for what is transpiring in the here and now. It may give insight into what needs attention, or it may represent the question to be answered. With this rune ask yourself: What does this rune tell me about how I have been or acted in the past that has led to the current situation? What elements or qualities either support or hinder my current situation? What from the past may I need to release?

Second position: This position represents the present. It is the energy of what is occurring in the moment with an understanding that the now is informed by what has occurred in the past. This can indicate the core of the current situation needing resolution or understanding. With this rune ask yourself: What lies at the heart of my current situation? What strength or ability can I draw upon at this time? What action or movement is called for today?

Third position: This position represents the future. It is an indication that, given the past and present flow of energies, this seems to be the direction the situation is headed. It is that which is likely to unfold—not that which is guaranteed to occur. This is not a fixed fate, and will shift into a different movement if changes are embraced in the current moment. With this rune ask yourself: Is this an outcome that I am comfortable with? Is this outcome in alignment with my own vision and plans? If not, what might I do to change the outcome?

The Elder Futhark [3]

ᚠ	ᚢ	ᚦ	ᚨ	ᚱ	ᚲ	ᚷ	ᚹ
Fehu	**Uruz**	**Thurisaz**	**Ansuz**	**Raidho**	**Kenaz**	**Gebo**	**Wunjo**
(F)	(U)	(TH)	(A)	(R)	(C, K)	(G)	(W)
Cattle	*Aurochs*	*Thorn*	*Ash Tree*	*Wheel*	*Torch*	*Gift*	*Windvane*
Moveable wealth	Strength	Protection	Divine insight	Journey Passage	Illumination	Talent Contract	Joy
ᚺ	ᚾ	ᛁ	ᛃ	ᛇ	ᛈ	ᛉ	ᛋ
Hagalaz	**Nauthiz**	**Isa**	**Jera**	**Eihwaz**	**Perth**	**Elhaz**	**Sowilo**
(H)	(N)	(I)	(J)	(EI)	(P)	(Z)	(S)
Hail	*Needfire*	*Ice*	*Season*	*Yew*	*Dice cup*	*Elk horns*	*Sun*
Setbacks	Help	Inertia Pause	Harvest Cycles	Endurance	Destiny Existence	Divine protection	Vitality Success
ᛏ	ᛒ	ᛖ	ᛗ	ᛚ	ᛜ	ᛞ	ᛟ
Tiwaz	**Berkana**	**Ehwaz**	**Mannaz**	**Lauguz**	**Ingwaz**	**Dagaz**	**Othila**
(T)	(B)	(E)	(M)	(L)	(NG)	(D)	(O)
God Tyr	*Birch*	*Horse*	*Mankind*	*Lake*	*God Ing*	*Day*	*Home*
Justice Courage	Beginnings	Loyalty Partnership	Society Humanity	Fluidity Emotions	Hearth Fertility	Well-being Dawn	Ancestral wealth Heritage

Further Exploration on Runes

Nordic Runes: Understanding, Casting, and Interpreting the Ancient Viking Oracle by Paul Rhys Mountfort. Destiny Books, 2003.

Northern Mysteries and Magick: Runes & Feminine Powers by Freya Aswynn. Llewellyn Publications, 2002.

Rune by Bianca Luna. Llewellyn Publications, 2012.

Taking Up the Runes: A Complete Guide to Using Runes in Spells, Rituals, Divination, and Magic by Diana L. Paxson. Weiser Books, 2005.

....

3 Adapted from *Magical Alphabets,* Nigel Pennick (York Beach: Red Wheel Weiser, 1992).

Personal Guidance and Intuitive Reflections

January 25: With what animal do you have a particular connection?

January 26: Which animals (if any) are you afraid of?

January 27: What is your sense of your instinctual side?

January 28: Reflect upon a time in your life in which you had a significant animal encounter.

January 29: Meditate upon the rune that corresponds to the first letter in your first name, allowing a picture to emerge from the symbol that speaks to you of its message.

January 30: What is your sense of the difference between higher realms, the underworld, and the earthly plain?

January 31: To which rune symbol are you particularly drawn?

The Solid Hynni of Grounding

When you find yourself in times of uncertainty or upheaval. When your body is struggling and tired. When all around you feels hopeless and dark, this is the time to activate the Hynni of Grounding.

This Hynni symbol represents the groundswell of energy we can draw up into our-selves for strength.

Preparation: Find a spot where you will not be disturbed. You may want to have a set of runes close by. Get into a comfortable position. Place your hands low on your abdomen by the hip bones. Begin to breathe deeply and slowly, visualizing the breath moving in and out of your body as the color red. Be aware of nothing but your breath and allow the tension to fade from your body.

Hynni: Begin to become aware of your body—this body that has carried you through so many experiences. It has been with you from the beginning and will be with you through to the very end. It is yours and it is a miracle. As you breathe, become acutely aware of the movement of your body. The rise and fall of your torso. The sensation of your diaphragm inflating like a balloon. Imagine that each breath is filling you with health and vitality.

Expand your awareness to encompass the earth. Become aware of the breath of the earth—the slight pulse like a minute sigh—and all its wonders. The miracle of its creation. The gift of its abundance. You and the earth are one. Allow this awareness to fill you. Both your body and the earth have the innate capacity to renew. In the times of greatest devastation there still lies the potential for growth. That which seems barren can come to full life once more—sometimes naturally, sometimes with care and attention. Become aware of all the ways you take care of your body, providing it with the nourishment and rest it needs. Your body may even send messages about some of the ways you can care for it differently.

Begin to focus on the grounding symbol, visualizing a golden light that carries the intent of the symbol moving through your hands and into the base of your spine. As you do, imagine the energy of this symbol soothing your fears, allowing any messages of doubt to rise to the surface. Meet those doubts and hear what each one has to say, responding to each doubt with the message "I am safe. I am supported." As you do, feel the unquestioned solidity of your place in the world. All around you may have turned to ash, or this may be a time of uncertainty, but you are here, and that in itself is a miracle. From that miracle all is possible.

With an open heart and open mind, invite an animal guide to come to you. This guide may have a message for you in how it moves through the world physically, through its nature or by what it symbolizes in different traditions. Know that whichever animal guide comes to you, it carries a perfect message for you in this moment.

When you have heard the message from your animal guide and feel filled with strong, healthy energy, begin to bring your focus back once more to the room. Take three deep, centering breaths, allowing each breath to bring you more fully back into the room. When you feel present once more, you may want to touch your feet to anchor yourself in conscious awareness. If you choose, reach into your rune bag and pull out a single rune that can give guidance on what may be of most significance for you to remember at this time of your Hynni meditation.

Part Two

Cycle Two
February 1–March 14

Gifts from the Inner Child
"Love Is the Highest Law"

PRESCRIPTIONS

Go through this section if you are experiencing any of the following:

- Overwhelmed by emotions
- An inability to identify or experience emotions
- Excessive or extreme reactions to current situations
- Difficulty in relationships with others
- Discomfort or shame regarding sexuality

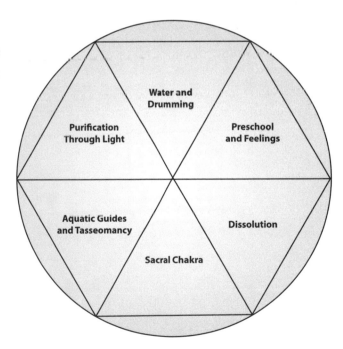

Seven

. . . .

Mythological Reflection on Purification Through Light

For the ancient European peoples, the midway point between the Winter Solstice and the Spring Equinox was a time when the first inklings of the thaw to come were evident. Not just in the ground, but all nature around them began to show evidence of coming back to life. There must have been a feeling of blessed relief to realize that the worst of winter was behind them, and that energy could now be put into preparations for the planting soon to come. Much of the focus at this time was about clearing out the dankness of the dark months. It was the time to air out the living quarters with central hearths, heavy with smoke from the winter months, allowing freshness to waft through once more. Life was opening up and there was flow once more.

The name of the month, February, is derived from the Latin *februa*, which means "purification" or "cleansing." Celebrations at this time focused on the energy of purification and love—seeing the world as new and pure, full of potential and hope. Candles, a symbol of purification, played a large part in the celebrations of this time of year. The delicate light of a candle has always symbolized a beacon of hope in a time of dark—the glow that can cast away all heaviness and nurture the tentative stirrings of expansion.

This was a time of dedication—a recommitment. In ancient times this would be a time for rededication of temples, or a more unconscious dedication to the work ahead—preparing the land for the planting of the coming year's harvest (and may it be a bountiful one!). In contemporary times we too respond to the coming light with hope and optimism. The call of the outdoors speaks to us, and we feel ourselves reawaken. This is a good time to begin to think about what one wants to bring to fruition in the coming year and start to make the initial preparations to manifest that vision.

This is also a time of awakenings and beginnings. It is not just evidenced in the first peeks of life poking through the still cold earth. Animals also respond to the warmth and growing light. The hibernating beasts (and bees) start to stir. Even now we look to the infamous groundhog to tell us if we have truly seen the last of winter's hardship, or whether we still have some weeks of harsh, cold weather ahead. This tradition has its roots in northern Europe, originating with a hedgehog's weather determination and becoming Groundhog's Day in the United States in 1887. In Celtic tradition, the awakened hibernating beast is the snake and is the goddess Brigit, also known as St. Brigid, who meets the snake stating, "I greet the snake and the snake greets me. I will not harm the snake nor will he harm me." As a goddess of healing, smithcraft, and inspiration, she was honored at this time of year with many traditions, including weaving a Brigid's Cross out of wheat that was hung in houses and barns for purification. Many wells and springs were considered sacred to Brigit, and votive offerings to these waters were done in her name.

Main Themes for Cycle 2:
Love
Purification
New beginnings

Ancient Cultural Archetypes of Purification and Love

Hathor *(Egyptian)* is the cow-headed goddess of love and childbirth.
She was the nurturer of the god-child, Horus.

Anuket *(Egyptian)* is the goddess of the Nile and life-giving waters.

Bast *(Egyptian)* is the cat-headed goddess of protection whose festival
was a celebration of joy.

Artemis *(Greek)* or **Diana** *(Roman)* is the virgin goddess who presides over the wild places of nature. The twin of the sun god Apollo, she is a moon goddess. As the goddess of childbirth, she can be called upon for purification, particularly in anticipation of labor.

Aphrodite *(Greek)* or **Venus** *(Roman)* is the goddess of beauty and love in all forms.

Eros *(Greek)* or **Cupid** *(Roman)* is the god of desire. In some myths he is the son of Aphrodite.

Februa *(Roman)* is a goddess of purification.

Coventina *(Roman)* is a goddess of wells and springs.

Brigit *(Celtic)* is the goddess of poetry, healing, and smithcraft. Her domain is the hearth whose fire prepares the healing herbs, forges metal, and inspires poetry through the "fire in the head." Many ancient wells and springs were dedicated to Brigit.

Boann *(Celtic)* is a river goddess who is said to have created the River Boyne by shifting the flow of water in the Well of Segais (the Well of Wisdom). Her lover is the Dagda, the High King of the Tuatha de Danaan tribe and a god of abundance.

Aengus *(Celtic)* is the son of the Dagda and Boann. A god of love and poetry, he saved his lover who had been magically turned into a swan by turning into one himself.

Sulis *(Romano-Celtic)* is a goddess of water and springs, particularly those that one could immerse oneself in in order to heal and purify.

Freya *(Norse)* is the much beloved goddess of birth and fertility. Like Aphrodite or Venus, she was called upon in matters of love, beauty, and sensuality.

Personal Mythological Reflections

February 1: Do you find yourself impacted by seasonal affective disorder?

February 2: How do you respond to new beginnings? Is it with excitement or resistance?

February 3: Reflect on a time in your life when you felt hope and optimism.

February 4: In what ways do you celebrate or acknowledge the release of winter's hold?

February 5: What does purification mean to you?

February 6: How do you prepare yourself for new ventures?

February 7: Reflect on the ways that you are loving to yourself.

Eight

....

Elemental Reflection on Water and Active Reflection on Drumming

Water: Going with the Flow

As much as we are of the earth, we are of the water. It is said the human body is 75 percent water. We rest in the waters of life in the womb before arriving in the world. We live on an earth whose surface is two thirds covered by water. It is absolutely necessary for our survival. Though we can go weeks without food, we can only go days without water.

If we do not have enough water in our systems, it can lead to dehydration, which can be a very serious condition. Symptoms of dehydration include fatigue, dizziness, weakness, and headaches. The cells in our bodies need water in order to function properly and keep us in good health. With sufficient water, a normal, healthy cell can be likened to a grape—round and plump. A 5 percent loss of water in the body is considered to be moderate to serious dehydration, and can result in symptoms of grogginess and nausea. Severe and dangerous levels of dehydration can occur with a 15 percent water loss, causing a myriad of health issues in all parts of our bodies, particularly our vital organs. A loss of more than 15 percent of water in our bodies is usually fatal. There is no question that one of the simplest and best things we can do for ourselves is ensure that we are adequately hydrated.

Water has been used throughout history as a symbol of purification. In ancient times people would travel to sacred wells and springs for blessing or purification. Offerings would be deposited into the water, or ribbons placed on nearby trees to elicit Divine blessing, generally for a specific purpose such as safety in childbirth or regaining health. Immersion into sacred waters was believed to literally wash away the dirt of the soul, allowing the person to arise cleansed anew.

Since 1999 Dr. Masaru Emoto has studied the effects of human consciousness on water and published his findings. Dr. Emoto claims that not just nourishing to the physical body, water crystals actually change their structure depending on the message the crystals contain. The crystals of polluted water look completely different than those of water that has been blessed. Symbolically, water is connected to emotions. Our feelings are meant to flow through us, not become stuck or blocked like logjams that impede progress or cause turbulence. Dr. Emoto's findings link emotions and water far more directly than had been previously thought. Not just symbolic of emotions, water actually carries emotional energy in its very structure. When we imbue water with emotions such as love, compassion, and peace, the concept of holy water takes on a completely different meaning. Traditionally, holy water is water that has been sanctified for use in specific rituals, or for a specific purpose such as protection and healing. Dr. Emoto's research indicates that intention can shift the composition of water to carry the resonance of the intended emotion—a different form of sanctification. This positively charged holy water, whether we drink it in or immerse ourselves in it, is healing and purifying.

Water is the element that flows. It allows for movement in our lives and teaches us how to recognize our own cyclical rhythms.

Messages that help to connect us to the element of water are:
I go with the flow.
I release with ease.
I move through my life with fluidity.
My emotions run clear.
I am cleansed by the blessings that surround me.

 Further Exploration on Water
The Hidden Messages in Water by Dr. Masaru Emoto. Atria Books, 2005.

The Miracle of Water by Dr. Masaru Emoto. Atria Books, 2010.

Water: The Ultimate Cure by Steve Meyerowitz. Book Publishing Company, 2000.

Your Body's Many Cries for Water by Fereydoon Batmanghelidj. Global Health
  Solutions, Inc., 2008.

Drumming

The drum is one of the most ancient of instruments. Even without specific construction, a drum can be created as long as one has something to strike and something to strike with. Any toddler let loose amidst the pots and pans knows this joy. There is something about the sound of a drum that awakens the deeply primal. Deceivingly simple, drums offer the potential for complexity that has touched areas of human interaction from communication to creative expression.

One of the earliest findings of a constructed drum is the alligator drum found in China said to date between 5500 and 2300 BCE. There are many examples found in cultures all over the world of drums constructed of animal skin stretched tightly over a solid material that serves as the base. Different skins, sizes, shapes, and bases produce a fantastic range of sounds. Some common types of drums are bongo, djembe, doumbek, frame drum, and timpani (or kettledrum).

At an indeterminate time in history the realization that one could bind several drums together, allowing one musician to play several drums, thus producing complex sounds and rhythms, becomes evident. The drum kit, that rock and roll standard, came into being as we know it today in 1930s America as musicians experimented with the placement of different size drums. Most of us know the drum as one of the key anchors of any rock song. Just picture the iconic image of a drummer with the sticks held high chanting, "One, two, three, four." Not just the anchor for the band, the driving beat of the drum can connect us to pure emotion. The guitar may thrill us, but the drum captures us. If you ever find yourself bobbing your head or tapping your toe, you have been snared by the drum.

In many ancient cultures the drum was used for distance communication. The beat of the drum pulsed a message that imitated the pitch and inflections of speech across miles from village to village. A particular rhythm of drumming called *shamanic drumming* has become popular in modern times. Shamanic drumming echoes the heartbeat and is a powerful tool to shift our perception, allowing for soul journeying and altered states of consciousness.

Contemporarily there has been a resurgence of drumming circles. To be in a circle of drummers, feeling the group rhythm flow through your body and contributing your own unique beat, carries within it a beautiful teaching about the necessity of the individual in relation to the community of others. It is an experience carried in the body and the soul, requiring little in the way of equipment for participation. Whether as a part of a drumming circle or in solitude, the drum opens up the flow of its rhythms and the sway of our bodies as we become caught up in the beat that connects it to our own heartbeat and the heartbeat of the earth.

Personal Elemental and Active Reflections

February 8: What in your life do you try to control, and where do you allow flow?

February 9: Reflect on a time you spent near water (an ocean, lake, or river) and how that made you feel.

February 10: Are there any bodies of water that make you anxious?

February 11: Have you ever been aware of the beat of your heart, or the pulse of the blood in your body?

February 12: If you could tap your own rhythm, what would it sound like?

February 13: When in your life have you lost yourself to someone else's rhythm?

February 14: Where in your life do you follow your own drumbeat?

Further Exploration on Drumming

Drumming the Spirit to Life: Let the Goddess Dance by Russell Buddy Helm. Llewellyn Publications, 2000.

Sacred Drumming by Steven Ash and Ash Renate. Sterling, 2004.

The Way of the Drum by Russell Buddy Helm. Llewellyn Publications, 2001.

Nine

·············

Developmental Reflection on Preschool Age and Psychological Reflection on Feelings

Three to Six Years of Age

The ages between three and six years old can be a wonderful, adventurous time for children and parents alike. In this stage of development children have the ability to motor under their own power. They are decidedly mobile and infinitely curious. The world has opened up for them and they want to know all about it. They are able to communicate about their experiences and ask questions about the new things they encounter.

It is a joy to see the world through the eyes of children this age. For parents, it is important to be aware of how one responds to this vision and how that is expressed. Children of this age are still very fluid in their sense of time. If they are compelled to sit and stare at a snail for fifteen minutes, that is what they will do. More often than not, parents operate from a different sense of time. With many of life's daily duties needing attention, parents are often caught in a strong awareness of time (i.e., the lack of sufficient amounts of it). Taking fifteen minutes to ponder a snail may bring up feelings of impatience. A parent who is able to carve out the time to plop down beside the child and enter into the snail exploration will be given a gift of wonder. Children also often operate from a place of fearlessness, and this is the time parents need to step in with guidance and boundaries. Messages like looking both ways before crossing the road can feel like a broken record in an attempt to instill a directive of healthy caution in response to a child's innate impulse to explore and find their way in the world.

This is a time of early budding independence and extraordinary learning. Children of this age are beginning to envision who they are and the elements that contribute to that. They are beginning to develop a sense of being male or female, of being like Mom or Dad, of their place in the family, and of what they can do. Often, kids of this age want to muck in and be involved. They don't have a sense of not being able to do something. If Mom is painting, they want to paint. If Dad is gardening, they want to garden. This is a wonderful opportunity for parents to encourage children to contribute and be a part of activities in a directed and age-appropriate way. Involving kids in helpful activities at this age lays the foundation for helpful kids in later ages. It teaches them how to be in the world as they test out what being grown-up is all about, and allows them to explore who they are and what they enjoy.

How often have you been asked the question, "What did you want to be when you were a kid?" This is the age that thoughts, no matter how generalized, about being an adult come into play. Literally. Kids learn through play. The earliest inkling of specific traits, characteristics, and preferences become evident here. This is the age of imagination and fantasy—both extremely important activities for children. If encouraged, these activities evolve into beneficial qualities that enhance problem-solving skills, creative thinking, and visioning as adults. Imagination is an active process of creation that is supported through play. As adults, we can often be surprised by how engaged children become in their play. Give a child a few carved blocks, and within minutes he or she will have built a castle with a whole story revolving around it. Often they can be immersed in that play for hours. This is important work for a child. Many adults have lost the ability to exercise their imaginations, and thus, become stuck when trying to activate change. They literally cannot envision a different scenario. Ask a child to problem solve (i.e., "How are you going to get the dragon from the top of the castle to its cave again?"), and he or she will come up with five different possible options. No matter if the solutions appear to be slightly loopy to adults (i.e., "This hot air balloon will swing down and scoop it up!"), the important thing is that their brains are exploring different possible routes, rather than giving up and saying, "I don't know," which is a refrain often heard in adults.

This is the age of the infamous "Why?" It is an awesome thing to be on the answering end of this question, which children seem able to take to the *n*th degree. Every answer becomes the opportunity for a new version of the why question, and more often than not, there comes a point that the adult simply doesn't have the answer anymore. This is another way that children are exploring the world. They are trying to figure it out and put the building block pieces together. One of the best ways to respond to why questions, especially when they get to that inevitable whacky extreme, is to turn it around. Ask the child, "Why do you think that people have feet instead of flippers?" Guaranteed that child will have an answer.

In healing work there is a very powerful modality called *Inner Child Work*, which helps to address current issues and emotional blocks, by reconnecting one to that aspect of self that still responds to the magic and wonder of the world; that is in touch with his or her own experiences and perceptions of the world; and that is in touch with emotions and not constricted by inner messages of shame. It is this age that, more often than not, carries the imprint and memory of the original pain that set us on the course to disconnection with self and potentially limiting adaptive behavior. Reconnecting to the Inner Child (hearing his or her needs, celebrating his or her vision of the world, encouraging his or her expression of self) opens up a wealth of energy, vitality, creativity, and joy that we can reclaim as our adult selves. This age offers the gifts of exploration, imagination, and curiosity. It opens us to the experience of being in the moment and seizing the full adventure of what that moment offers. All of these are significant attributes to have access to, regardless of how old we are.

Connecting with Your Inner Child

We all have, within us, an Inner Child. This aspect of self may be buried deep below the surface in our unconscious minds, but it still influences us on a daily basis.

- Do you ever have anxiety toward authority figures, including bosses?

- Do you ever have strong emotional reactions to certain situations?

- Do you ever feel ashamed?

- Do you ever stop an impulse in yourself to do something silly or fun?

- Do you ever feel that "should" is the most used word in your inner vocabulary?

All of these (and many more) are indicators that your Inner Child is in there, trying to communicate with you. As adults, rather than take a moment to listen to what that aspect of self has to say to us, we tend to push the feelings away, and enlist well-worn coping mechanisms that, more often than not, have become outdated and dysfunctional. Rather than explore the anxiety, we become timid and self-effacing. In response to intense emotions, we withdraw and cut ourselves off from others. We feel shame and try to please other people. We attempt a myriad of other ways to push the uncomfortable feelings away, effectively shutting our Inner Child behind a door once more.

Connecting to the Inner Child does not mean that we give ourselves license to behave however we want, regardless of consequences. Connecting to the Inner Child does not mean we give ourselves ice cream for breakfast, or stay up until three a.m. watching movies despite having to work in the morning. It does not mean that we confront the police officer who has stopped us for inadvertently speeding with the declarative statement, "You're not the boss of me!"

Connecting to the Inner Child means listening to the deep inner messages, knowing that they have validity. It means allowing for the possibility of making a different choice. It is acknowledging, that in the desire for breakfast ice cream perhaps there has been a lack of joyful experiences in the last while, and looking at other ways to encourage joy in life. Or realizing that, in truth, it is not the police officer you are annoyed at, but the fact that you ignored the inner nudge that told you to slow down. Or soothing the voice of inner anxiety with understanding ("You made a mistake. That doesn't make you a mistake.").

There are many wonderful ways to reconnect with your Inner Child:

- Find a photograph of yourself as a child and display it in a place where you see it often.

- Make a timeline of your life from birth to adulthood, and write down significant life events.

- If you have any childhood mementos (a stuffed animal or picture you drew), bring it out of storage.

- Ask family members what they remember of your personality when you were a child.

- Allow yourself time to engage in fun activities that you enjoyed as a child (climbing, coloring, dancing).

One of the most powerful ways to engage with your Inner Child is through meditation. Breathing deeply into the body, allow yourself to see an image of yourself as a young child, and in meditation, pay attention to how that child responds to you. In a meditative state begin to dialogue with that child, asking him or her about their hopes and dreams, and fears and hurts. Make a commitment to listen to that child, and to validate his or her voice. An adult has an understanding of society's rules of engagement and responsibility. The adult has to be the one, ultimately, making the healthy choice, but taking a moment to allow the Inner Child to express itself is what creates choice rather than obligation. That shift in itself makes a huge difference in how we operate in the world. We all have that Inner Child within us. Embracing that aspect of self and seeing the world through his or her eyes always serves to bring a full spectrum experience to our lives.

 Further Exploration on the Inner Child

A Gift to Myself by Charles L. Whitfield. Health Communications, Inc., 1990.

Healing the Child Within: Discovery and Recovery for Adult Children of Dysfunctional Families by Charles Whitfield. Health Communications, Inc., 1987.

Homecoming: Reclaiming and Championing Your Inner Child by John Bradshaw. Bantam, 1992.

Inner Bonding: Becoming a Loving Adult to Your Inner Child by Margaret Paul. HarperOne, 1992.

Recovery of your Inner Child: The Highly Acclaimed Method for Liberating Your Inner Self by Lucia Capacchione. Touchstone, 1991.

Running from Safety: An Adventure of the Spirit by Richard Bach. Delta, 1995.

Feelings

We live in a world that elevates logic and reason far above emotion and feelings. Ever since philosopher Descartes proclaimed, *"Cogito ergo sum* (I think, therefore I am),"* we have prioritized a rational, deconstructive approach to life, and relegated the murky, irrational emotional realm to the depths. We make decisions based on the evidence before us regardless of what our hearts or guts may be trying to tell us. It is true that we cannot move through the world as raw, exposed emotional nerves, but looking at the current climate with rampant dependence on pharmaceuticals to alleviate anxiety and depression, or even the alarming state of the earth at this moment in history, it appears that appealing largely to reason has not done the trick either.

The issue that philosophers, such as Descartes, had with emotions is that emotions are subjective and mutable. In other words, they can have a tendency to shift with the wind and, as such, are undependable. Several people can have different feelings in response to the same event, so how do we know which feeling is real? To make things even more complicated, as humans we have a preference over feelings themselves. Happy, joyful, uplifted, grateful, and loving are good. Sad, hurt, afraid, anxious, and fearful are bad. We spend a lot of time consciously, or unconsciously, trying to make sure that we fill our lives with the good feelings. We strive to eliminate the possibility of experiencing the bad feelings, even if that means blatantly ignoring when one of the more uncomfortable feelings steps right up to introduce itself. "Hurt? What hurt? Who's hurt? Nobody is hurt here. I'm fine."

It is helpful to remember that feelings are simply energy that have the capacity to move through us, if we allow that flow to happen. They are neither good nor bad, any more than a right foot or left ear is good or bad. Feelings are literally a tool through which we can understand more about ourselves as we view our experience of the world filtered through their expression. If I am aware that I feel anxious every time I approach water, that gives me information about my perception of water—that there is something I find threatening about it. That can actually open me up to learning something I may have forgotten about, perhaps a scary experience around water as a child. The water itself is not bad, nor is the emotion. But listening to the emotion may offer a helpful message. "Remember that time you dove in the water without looking, and the water was shallower than you thought and you cracked your foot on the bottom of the pool? Well, this time, how about enjoying the water but take your time and be safe?" When we are able to listen to the messages of our emotions, it gives us a sense of our own personal growth, including what we have released of old pain.

In order for us to fully experience our lives, we need to be open to a full range of emotions and develop a language around them in order to be clear with ourselves and with others. This is called *emotional fluency,* and it recognizes that the language of emotions is as significant and eloquent a language as any other. If we stumble while walking down the street, crashing to the sidewalk, and respond to the question, "Are you okay?" with the response, "Sure, fine," it likely does not accurately reflect our actual emotional response. It may indicate a disconnection from the inner experience of hurt, confusion, surprise, shock, embarrassment, or anger at the fall, and at the same time, gratitude, wonder, and openness at a stranger's kindness. Humans are complex beings, and we rarely, if ever, experience a single straightforward emotion. Acknowledging this complex of emotions is what contributes to emotional fluency.

Emotions also shift constantly. There are some overarching constants that we can rely on. I can know without a doubt that I love my child. But even within the context of that love, there can be some days when frustration or sadness is far more prevalent. Emotions can shift day to day, even hour to hour. Knowing this helps us to not become too attached to a certain feeling. It is important to honor our feelings and listen to what they have to say, but when you feel them shift, it is also important to allow that to happen. Not to hang on to anger that feels like it is dissipating, for example, because one feels entitled to feel angry or is told one "should" feel angry.

In the exploration of our inner lives, it is the Inner Child who is the keeper of our emotions; the inner aspect of self and our emotions are one and the same. The work of connecting to our Inner Child is literally opening up to embracing our emotional life.

There are hundreds of feelings; however, they tend to fall into certain camps. Designating certain feelings as good and bad (or pleasant and unpleasant) is an initial approach to categorization. In the category of unpleasant emotions, we have the further distinctions of sad, angry, hurt, and afraid. There can be many variations of angry—irritated, frustrated, annoyed, piqued, or furious. And many variations of sad—inconsolable, melancholy, grief-stricken, despairing, bitter. Each of them have a slightly different sense, intensity, and connotation. But it is easy to see how they all fall under the same general umbrella of angry or sad. Similarly, in the category of pleasant emotions, we tend to focus on being happy, but there is a huge range of emotions in this category that uplift, creating an inner sense of optimism and positivity about ourselves, others, and the world.

There is one emotion that does stand apart from the others, a core unpleasant emotion that can be experienced as hooked into or connected to the others. That is shame. Often, when we experience one of the other unpleasant emotions, there is this undercurrent emotion of shame that makes it very challenging for us to begin to explore the initial emotion. We feel anger at a comment someone has made to us that is immediately followed by shame around feeling angry in the first place, or shame around the sense that the comment has validity. One of the complicating factors around identifying the emotion of shame, is that it has become interwoven with the experience of guilt. Often, people refer to feeling guilty, when what they are actually feeling is shame.

Guilt and shame tend to develop in children at the age of three to six years, and these two very different emotions get confused. One can be helpful and directive, and the other is debilitating and soul-destroying.

Guilt is the sense that we have done something wrong. It is our conscience. It helps us to keep our choices and actions in alignment with who we know ourselves to be, and with what we understand to be generally accepted societal rules and guidelines. If you are feeling guilt, ask yourself "What have I done that perhaps I could have done differently? What different choice or action could I have taken?" If there is an answer to these questions, then you are experiencing guilt. Guilt guides us to make amends, or to know that we can make a different choice in the future. It is connected to what we do (our "Doing-ness"), and so it is possible to address it in the world out there.

Shame carries a very different message. It tells us that there is something inherently wrong with us. It is not about a choice we have made, but about who we are (our "Being-ness"). Shame tells us we are flawed, and thus, unlovable. Shame stops us in our tracks and sets the stage for isolating us from others. If you ask yourself the same questions as with guilt, but are not able to identify what different choice or action you could have made, then it is likely you are experiencing shame. It is not about what we have done, but the belief that no matter what we do, we will be rejected. Because we often experience shame as related to other emotions, we are ashamed of ourselves for the feelings we do have. This becomes a very convoluted path. To protect ourselves from feeling shame, we reject or repress other emotions, cutting ourselves off from our authenticity and truth.

We have a natural impulse for self-protection and an innate need to be accepted by others. In many ways this harkens back to survival. We learned early in the evolution of humankind that our survival depended upon being accepted by the group. Isolation was a threat. Psychologically, if we carry a deep, core, inner message that we are flawed (shame), we create ways of ensuring that nobody else is able to see this flaw. On a deeply unconscious level, we do not entertain the possibility that perhaps we are not actually flawed, and test out that hypothesis. Instead, we develop innumerable coping mechanisms to shield us from feeling shame. A coping mechanism is any internal reaction that takes us away from listening to our emotions and/or experiencing shame. There are two main unconscious approaches to protecting ourselves in this way: defenses and subpersonalities.

Picture yourself as a castle. Your inner life, your feelings, and your truth are all represented by this exquisite structure. It is filled with beauty and wisdom that is precious to you, but because you do not trust that others will see it the same way, you need to employ ways and means to keep it safe. You need to employ a defense system.

Defenses are how we keep others at a distance. They are like internal archers on the ramparts and crocodiles in the moat. There are innumerable defenses that we can use for that purpose. There are physical ones, such as isolating and withdrawing, that effectively remove us from the situation that triggers shame ("Pull up the drawbridge."). There are emotional ones, such as using tears or anger, to divert others from seeing what is really going on within ("Ready the archers."). There are mental ones, such as justifying, blaming, intellectualizing, denying, and minimizing, that attempt to control the feeling of shame ("This isn't the castle you want. You want the castle three hectares to the north. This is just a little insignificant castle."). There are even spiritual defenses, such as fantasizing or "blissing out" ("I don't hear barbarians at the gate. I only hear the lovely minstrels."). This is not to suggest that we don't have boundaries. Indeed, knowing where my castle stops and your castle begins is important information to have and respect. However, defenses that stop us from letting people see who we really are need to be addressed for our own emotional health.

When there comes a time that we absolutely must exit the castle walls, we employ subpersonalities (or armor) to ensure we are protected outside our own gates. These are roles we take on to make sure others perceive us in a way we hope will make us acceptable. Many of the roles that are commonly present are familiar, such as: people-pleaser, approval-seeker, perfectionist, caretaker, fixer, and martyr. These are not who we are, but who we allow others to see of us. There certainly can be an aspect of each of these roles that resonates with our inner truth, the part that strives to do our best or that genuinely cares for others. But, with subpersonalities, what others think becomes more important than how we feel. We continue to take care of others long past when we reach our own exhaustion because we are afraid the other person may feel we don't care enough. Or, we push ourselves higher and higher in our goals, never allowing a moment to celebrate what we have already accomplished. We all have to find the role we play in the world, but these subpersonalities often become armor that traps us within, carrying a cost to our own truth and self.

Befriending our emotions, all of them, is integral to knowing ourselves, validating ourselves, and coming to a place of health and wholeness. Owning our emotions allows us to interact with others with openness rather than defensiveness, and authenticity rather than role-playing. In listening to our emotions, we do need to determine whether they are healthy and appropriate given the circumstance. There may be times that we map an old experience with unresolved, unconscious responses upon a new situation. This is the difference between carrying baggage and honoring our story. Our past will always be our past. It is our story, and no amount of denial or rewriting can change that. But, we can eliminate the pain of the emotional charge that remains attached to the past, when we allow the emotions we experienced from the past to flow through and out of us. Connecting to the Inner Child and allowing the old pain to be expressed clears out the emotional silt, allowing the flow of our emotions to run clear and current. Our emotions need to be present and current, responsive to what is in front of us in the moment. It is what underlies true emotional healing.

What Are You Feeling?

Fear	Anger	Guilt	Depression
Pride	Jealousy	Anxiety	Resentment
Envy	Frustration	Shame	Grief
Disappointed	Bored	Irritation	Regret
Sadness	Afraid	Vulnerable	Worried
Embarrassed	Trapped	Misunderstood	Lonely
Empty	Annoyed	Betrayed	Exposed
Apprehensive	Dissatisfied	Disgusted	Fatigued
Certain	Determined	Comfortable	Fascinated
Relaxed	Optimistic	Loving	Joyful
Surprised	Happy	Hopeful	Enthusiastic
Trust	Confidence	Excitement	Contentment
Appreciative	Patient	Sexy	Ecstatic
Optimistic	Tender	Open	Social
Grateful	Relief	Generous	Curious
Awe	Wonder	Expansive	Resolved

Further Exploration on Feelings and Subpersonalities

Discover Your Subpersonalities: Our Inner World and the People in It by John Rowan. Routledge, 1993.

Embracing Ourselves: The Voice Dialogue Manual by Hal and Sidra Stone. New World Library, 1998.

Healing the Shame That Binds You by John Bradshaw. Health Communications, Inc., 2005.

Letting Go of Shame: Understanding How Shame Affects Your Life by Ronald and Patricia Potter-Efron. Hazelden, 1989.

The Language of Emotions: What Your Feelings Are Trying to Tell You by Karla McLaren. Sounds True, 2010.

 Personal Developmental and Psychological Reflections
February 15: Reflect on your earliest memory.

February 16: As a child what did you want to be when you grew up?

February 17: What gave you great joy as a child?

February 18: How were you supported in your hurts and fears as a child?

February 19: How do you experience shame?

February 20: How do you stop yourself from experiencing uncomfortable feelings?

February 21: In what ways do you act with others that feel different from your inner truth?

Ten

Alchemical Reflection on Dissolution

"Its mother is the moon."
FROM *THE EMERALD TABLET*

DISSOLUTION ASSOCIATIONS[4] "THE BLACK PHASE"

Element: Water • **Metal:** Tin • **Planet:** Jupiter
Symbols: Queen, Luna, Green Lion, Goose
Dream Imagery: Floods, acid, baths, drowning, melting, aquatic animals

Often, the first response to the great loss that precipitates calcination is shock. It is a survival response that allows our systems to keep functioning. We are able to go through the motions in a state of disbelief or denial, getting done what needs to be done. We make necessary arrangements, often feeling like we are moving through life like a robot. We feel that what was inside has been reduced to ash and there is no life. *Dissolution* is the first movement toward coming back to life. It is the application of life-giving water to start the process of reanimation.

---

4 Dissolution Associations adapted from *The Emerald Tablet: Alchemy for Personal Transformation,* Dennis William Hauck (New York: Penguin/Arkana, 1999).

Chemically, the stage of dissolution involves bathing the resulting ash with water. It is referenced in the alchemical axiom *"Solve et Coagula* (Latin for dissolve and bind)." When a substance, such as ash, is dissolved in water its crystalline structure disintegrates. Alchemically, this brings it to a purer state (granted in a watery form), which can then be worked on further.

Psychologically, this is the stage of tears. The emotional response to the situation starts to come through. Like water, this can move through us in waves. It is important to allow this ebb and flow to occur, trusting that, however painful it is in this moment, it will pass. In so many cases the impulse is to shut down the feelings. We think we have to be strong and put on a brave front, or we need to shield others from our feelings. There may indeed be situations that are not appropriate to allow our tears free reign. In these situations, the technique of *bracketing* is very helpful. Bracketing is an internal mechanism when we place boundaries around our emotions, acknowledging that they are there and need to be heard, but recognizing that this is not the time. Bracketing tells the emotion "I know you are there, and I will listen to what you have to say in a moment, but right now I need to put you aside." It is very important with bracketing that we do actually go back to the emotion, taking the time to reconnect to what was going on inside when there is a moment to do so. That is the difference between bracketing and "stuffing"; the difference between acknowledging our emotions (when we are able to do so) and repressing them.

Dissolution is connected to the unconscious, the material from the past, and old wounds. Most are familiar with the terms conscious and unconscious, but what exactly constitutes these delineations? And how do they interact with each other?

From a very basic approach, our psyches consist of several different layers. When looking at alchemy as a psychological and spiritual process rather than as a chemical process, it opens us to an awareness of the interaction of all these layers. The alchemical axiom "as above, so below; as within, so without" can be applied psychologically to indicate the awareness of the different aspects on our inner life, and how what we experience inside impacts on how we respond to the world around us. It allows us to begin to experience ourselves as multi-dimensional beings.

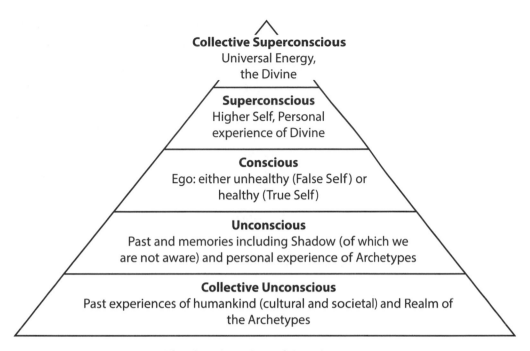

The Five Dimensions of Consciousness.

The *unconscious* (or personal unconscious) is the container of all that we have experienced. We remember absolutely everything, but it is impossible for us to function in the world if we remember everything at all times. The unconscious is the handy storage unit of memory allowing just the most present or salient information to remain in our conscious awareness. There is a subcategory of the unconscious—the shadow. This stores the past material that seemed at some time to threaten us. The shadow consists of what is deemed too painful, what triggers feelings of shame, or what has been rejected by others and so is rejected within ourselves. We store old wounds in our shadow, but sadly, we often shut much of our beauty and strength in there as well. The less we are aware of our unconscious and the shadow, the less we are able to share our True Self with others.

Carl G. Jung coined the term *collective unconscious*, which was as revolutionary in psychoanalytical circles at the time as Darwin's theory of evolution was in his. Jung proposed that, similar to one's personal memories that are contained in the personal unconscious, we as humans carry the traces of all that has occurred since time immemorial in a collective unconscious. Being faced with a huge, snarling dog triggers the fight-or-flight instinct, which is connected to the collective unconscious memories of threat to survival. We don't need to have someone tell us what the best approach in such a situation would be. We don't have to have had a previous personal experience of a huge, snarling dog. When faced with such a situation something deep and instinctive arises in us, and that, Jung would say, comes from the collective unconscious. Not only would I experience the fight-or-flight impulse, but every single human on earth would. Whether I choose to fight or flee is dependent upon my own personal unconscious material, including what I have been taught, what I have observed in others as an acceptable response, or what self-perceptions I carry. It is also in the collective unconscious that we carry the traces of past glories and cultural shame. The pain of slavery may not be the personal experience of a modern African American, but the trace memories of that cultural legacy are carried in the collective unconscious and still have the power to impact on a personal experience. Some also respond to remnant memories of a "Golden Age." The continued fascination with Atlantis and Lemuria may come from this deeply unconscious resonance of a time that we, as humans, lived in harmony and beauty with others and with the earth.

The collective unconscious is the holding place of the archetypes, a subject on which Jung was extremely eloquent. Archetypes in and of themselves are empty vessels. Some key archetypes are: mother, father, lover, child, warrior, ruler, and sage. An archetype does not have a particular presence or energy, and it does not look or act a specific way. It is just a form or a template to be filled with our own impressions. It is not until an archetype moves into our personal unconscious, by becoming activated by our own personal experiences, that it begins to take on a particular shape. As humans, we all contain the mother archetype within us, but my personal experience of mother will be very different than any other person. My experience of mother, from my own mother and from other presentations that I encounter (including books I read or movies I see), allows my mother archetype form to take shape.

Archetypes are extremely complex. They will be filled with both positive and negative perceptions. I may experience mother as both nurturing and suffocating. Both and neither are completely true. What is important is how my perceptions either support me or hinder me. Jung taught that what we do not know of ourselves will insist on making itself known, often in troublesome ways. Self-destructive life choices, nightmares, or problematic relationships are some of the ways that negative archetypal material may manifest in our lives. Healing comes with knowing how the archetype has been activated—what I have filled the vessel with—and releasing negative, limiting associations. This is the psychological alchemical journey to achieving the Philosopher's Stone.

The *conscious* is what we know of ourselves and allow the world to see. The more we are aware of our own depths and complexities, the more our conscious will be a reflection of our True Self. When we close ourselves off to our inner experiences, all we are able to present to the world is a *persona* (subpersonality or false self). It is a mask we show the world. Healing is the movement from false self to True Self, from subpersonality to authenticity. Jung referred to this process as *individuation*. It is the process through which we step into our own individual, unique expression of a human life in the context of living in society with others.

When we are in dissolution we have been dropped into the pool of our unconscious. What is beautiful about this is that we no longer have a two-dimensional self-perception. We know that we are not just the persona we show to the world. There is more to us going on under the surface. It may feel like we are drowning at first, but it is important to allow the process to unfold. If we do not allow our emotional responses to situations of great upheaval to have expression, or if we do not begin to explore the old wounds that have never properly healed, we run the risk of *petrifying*. Rejecting dissolution and turning our emotions to stone will absolutely set the stage for another round of calcination. It is better to take a deep breath and dive into the depths.

There is, in this stage, an underlying message that will become more evident as we continue along the alchemical path of healing. If there are depths that I have not previously explored, then that means there are heights I have not necessarily explored either. Just as it is important for us to develop emotional fluency, and to expand the language that reflects the variations of our emotional experience of the world, it is important for us to develop multi-dimensionality; to see ourselves as multi-faceted and complex, having many varied perceptions of a single event. Yes, this makes life far more convoluted, it takes more time to sort through a response to an event, and it may not be easy, but it is a more accurate reflection.

Though not a recognized term, I have coined the term *collective superconscious* to illuminate the highest vibration of the psyche's experience. It reflects Jung's concept of the collective unconscious, but from the perspective of spiritual, rather than human, experience. The collective superconscious is the Divine, the All, God, Universal Energy. It is the force, movement, and structure that underlie everything in existence. The ancients tended to personify this energy as a way to make it more approachable, and perhaps, understandable. Similar to the archetypes we find in the collective unconscious, there are archetypes in the collective superconscious. The ancients called these the gods. For example, the archetype of justice is reflected in Ma'at *(Egyptian)*, Skadi *(Norse)*, Zeus *(Greek)*, and Jupiter *(Roman)* to name but a few. It is a truth of humankind that we may not agree on what the Divine is, but everyone has a concept of "that which is greater than myself," and it is a sad truth that many lives have been lost because of this. The Divine is what is impossible to put into words, but that we, as humans, have been trying to do for thousands of years.

What we end up describing, instead, is always the superconscious—our own personal experience of the Divine. Just as when we start talking about "what a mother is," we need to know that we speak from our own perceptions that are going to be different than someone else's; when we talk about the Divine, we have moved into our own reflection of what that is. That is not to say that there is not a solid truth to what is Divine, but it is so all-encompassing, that we as humans cannot truly and completely reflect it. If the Divine is "all there is," then the moment I say "it is this," I have drawn a line between what it is and what it is not. And it is All, so I have missed the boat. All I end up describing is my own experience. This is perfectly fine, except when we believe and insist that our own experience is the whole experience. With the superconscious, what we are connecting to are aspects of the collective superconsciousness—values such as empathy, love, understanding, light, forgiveness, and so on. The superconscious gives us access to our Higher Self, which itself connects to the Divine (collective superconscious). The Higher Self contains the blueprint of our own personal lessons, so that we can appreciate an objective perspective on our life's journey. It is this we will explore as we continue along the path of alchemical healing.

At this point along the journey, awash in dissolution after finding yourself flooded with emotion, or experience dropping into the memories of the past, what is needed more than anything is gentleness. We do not benefit from throwing ourselves unprotected into the raging, stormy seas. If anything, this will cause us to instinctively reach for the coping mechanisms we have relied on to keep us safe in the past, even if they are not really working for us anymore. In cases of extreme emotional discomfort, we will employ addictions or other methods of escape. Internet surfing, emotional eating, or compulsive shopping are examples of the many methods easily at hand for taking ourselves out of our emotions, avoiding the stormy seas, and pushing painful emotions back into the murky depths. When we expose a raw wound on our bodies, we don't leave it exposed at risk of further damage, nor do we aggravate it through rough handling. The pain is a message that attention and care is needed. We have a natural response to attend to that wound in the least inflammatory way possible, carefully washing and cleaning out the damaged area. Our emotional wounds require nothing less than the same delicacy and gentleness.

Once we are ready, and the pain has subsided at least a bit, we are ready to take stock of what damage has been done, and what further efforts need to be put forth for full healing to occur. The next stage, *separation*, helps us to begin to enter into the sorting out process. For the time being, in dissolution, all we need to do is to feel.

Personal Alchemical Reflections

February 22: Reflect on a time when you may have shut down your feelings to a situation.

February 23: What words do you associate with the term unconscious?

February 24: Who are the people with whom you share your true feelings?

February 25: Is there anything in your experience that feels "too painful" to look at?

February 26: What are some ways you take care of yourself when it feels you are drowning?

February 27: What have you always wanted to do that you have not allowed yourself to?

February 28: Is there a memory that you would never think of telling anyone?

Eleven

Energetic Reflection on the Sacral Chakra

SACRAL CHAKRA ASSOCIATIONS [5]

Name: Swadhisthana • **Location:** Center of abdomen, below navel
Color: Orange • **Tone:** D • **Gland:** Testicles and ovaries
Body: Sexual and reproductive organs, large intestine, spleen, and bladder
Yoga Path: Tantra • **Symbol:** Six-petalled lotus • **Stones:** Goldstone,
Carnelian, Fire Opal, Orange Calcite

The sacral chakra is located in the center of the abdomen, just below the navel. As with the other chakras from the sacral to the brow chakra, it opens both to the front and the back. It is connected to the digestive system (particularly the large intestine) and the sexual organs.

Physically, a blocked sacral chakra can manifest as frequent urination, lower back pain, menstrual cramps or pain, endometriosis, prostate issues, or groin pain. We often carry fear and anxiety deep in our lower abdomen. The tension caused by carrying this fear can cause clenching and tightening of muscles that results in pain.

The sacral chakra is the seat of our emotions. Being balanced in this chakra does not necessarily mean we have to keep our emotions in check at all times. It means that we are

---

5 Sacral chakra associations adapted from The *Chakra Handbook: From Basic Understanding to Practical Application,* Shalila Sharamon and Bodo J. Baginski (Wilmot, WI: Lotus Light Publications, 1991).

able to accept our emotions, both the pleasant and unpleasant ones. We are able to listen to what they are trying to convey to us, and we are able to let them go once the message has been received. Sometimes that feels like we are being swept away by a certain emotion, but we know that, as we work through it, balance will be restored once again.

This chakra also communicates to us about our feelings toward others. A chakra of relationship, the sacral chakra helps us to honor and recognize the balance between opposites, most eloquently illustrated in the opposing energies of masculine and feminine qualities. This has little to do with whether one is a man or a woman, but rather with energetic qualities. This duality is the first division of the All, beautifully symbolized in the yin-yang image. It denotes the necessary interplay of opposites to create movement: light and dark, reason and emotion, active and receptive, outwardly focused and inwardly focused. There is a dance between these opposites, and in order to achieve wholeness, we need to be well versed in both parts.

The balance of opposites includes understanding the balance between "my perspective and yours." When we are imbalanced in this area, we can become enmeshed with others. Who I feel myself to be flows so directly into another that I lose the differentiation of self. The black and white of the yin-yang becomes, instead, a large grey mass.

One of the biggest issues in the sacral chakra is that of sexuality. It can be such a challenge to accept that we are sexual beings, that we have sexual preferences and to share that appropriately, knowing that our sexuality is as much a part of us as our minds or our spirits. To open ourselves to a sexual relationship with another is to expose ourselves to intimacy and allow ourselves to be vulnerable. If we are shame-based, intimacy is experienced (often unconsciously) as extremely threatening. There is much shame particularly around sexuality in our culture that compounds the issue. Sexuality is meant to be experienced with joy. It is meant to be the human, physical expression of union. Symbolically, it is the resolution of opposites that can open one to the experience of unity. It connects us to the most wonderful of emotions of Spirit, promoting a healthy, flowing sacral chakra.

Messages that help to balance the sacral chakra are:
My emotions help to guide my healthy choices.
I am able to share my feelings with others.
I am comfortable in my sexuality.

 Personal Energetic Reflections

March 1: The color orange makes me feel …

March 2: Have you ever felt that you "lost" yourself in another person?

March 3: How comfortable are you connecting and sharing with other people?

March 4: How do you release tension in your lower back or abdomen?

March 5: Reflect on what intimacy means to you.

March 6: In what ways do you embrace your sexuality?

March 7: Reflect on what it means to you to be a man or a woman.

Twelve

Guidance Reflection on Aquatic Guides and Intuitive Reflection on Tasseomancy

Aquatic Guides

It goes without saying that aquatic guides are at home in the realm of water, although some of them may be as comfortable on the solid earth as they are in watery fluidity. Their ability to thrive in this very different environment gives them a unique perspective, and thus their messages and guidance take on a different slant.

Being at home in the element symbolically associated with the unconscious and emotional realms, these creatures help us to identify and move through what is hidden in our own depths. They can connect us to our hidden fears, our deepest desires, and that which we have kept in the corners of our own unknown. When an aquatic guide comes into your life, spirit is there—in the life-giving waters that enfold and support, regardless of the challenges being faced. They guide us in moving through our emotions, in exploring our creativity, and in bringing wisdom to those aspects of ourselves we have been afraid to recognize. They reflect to us how to be at home, at peace, and to flourish in those environments that are unfamiliar, yet which have an exquisite beauty in themselves.

In many ways, we resonate with those environments that, at first blush, appear to be disconcertingly unfamiliar. Our first home, both from a collective unconscious and a personal unconscious perspective, was water. Billions of years ago some forward-thinking water creature took a tentative foray onto solid ground. Each individual who walks upon this earth made the same journey from the waters of the womb to the solidity of the world outside. Aquatic guides open us to reclaiming comfort in swimming through the waters that we once called home. They reawaken tools for moving through experiences that were once second-nature to us.

Those aquatic guides that are as comfortable on land as they are in water hold a special message. They teach us how to draw upon the interplay of resources that allow ease of movement between the unconscious and conscious aspects of self. They offer insights into the balance between being and doing.

As with animal guides, becoming familiar with the traits and characteristics of an aquatic guide that has presented itself is important. Meditating on your aquatic guide while in its familiar element creates a particularly powerful connection. Baths or pools are wonderful places to meditate with one of these guides. Experiencing the gentle flow of water around your own body brings your own consciousness into alignment with that of your guide, and helps you to flow with their messages.

Some Common Examples of Aquatic Guides

Alligator Balance of doing and observing	**Barnacle** Tenacity, Obstacle	**Beaver** Industry, Teamwork, Protection	**Clam** Digging deep for answers
Conch Spiritual calling	**Crab** Intensity, Emotional release	**Crayfish** Moving forward in spite of fear	**Dolphin** Rhythm, Freedom
Eel Creative life force	**Frog** Transformation, Adaptation	**Goldfish** New opportunities	**Hermit Crab** Freedom, Mobility
Hippopotamus Intuition, Protection of young	**Jellyfish** Acceptance, Faith	**Koi** Peace, Prosperity	**Leech** Detoxifying, Trust hidden processes
Lobster Ability to transcend	**Manatee** Gentle, Loving, Childlike	**Manta Ray** Taking it slow, Knowing differences	**Octopus** Skilled in many things, Evasion
Orca Grace, Strength, Freedom	**Otter** Playfulness, Curiosity, Creativity	**Platypus** Value of uniqueness, Belief in improbable	**Porpoise** Good fortune
Salmon Wisdom, Persistence	**Sea Dragon** Wonder, Magic	**Seahorse** Patience, Grace, Balance	**Seal** Play, Imagination
Shark Survival, Reactive response	**Starfish** Regeneration	**Walrus** Individual, Fierce mask	**Whale** Creativity, Listening to own song

Tasseomancy

Tasseomancy (also sometimes known as tasseography) is the specific method of divination that looks for symbolic meaning through sediment left in cups from tea leaves, coffee grounds, or other liquid beverages. As a form of divination, tasseomancy is fairly new. There is some evidence that its roots lie in the fourteenth and fifteenth centuries with European fortunetellers who read the splatter of wax. In the seventeenth century China introduced tea to Europe, and tea leaf reading soon followed. Cultures in areas of eastern Europe that developed more of a taste for coffee than tea, developed a method of reading coffee grounds instead.

With either tea leaf or coffee ground reading, the individual drinks from the cup until a small amount of liquid is left where the sediment floats. The cup is turned upside down on a saucer and turned three times to loosen the sediment in the liquid. The cup is then turned upright again, and the resulting patterns are searched for recognizable simple forms or shapes.

Traditionally, cups are read clockwise, from the handle spiraling out and down to the bottom of the cup, with the symbols found nearest the handle at the top of the cup indicating the present, and those at the bottom of the cup indicating the far future. The handle itself represents the current day. Some readers divide the circle of the cup into twelve, giving a yearly structure to the reading. Other readers forego the importance of timing and read the symbols close to the rim of the cup as having more importance than those closer to the bottom of the cup.

In the late nineteenth century special cups designed specifically for tea leaf reading were produced in England and the United States. These beautiful cups are marked with positional placement for ease of reading.

There is an element of ritual involved in tasseomancy that makes it a particularly beautiful method through which to receive guidance and messages. The requirement of taking the time to drink the beverage before beginning the reading allows the space for entering into communion with one's Higher Self. The pause is an invitation for reflection, each sip bringing one into close connection with one's inner worlds. Once the beverage has been consumed and one is ready to begin to discern the symbols, there is often a peace and inner calmness that comes from having taken the time to open up to intuitive eloquence.

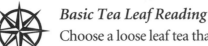

Basic Tea Leaf Reading

Choose a loose leaf tea that you enjoy and make yourself a cup of tea, letting the leaves float free in the boiling water. When the tea has steeped and cooled, take your time enjoying your tea, holding the intention of connecting to your Higher Self and intuitive guidance.

If there is a particular issue or situation you would like clarity for, allow yourself to ponder that situation as your drink your tea. I find the best method is to focus on clearing my mind of anything specific, trusting that the Divine knows what I need far better than I can possibly consciously know. What I need to know, the Divine will reveal.

When there is just a little tea left in the cup and the liquid is mostly made up of the leaves, place the cup upside down on a saucer and turn the cup clockwise three times. You can place a napkin on the saucer to catch any remaining liquid. After the turns replace the cup in an upright position. You are then ready to begin reading.

If your cup has a handle, begin there. Work clockwise around the cup, making note of any symbols you see. The cup can be approached as a cycle, seeing the area closest to the handle as closest to this moment and moving away from the handle into the future. Pay attention to whether the symbol appears near the rim, the middle, or near the base of the cup. Symbols near the rim indicate the presenting situation, symbols near the middle of the cup indicate influences on the situation, and symbols near the base of the cup indicate possibilities of outcome.

Tea leaf reading is very subjective. There are no right or wrong answers. What is important is how the symbol speaks to you. Relax into the enjoyment of the experience, and let your imagination and intuition flow.

Some Common Tasseomancy Symbols

Acorn Success	Angel Positive messages	Anvil Effort, Industriousness	Apple Achievement	Bean Financial concerns
Bell Unexpected news	Birdcage Obstacles	Boomerang Treachery	Bouquet Love	Bridge Opportunity
Chair Visitor	Clover Prosperity	Crescent Journey	Dot Amplifies nearby symbols	Egg Prosperity
Fairy Enchantment, Joy	Foot Decision	Flag Warning	Hand Friendship	Hoe Hard work
Horn Abundance	Key New openings	Knife Broken relationships	Lock Obstacle	Number Indicates time frame
Oar Worry	Pear Comfort	Pillar Support	Pyramid Solid success	Question Mark Hesitancy
Rainbow Happiness	Spoon Generosity	Steps Improvement	Table Gathering	Telescope Adventure
Umbrella Shelter	Urn Wealth	Wheel Completion	Wishbone Desires come true	Wreath Happiness

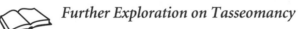

Further Exploration on Tasseomancy

Tea Leaf Reading Guide: What You Already Know by Sandy L. Pitzel. Outskirts Press, 2011.

Your Future in a Cup: Channeling with Coffee Grounds—A Beginner's Guide to Divination by Magzcha Westerman. Trafford Publishing, 2005.

Personal Guidance and Intuitive Reflections

March 8: Do you have an affinity to a particular fish, water mammal, or sea creature?

March 9: How do you respond to unfamiliar environments?

March 10: Are there any aquatic animals you fear or to which you have a strong aversion?

March 11: Do you respond differently to creatures that live on both land and water to those that live in water alone?

March 12: Reflect on what simple symbols you are aware of that show up in your life.

March 13: How might a single symbol mean numerous different things?

March 14: How might consecutive symbols tell a story?

The Loving Hynni of Ebb and Flow
When you find yourself in times of intense emotion. When you are flooded with memory or waves of feeling. When all around you feels in flux, this is the time to activate the Hynni of Ebb and Flow.

This Hynni symbol represents the gentle movement of waves that carry us through times of chaos.

Preparation: Find a spot where you will not be disturbed. If it feels right, this hynni is best experienced in water, such as a bath or pool. Create a soothing atmosphere with subdued lighting. If you choose, prepare a cup of loose leaf tea, making sure there is a saucer handy. Begin to breathe deeply, visualizing the color orange. Allow any tensions in your body to slip away. Allow the refreshing energy of orange to fill your every cell. Take some time in this inner space, sipping your tea and connecting to your inner being. When you get near the bottom of the tea, turn the cup upside down on the saucer, turn it three times counter-clockwise, and turn it upright again. Make note of the first three symbols you discern in the pattern of the leaves and put the cup aside.

Hynni: Bring your awareness to your lower abdomen, placing your hands just above your pelvic bones. As you breathe, connect with the flow of your body. Be aware of the blood coursing through your entire system, and the pathways that allow it to reach every single part of you. See the blood that flows as vital and healthy, nourishing and strengthening you.

Gradually expand your awareness to encompass the earth. Reach out with a sense of flow to the streams, rivers, lakes, and oceans. Allow yourself to be taken on a journey from the tiniest brook to the most magnificent waterfall, exploring above-ground waterways and hidden subterranean passageways. You are a drop, and yet you are part of the whole network of water that brings nourishment to all forms of life.

Become aware of any places in your body that feel stuck or blocked. What does it feel like in that space in your body? What emotions are you aware of flowing through that part of you? As you become more aware of this energy, contemplate the three symbols that appeared to you. What messages might they have for what is going on within you at this time? What insights or new perspective might they offer? Allow yourself to explore both the current connections and how those connections might have relevance to what has happened in the past, and what may still have a hold on you.

Begin to visualize the ebb and flow symbol, visualizing a golden light that carries the intent of the symbol moving through your hands into your abdomen. As you do, feel the messages of love and acceptance for all you are, all you do, all you hope to achieve, and all you have attempted in the past. Be aware of any hindrances to the flow—any shards of anger or hurt, any shoals of resentment or betrayal. Allow the watery flow of the hynni to pulse over the sharp spots with love, gently washing them away.

With an open heart and open mind, invite an aquatic guide to come to you. This guide may have a message for you in how it moves through the world physically, through its nature, or by what it symbolizes in different traditions. Know that whichever aquatic guide comes to you, it carries a perfect message for you in this moment.

When you have heard the message from your aquatic guide and you feel filled with gentle, loving energy, begin to bring your focus back once more to the room, the bath, or the pool. If you are in water, you may want to splash a little to bring your presence fully back to your body. Know that any negativity or blocks you may have held have drained away, and that you come to conscious awareness truly cleansed and purified once more.

Part Three

Process Phase One
March 15–21

Waxing Moon:
Innocence and Openings
"Experience the Adventure"

PRESCRIPTIONS

Go through this section during any Waxing
Moon Phase or if you are experiencing any
of the following:

- Cynicism
- Inability to start a new project
- Anxiety around new beginnings
- Overwhelmed with responsibility
- Lack of joy for life

Thirteen

Waxing Phase of Innocence and Openings

There is an energy of hope and optimism at the beginning of each moon cycle. The delicate arch of the new moon that hangs in the sky, waxing quickly into crescent, holds the promise of how it will be filled and with what. It is a pure potential holding space for the full moon to come.

The waxing moon is symbolized by the Maiden, that youthful energy that is autonomous and free unto herself. This concept comes from a time when crossing the threshold of menarche placed a weight of responsibility upon a woman's shoulders—childbirth and rearing. The Maiden is sometimes referred to as the virgin. This is not a reference to her sexual innocence, but means "beholden to no man." The Maiden is still guided by her inner compass, and is free to follow where her heart guides her.

The waxing moon inspires us to connect with a sense of adventure and curiosity. It is the ability to see the potential of what can be created and to allow our imaginations to soar. Later in our lives, when we have been buffeted by the winds of experience, we can sometimes look back on the time of youth with yearning. For many, it is a time of innocence and care-free engagement with the world. Concerns are not overly pressing, and days seem to stretch, for better or worse, depending on what lies ahead and what we are anticipating.

The archetypal energy in this phase reflects the excitement of new beginnings infused with enthusiasm to see what the future will bring. It is the time to explore dreams and plans, unencumbered by shoulds and oughts. The sight of the slowing, growing moon in the sky guides us to see the slow progress in our own goals and ventures. It takes time to bring dreams to fruition, and as we continue to move through the waxing phase to fullness, concretization and fine-tuning will occur.

It all starts with a dream.

Main Themes for Process Phase 1:
Autonomy
Innocence
Curiosity

Ancient Cultural Archetypes of Innocence

Artemis *(Greek)* or **Diana** *(Roman)* is a moon goddess of the wilderness and wild animals. She is Apollo's twin sister—the moon to his sun.

Hebe *(Greek)* or **Juventas** *(Roman)* is the daughter of Zeus and Hera whose role was to serve ambrosia to the gods of Olympus.

Persephone *(Greek)* or **Proserpina** *(Roman)* is the daughter of Demeter who, when gathering flowers in a field, was taken by Hades to be his wife in the underworld. She is also referred to as Kore, which simply means "maiden." Persephone bridges a dual role, stepping into Maiden in the spring and becoming Queen of the Underworld in the fall.

Selene *(Greek)* or **Luna** *(Roman)* is a moon goddess whose name means "the moon."

Blodeuwedd *(Celtic)* is a spring goddess created out of flowers by the magician, Gwydion, to be the wife of Lleu Llaw Gyffes. She too fulfills a dual role. An encounter with Gronw Pebr, and all that transpires from that, leads to punishment by Gwydion who turns Blodeuwedd into an owl. As "flower face" she embodies acquiescence, and as the owl she represents hard-won wisdom found in the dark.

Personal Waxing Phase Reflections

March 15: What dreams for your life did you have as a child or teenager?

March 16: What activity or activities did you love most as a child or teenager?

March 17: What messages about the world do you remember believing as a child or teenager?

March 18: Reflect on an adventure you experienced when you were young, and what opened you to that experience.

March 19: What do you do purely for the experience itself without any attachment to goal or outcome?

March 20: In what ways have you become jaded or cynical?

March 21: If you had the potential to achieve anything you wanted, what would it be?

The Joyous Hynni of Openings

At the cusp of a new venture. When you are exploring new ways of being. When you feel the need for a burst of optimism, enthusiasm, or openness to embracing the adventure of life, this is the time to activate the Hynni of Openings.

This Hynni symbol represents the sliver of new possibility and the potential for how it will be filled.

Preparation: Find a spot where you will not be disturbed and eliminate all possibility for distraction. Get into a comfortable position. Begin to breathe deeply and slowly, focusing on the breath moving in and out of your body. Allow the tension to fade from your body. Be aware of nothing but your breath.

Hynni: As you breathe feel yourself become lighter, the years dropping away from you. With each inhale connect with any situation or experience that has, at some point in your life, weighed you down. Perhaps you have experienced a great hurt or a relationship that shifted how you view the world in some way. Hold space for each of these moments, and as you exhale, release them. Feel the energy they held in your body dissipating, creating a space of openness and potential instead.

As you breathe, releasing any heaviness from the years of experience, you find that images of yourself in youth come more and more to the fore. Perhaps a favorite, secret spot or your room when you were growing up. Begin to focus on the energy of your youth. What you looked like, what you were interested in, and the people with whom you engaged, such as close friends and confidants. As you begin to resonate with the energy of your youth, connect with the sense of three qualities that feel reflective of this energy. Some examples are:

- Adventurous

- Trusting

- Inquisitive

- Fearless

- Confident

- Carefree

- Resilient

- Optimistic

- Fun-loving

Focus on the three qualities you resonate with the most, and breathe them into expansion in your body, starting with your toes and moving all the way up to your head. Feel the pulse of these energies filling every corner and every cell, energizing and revitalizing you.

These qualities are a part of you. They have been there in the past and they are here in the now. From this space reflect on a current situation that may be challenging you. Where in your life currently do you feel discouraged, defeated, drained, or stuck? Where in your life do you need new vision or an opening to a new approach? Allow the whole sense of that situation to unfold, but through the lens of the qualities that now move through you. Be aware of how your response shifts in this light. Pay attention to any messages that arise for new pathways or methods of approaching the situation are open to you that you may not have seen before.

Place your hands on your heart, and begin to focus on the openings symbol, visualizing a golden light that carries the intent of the symbol moving through your hands and into your heart. As you do, feel the expansive unfolding of possibility, creativity, and hope flow from you in waves. From this place life is an adventure and there are no mistakes. Only the joy of discovery.

When you are ready, take three deep, centering breaths and open your eyes, filled with the promise of potential.

Part Four

Cycle Three
March 22–May 2

Nurturing Empowerment
and Self-Esteem
"You Are Whole Within"

PRESCRIPTIONS

Go through this section if you are experiencing any of the following:

- A shaky sense of self-esteem
- Inflated guilt over little incidents
- Challenges or uncertainty while in the company of others
- Feeling not in control of one's own life or choices
- An inability to establish healthy boundaries

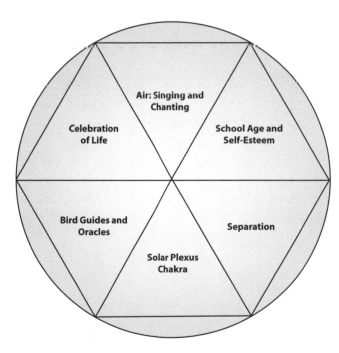

Air: Singing and Chanting

Celebration of Life

School Age and Self-Esteem

Bird Guides and Oracles

Separation

Solar Plexus Chakra

Fourteen

Mythological Reflection on the Celebration of Life

There may be snow on the ground, and even thoughts of a last blast or two of winter weather coming in, but there is a definite turn in the air. By this time in the year we know a corner has decidedly been turned, and there is renewed positivity of warmth and ease. The melting of the ice sparks a melting inside, inspiring festivals celebrating life springing forth once more.

The Spring Equinox marks a time when day and night are in equal balance. From a symbolic perspective it is the triumph of life over death. We can now feel the difference in the sun's strength, and at this point in the sun cycle, we know that the days to come bring more light than dark. The reawakening of life is evident in nature all around. In ancient days before controlled production, eggs became readily available at this time. The increased daylight hours trigger hens to begin laying, as left to their natural biochemistry, hens will not produce eggs when there is less than twelve hours of sunlight. In the past this in itself was cause for celebration—a welcomed change to root vegetables and scarce meat supplies. This may contribute to the meaning behind the significance of eggs and their use in celebrations at this time of year. As a symbol of fertility, there is a long tradition of coloring or burying them, beckoning forth intentions of prosperity and abundance. The Spring Equinox also marks the return of the bees from dormancy—another promise of new life. The fruit trees touch us with their beautiful flowers and delicate, sweet scent bringing visions of the fruit laden branches to come.

Many myths associated with this time focus on regeneration, resurrection, and renewal. The celebrations contain the implicit message of reliance and resourcefulness, the ability to deal effectively with challenge, and to withstand whatever obstacles have stood in one's path. Oftentimes the descent to the underworld (the cold hand of winter) has required sacrifice. The beauty that abounds at this time of year is a testament that the sacrifice has been worth the effort. The hard-won knowledge acquired is that one does have the capacity of strength within to be equal to the task of the work in coming months. With that knowledge comes renewed energy and an eagerness for what lies ahead.

Many of the ancient tales give us the image of the Green Man. That iconic face, surrounded by or made from leaves, is most often recognized in contemporary times as a garden plaque or containing a spout for a garden fountain. As with any archetype, this particular energy is known by many names, depending on the culture. He has been Cernunnos, Herne, Pan, Jack in the Green, John Barleycorn, and Robin Goodfellow, to name a few. The underlying truth that connects them all is that the Green Man represents reawakened life and the return of vegetative abundance. It is the recognition of reawakened life within that provides the receptive foundation to build upon. With attention, work, and effort in the days to come abundance is sure to be the culmination. At this time we celebrate that opportunity.

Main Themes for Cycle 3:
Renewal
Resurrection
Preparation

Ancient Cultural Archetypes of Reawakened Life

Pan *(Greek)* or **Faunus** *(Roman)* is a nature god connected with flocks, wild places, and rustic music.

Eos *(Greek)* is a goddess of the dawn.

Sylvanus *(Roman)* is a nature god connected with woods, fields, and flocks.

Aurora *(Roman)* is a goddess of the dawn.

Flora *(Roman)* is a goddess of spring and flowers.

Maia *(Roman)* is a goddess of spring and rebirth. Her name means "she who brings increase."

Cernunnos *(Celtic)* is a god of nature and fertility.

Eostre *(Germanic)* is a spring and fertility goddess. Her name gives us the English word for Easter.

Iduna *(Norse)* is a goddess of youth and spring whose name means "she who renews."

Personal Mythological Reflections

March 22: What makes you feel alive?

March 23: Reflect on lessons you learned from a time of hardship or obstacle.

March 24: What qualities of strength do you recognize in yourself?

March 25: In what ways do you celebrate having come through a challenge?

March 26: What sacrifices have you made in your life to achieve a goal?

March 27: Reflect upon what you wish to "plant" for future fruition.

March 28: In what ways do you prepare yourself for change?

Fifteen

Elemental Reflection on Air and Active Reflection on Singing and Chanting

Air: The Fresh Breeze of Clarity

If there is one element that connects us to this season it would be air. We feel the shift in temperature in the breezes that blow across our skin. We feel compelled to open windows and doors to allow the air to move through that has felt shuttered and stifled. Air is the great clarifier. It animates that which has become still, brushing away the cobwebs, clearing out the stagnant, and bringing fresh perspective.

If breath is what connects us to our bodies, it is through the medium of the element of air. Air animates us and helps bring us to a sense of center within ourselves.

The element of air is about differentiation and discernment. It is associated with the mind and our ability to see past the illusions (or cobwebs) that have cluttered our thinking. In tarot air is associated with the suit of swords, which is the tool of differentiation. From a symbolic perspective, a sword cuts away what is useful from what no longer serves. We carve away the unwanted bits, so that what remains is that which serves to enhance and support our purpose. Air has a similar ability to move in whatever direction it needs or chooses. It is, for the most part, unencumbered and can explore in whichever area suits the need. It can focus on the healthy or the unhealthy, the helpful or the hindering.

With its ability to move great distances with great force and speed, air connects all in this world in a very different way than water or earth. There are many islands with wondrous flora because of what has been carried across expansive waters on the wind. It is this transporting quality that links air with the bridge of communication. Through touch we connect earth-wise. Through tears we connect water-wise. But with the words that travel from us to another through the element of air, we connect air-wise, creating sounds that carry our message to another via our breath.

Discernment, clarity, choice, and communication are all embodied in the element of air.

Messages that help to connect us to the element of air are:
I communicate clearly.
I am open to a fresh perspective.
I am able to discern the truth.
I experience freedom in my life.

Singing and Chanting

Using the air in our bodies to create sound is a wonderful way to connect to the element of air. Our bodies themselves become instruments when we pull air across our vocal chords creating different tones, notes, and nuances of intensity.

Sound has been used to transform, inspire, and uplift for centuries. One can imagine that, at the very dawn of humankind, if one could make sound to communicate, one would make sound to celebrate. Intentional sounds, such as chanting or toning, have the ability to create an altered state of consciousness allowing us to rise above the physicality of our bodies and experience a higher vibration—a connection to spirit. As such, sound has been used both as a healing tool and as a means through which to connect with the Divine. Even listening to such sounds, as opposed to creating them, has the ability to shift our consciousness, impact our energy, and heal us.

There are three main modes of working with sound, from the simplest to increasingly complex. Even within those three delineations there can be extraordinary and beautiful levels of complexity.

Toning is a method of holding a single, prolonged note. In Eastern tradition, certain notes are associated with the different chakras, along with seed sounds or vowel sounds, which resonate with the particular chakras and help to clear any blocks we may hold in those centers. Often, different vowels evoke different experiences in us and we can utilize those nuances intentionally. A round, thrumming type of vowel (ooooh) resonates on a deep level, bringing us more into our bodies and to a connection with the earth. A high, squeaky type of vowel (eeeee) tends to feel lighter, bringing us out of our bodies. It is interesting to play with different notes and sounds to get a sense of what effects they have physically and emotionally.

Chakra Toning Chart

Chakra	Note	Seed Sound	Vowel Sound
Root	C	Lam	"oh" (as in "rope")
Sacral	D	Vam	"ah" (as in "dot")
Solar Plexus	E	Ram	"o" (as in "rose")
Heart	F	Yam	"ah" (as in "father")
Throat	G	Ham	"eh" (as in "pet")
Brow	A	Ksham	"ee" (as in "see")
Crown	B	Om	"m" (as in "hem")

Toning is the most abstract of the vocal methods, and a beautiful way of working with breath and air. To tone, simply inhale, and on the exhale allow the breath to leave your body riding on the wave of a certain note, while wrapped around the energy of a certain sound. Allow the tone to sustain as long as it takes your breath to be expelled.

Chanting can be considered more formalized toning. A chant is a combination of repetitive tones and sounds (words). Chants can be very short and simple, involving limited notes and a simple core concept expressed in few words, or they can be highly complex structures, consisting of multiple layers and musical phrases. Chanting has been a part of spiritual practice for centuries. In Western culture, the best known example is that of the "Gregorian Chant" practiced in the Roman Catholic Church in the ninth and tenth centuries. Contemporarily, we tend to be more familiar with the tradition of Eastern Buddhist chants. Chants are a large part of Pagan celebration, and there are many simple, well-known chants that are fairly easy to find on compact disc. One of the best ways to work with chants is to create your own, writing words of meaning and playing with sounds that resonate with the energy of the words.

Singing takes the combination of notes and words to yet another high level of complexity. The variations of songs are truly endless, and different genres of songs touch us in different ways. As William Congreve said, "Music hath charms to soothe a savage beast, to soften rocks, or bend a knotted oak." Singing has more of a tendency to take soundwork out of the impressionistic and symbolic into the more realistic and concrete. We sing words that connect us to all the shades and examples of life's experience. Singing, or its nonverbal counterpart, humming, is often an expression of an uplifted Spirit. As such, it can also be used as a tool to uplift and cheer the Spirit when the weight of sadness or depression sinks in. Some songs connect us to memories of the past, filling us with the happiness or melancholy for times gone by. Music is evocative and always has the power to shift our internal experience.

Working with sound adds emotional energy to intention. If we are holding a vision of manifestation, creating a chant or song around that vision and sending that vision upward to the universe with our voice through music connects us emotionally to that vision. If you are drawn to work more simply, toning a particular word repeatedly can create the same, powerful resonance as chanting or singing. For example, if you want to foster the energy of strength in response to a certain situation, toning the word "strength" will cue the unconscious to fill you with that energy. With each toning of the word, you will feel strength build within or you will become more aware of what other qualitative patterns may be interfering. Perhaps a shimmer of fear arises with each tone. This is important information to encounter, as you can then take a moment to address what the fear may be about, determining the best way you may have to release it, before moving into the toning once again. As with ripples on water, the more we tone, chant, or sing, the more the sound waves ripple through the airwaves, creating amplification and resonance.

Though working with sound definitely connects us to the throat chakra with the focus on our personal expression, it is our solar plexus chakra that is exercised with soundwork. To create effective force behind the toning, chanting, or singing, we must engage the diaphragm, expelling the air from the depths of our bellies. This activates the solar plexus chakra, connecting us to the core of our own beings and centering us in ourselves. Working with sound boosts confidence, releases emotional pain, combats depression, and can reduce stress. The simplest ditty remembered from childhood can have a positive impact on all aspects of being, and the most complex symphony can awaken the transcendent experience of awe.

 Further Exploration on Singing and Chanting

The 7 Secrets of Sound Healing by Jonathan Goldman. Hay House, 2008.

The Healing Power of Sound: Recovery from Life-Threatening Illness Using Sound, Voice, and Music by Mitchell L. Gaynor, M.D. Shambhala, 2002.

The Yoga of Sound: Tapping the Hidden Power of Music and Chant by Russill Paul. New World Library, 2006.

Personal Elemental and Active Reflections

March 29: Reflect on a time when you felt compelled to engage in a cleaning-out process or cleanse.

March 30: When faced with a difficult situation do you respond with heaviness, or are you able to move with ease through several possible scenarios to address the situation?

March 31: How clear is your communication about who you are or what you need?

April 1: Reflect on a song you remember from childhood and how it made you feel.

April 2: What resistances to singing do you hold?

April 3: When you sing are you aware of your feelings?

April 4: What songs do you associate with special or significant times in your life?

Sixteen

Developmental Reflection on School Age and Psychological Reflection on Empowerment and Self-Esteem

Seven to Thirteen Years of Age

These years of development see a shift from a family-oriented interaction to more exposure to society at large. Traditionally, this is the age that children move from spending the majority of their time in the family home and being cared for by parents or family-oriented caregivers, to entering a school environment and being exposed to the guidelines of group interaction on a larger scale. Over the decades, with the increased need for double-income families, this has changed. By necessity there is more of a dependence on day care. Children are being enveloped into group social interactions at a younger age. Regardless of the external circumstances of childcare and preschool social environments, there is a physical change that occurs around this age that marks the definitive entrance to a new stage of development.

Anthroposophy (developed by Rudolph Steiner) considers the onset of the loss of baby teeth as an indication that children have shifted in their capacity to learn on a different level. Steiner proposed that up to age seven, children learn primarily by empathy through direct engagement with the world and through play. As such, more formalized teaching is inappropriate and counter-effective. At around age seven children enter a different developmental stage indicated biologically by the loss of baby teeth. From this age to puberty, children learn through their feelings and imagination, allowing for a deep connection with the material on a visceral level. According to this theory, it is not until puberty that children are able to learn though critical thinking and application of the abstract concepts.

In this stage children are exploring their ability and competence. They have gained a certain level of autonomy from parents, and through this, they are able to get a sense of what they are capable of, making certain age-appropriate choices and beginning to put their own stamp on the world. A child of this age can certainly choose what clothes to wear or how to decorate a bedroom. Even certain simple meals and tasks can be delegated: making his or her own bed, feeding the family pet, or being responsible for certain household chores. This perspective is underpinned by the belief that we, as humans, have an innate desire to engage with the world and to experience ourselves as making a difference. We need to know that we are worthy simply because we are here. If this belief has been firmly established in our early years, it provides a solid foundation that we are able to stand as "human doings," taking pride and ownership in our ability.

When children move into a formalized school setting, there is an important shift that occurs. The underlying message in the educational system is that children are now being taught the information and the tools they will require when they move into the adult world. Part of the bump many children experience upon entering the school system is a bump of relevancy. How many parents have heard, "When am I ever going to need to know the capital of Liechtenstein?" Or, "Why do I need to memorize the multiplication table when there is a calculator on my cell phone?" There can be merit to these questions. If one looks at the development of the educational system as tied to the development of industrialization, the focus of education is about instilling standardized information—a factory-line type of approach to pedagogy. This does not necessarily take in the individual needs of each child, nor can it accommodate highly creative approaches to teaching. Many areas of education are looking at the limitations of an educational system that was created when the world looked very different than it does today. Beyond the possible limitations of the current public education system, the message being conveyed to children is "You are being offered exposure to a world that is larger than your home and neighborhood," and "You are being offered tools that can be applied in a broader context when you reach adulthood." Perhaps it is not about memorizing the capital of Liechtenstein, but about realizing that each country has a recognized center and how different each of them is! Perhaps it is not about getting to a final, correct numeric response, but knowing how to rely on one's inner resources to find answers. The education system provides a context for new learning opportunities, and so provides a canvas so that children can test their ability, develop new skills, and begin to see themselves as part of a larger world.

The school environment also provides an opportunity to learn negotiation with others that is of greater emphasis than in earlier years. Being in a class with many other children requires the development of social skills and cooperation. This can, at times, provide more of a challenge even than the material being taught. Many children struggle with group projects, not knowing how to balance input and teamwork. Again, an oft-heard complaint is, "We were given a group project and I had to do all the work." How to balance self with others can be a challenge. Learning how to communicate, compromise, or stand up for oneself if need be are all skills that can only be learned in the context of a group. A school environment provides situations for these skills to be developed. They are imperative in order to achieve successful interdependence and collaborative abilities in adulthood.

What can be a challenge to a child moving into a greater social structure is the potential for the implied coercion to conformity; that our sense of self and innate uniqueness and individuality needs to be repressed in order to function in a group. This is a dicey area as it is impossible in an educational setting for any teacher to give absolute, one-on-one attention to a group of thirty-plus children. There needs to be generalized guidelines that apply to all. But this does not mean that our individuality is of no importance. It is about finding the means through which to honor self in the context of the whole. This is a significant life lesson. Moving into the school setting can open children up to developing confidence in their own unique ability. But, if not supported and encouraged, children can develop a deep-rooted fear of making a mistake, leading to fear of failure and perfectionism. Being different or doing things in a different way is not a mistake. One may need to learn how to acknowledge group consensus at the same time as recognizing the validity of one's own particular perspective.

To see the school-age years as a testing ground and opportunity to explore personal, innate interests allows the child to understand that making a mistake does not mean he or she *is* a mistake. A child who is guided to explore his or her uniqueness at the same time as being involved in the company and activities of peers, is able to feel confident in a developing sense of self. It is a time to encourage the risk of action in exploring abilities, supporting continued efforts at achievement and, in the process, fostering the development of healthy self-esteem.

Empowerment and Self-Esteem

There is a crisis of self-esteem in our culture. Sadly, a huge number of individuals suffer from a lack of positive self-reflection, and carry an inner message that they are not worthy. There is an often unconscious belief that if others truly knew what was going on inside of them, they would be rejected. This is the message of shame and it is experienced in epidemic proportions. Many individuals have an enormous capacity to hold empathy and compassion for others, and yet are not able to direct that empathy and compassion toward themselves.

Empowerment and self-esteem are two different concepts, and yet, are intimately tied together. Empowerment is connected to ability and self-determination, whereas self-esteem is connected to a sense of personal worth and innate inner value. Self-esteem is the recognition of our value as a human being, which underlies the empowerment to express through doing. It is impossible to have one without the other. Shame inhibits self-esteem and thus inhibits a sense of empowerment.

Self-esteem is fostered when we are given messages that reflect our essence and the energy of our effort. Parents help children develop self-esteem when they support and encourage children in each stage of development. This does not mean that parents cannot guide or reflect when children make questionable choices. Feedback on the appropriateness of a choice is not the same as criticizing the essence of an individual. The message "that was a bad decision" is a completely different message than "you are bad." One is about doing. Constructive and appropriate feedback around our choices and actions fosters guilt, which can translate into a healthy conscience. The other is about being. Critical messages about who we are result in shame. When the message inherent in any feedback or guidance is "I care about you. I love you. I see and support the best in you and want to encourage you to see that in yourself," it promotes an inner dialogue that creates a solid foundation for self-esteem. As we are esteemed by our parents, so we are able to apply those messages to ourselves.

In many cases, for adults who have not experienced that reflection as children, what develops is a fierce *Inner Critic*. It is important to realize that those who do not have self-esteem themselves will not be able to foster self-esteem in others. It is also important to recognize that for many past generations, much of this self-reflective information simply was not available. There is a legacy of low self-worth that has trucked on through the ages from the "children are to be seen and not heard" parenting techniques of the past to current days. The fear-based and critical messages of much past generational parenting have contributed to the current crisis of self-esteem. The Inner Critic is the internalized, critical parent who continues to tell us that nothing we ever do is good enough. It continues to tell us that we are to be seen and not heard. It tells us that we are bad, or unworthy, or unlovable. It is harsh, berating, and devastating, but it serves a purpose. The Inner Critic wants us to succeed and be accepted by others; however, it is trying to achieve that goal in ways that are destructive to our sense of self. It is of utmost importance in the development of self-esteem to be aware of the Inner Critic voice. We do not need a coach on the sidelines hurling abuse at us each time we stumble. We do not need the message that tells us that we have to win at any cost to prove our worth.

On the other hand, the complete opposite guiding response is not helpful either. It is not beneficial to anyone to have a cheerleader say, "Oh sweetheart, stay down. This is too hard. I'll finish the race for you" when we stumble. It has been said that a growing issue in the current generation is the attitude of entitlement. One of the contributors to this stems from a well-intentioned fear of instilling low self-esteem. In the challenge to find the method to reflect feedback without criticism, many parents fall into the trap of becoming their child's friend rather than guide. The pain of seeing children struggle, (which often triggers a parent's own unresolved childhood pain) often leads to an urge to take away the source of the pain. Challenging teachers on grades, finishing projects for the child, or not asking a child to contribute to the tasks of the household enables an attitude of entitlement. And entitlement is not self-esteem. Underneath entitlement is a fragile self-esteem that suspects that one is not capable of achieving on one's own.

When we have self-esteem, we truly want the best for ourselves. We know we deserve the best for ourselves. And we know we have the tools within us to be able to achieve the best for ourselves. Removing the source through which one hones the skills of using those tools is as damaging to the development of self-esteem as criticizing fledgling attempts to become adept. When we stumble (and it is an absolute guarantee that we will) what we need is a cheerleader who sees our stumble and says, "Hey, sunshine! Pick yourself up. I know it hurts. I know it is hard. But try again. I know you can do it. I believe in you." We need the voice of encouragement to do our personal best, whatever our personal best may look like. This supportive voice is our Higher Self. It doesn't always tell us what we want to hear, but it always reflects the highest expression of our potential and ability.

When we have a solid sense of self-esteem within, we are able to operate from a place of empowerment. Empowerment is self-referential. In our culture we have long battled with issues of power, control, and inequity. There is a bully/victim dichotomy that continues to be rampant. When one tries to exert power over another, this is the bully. When one feels ineffective to establish boundaries or protect oneself, this is the victim. Both of these exhibit an inner experience of power in relation to the dynamic of the other. Empowerment comes from knowing who we are, knowing what our needs are, knowing what we want, and believing that we are able to actualize our own life's experiences. It has nothing to do with anyone else.

With empowerment comes the ability to stand in our truth and create appropriate boundaries for ourselves. We have accountability for our choices and decisions, even knowing that sometimes they may be mistakes. We are able to steer through difficult or painful times knowing that they may happen to us, but they do not define us. And perhaps most importantly, being empowered ourselves, we recognize how to empower others, allowing them to be accountable and responsible for their own feelings, choices, and actions as well. As our own light within shines brightly, so do we encourage others to shine their own lights as well.

Empowerment and self-esteem are the cornerstones to becoming a self-actualized person.

Further Exploration on Empowerment and Self-Esteem

Embracing Your Inner Critic: Turning Self-Criticism into a Creative Asset by Hal and Sidra Stone. HarperOne, 1993.

How to Raise Your Self-Esteem by Nathaniel Branden. Bantam, 1988.

Overcoming Perfectionism: Finding the Key to Balance and Self-Acceptance by Ann Smith. Health Communications, Inc., 2013.

Self-Esteem: A Proven Program of Cognitive Techniques for Assessing, Improving, and Maintaining Your Self-Esteem by Matthew McKay and Patrick Fanning. New Harbinger Publications, 2000.

The Six Pillars of Self-Esteem by Nathaniel Branden. Bantam, 1995.

When Perfect Isn't Good Enough: Strategies for Coping with Perfectionism by Martin M. Anthony, Ph.D. and Richard P. Swinson, M.D. New Harbinger Publications, 2009.

Personal Developmental and Psychological Reflections

April 5: What messages do you recall about your value and innate worth that you received from your parents in childhood?

April 6: Reflect on how accepted you felt in a circle of peers as a child.

April 7: In what ways were you encouraged to risk making mistakes while exploring your abilities as a child?

April 8: Reflect on how you work as part of a team or in a group setting.

April 9: Reflect on in which situations you may feel powerless.

April 10: In relationship do you hold the other's feelings in higher regard than your own?

April 11: What is your experience of your inner voice?

Seventeen

....

Alchemical Reflection on Separation

"The wind carries it in its belly."

FROM *The Emerald Tablet*

SEPARATION ASSOCIATIONS[6] "THE WHITE PHASE"

Element: Air • **Metal:** Iron • **Planet:** Mars • **Symbols:** White birds
Dream Imagery: Knives, scissors, hatchets, swords, dismemberment, surgery

Separation, the third alchemical process, involves the filtration of the dissolved substance, isolating the various components, allowing one to discern what is worthy of keeping, and discarding whatever is base or of no use. This is a sifting process much like panning for gold.

Psychologically, the previous two stages were mired in deep emotion—of shock, pain, betrayal, anger, fear, and sadness. In this stage the mind comes back into the fore in order that the emotional content can be explored and examined. This is the process of classification and analysis of material that was previously hidden deep in the unconscious. With that material having been brought into the light via the emotions, one is able to begin to

....

6 Separation associations adapted from *The Emerald Tablet: Alchemy for Personal Transformation,* Dennis William Hauck (New York: Penguin/Arkana, 1999).

sort through, prompting the possibility of arriving at a different perspective, or determining healthier responses.

This is an important stage in the process of moving from an emotional reaction to an event, to a tempered, considered, and adult response. An emotional reaction is fueled by unresolved content from the past. Having felt rejected in the past, any situation that carries an unconscious familiarity to the past experience will be reacted to with the same response. Allowing oneself to re-enter the past hurt, bringing the pain to the surface, and truly experiencing the emotions allows one the psychic freedom to explore current situations without the pull of the past. A current rejection can be examined purely on its own. Perhaps it truly was a rejection. On the other hand, perhaps the other person was having their own inner experience in which their apparent rejection had nothing to do with the situation (i.e., that person was just having their own bad day). Even more challenging is perhaps one inadvertently acted in a way that was perceived by the other as rejecting, which triggered the other person's defenses, which was then experienced as rejection. If you are operating from an unhealthy internal message that says "You are unworthy and you will be rejected," this is the only lens through which you will see the world. Rejection is expected, and rejection will most definitely be experienced again and again.

The stage of separation allows for the discernment to explore whether, in fact, our internal determinations are coming from a healthy or unhealthy place. Is the underlying message of worth helpful or destructive? It is in this stage that we are able to step back from emotions and take stock of what has contributed to our experience of the world. It is in this stage that we are able to choose to let go of what is no longer working for us.

This is a large part of what the psychotherapeutic process is all about. Generally speaking, clients reach out from a place of crisis—calcination—because truly speaking, who opens a phone book to look for a therapist when one feels that everything in life is going swimmingly? It is when situations or our inner life feel out of control that we tend to reach out for help. From that place of crisis there is a portion of the therapeutic process that is simply holding the space for dissolution. It allows the emotional content to flow: the tears, the fears, and the confusion. This can be quite a flood. It may be many sessions or many months that this content, which has never really been allowed to surface before, continues to rise and rise and rise to the surface. It can be disorienting and unnerving for a client, but it is imperative. It is the process of putting all the baggage on the floor in the space between client and therapist. Once there, it is time to roll up the sleeves and start the sifting process. What is mud and what is gold? What supports and what detracts? What is healthy and what is unhealthy?

Separation is the significant stage of self-examination. But it is important, at this stage, to recognize the higher purpose of the examination. Discernment and ownership are all part of the process. What is mine to own and what of the baggage can I give back? For example, when examining the painful ending of a relationship, where might I have made a different choice and what is truly the result of someone else's emotional issues and inner pain? Perhaps I was withdrawing and isolating, or smothering and engulfing, either one arising out of a fear of being abandoned. Perhaps the other person was critical and demanding, or uninvolved and dismissive, either one arising out of his or her own shame. One is mine, and owning it means I have the power to shift it. The other is baggage that is not my responsibility to address. That I can hand back.

Self-examination is just that—examination of the self. It is really never about the other person. However, if one does not already have a certain level of ego strength entering into this process, it can feel like torture—self-dissection rather than self-examination. The higher purpose of the examination is always to enable one to move into future situations with greater clarity and choice. It needs to be done with gentleness and understanding. It needs the guiding voice of the Higher Self, not that of the Inner Critic.

In alchemy the process of turning lead into gold starts with the *Prima Materia* (the First Substance), and works to transmute the Prima Materia into the Philosopher's Stone. The Philosopher's Stone is that which can never be destroyed. It is pure, eternal, beautiful, and of the utmost value. The key to the alchemical process—the secret—is that the Prima Materia and the Philosopher's Stone are one and the same! It is the same stuff, in different form. A diamond is really just a lump of coal that has been subjected to intense heat and pressure. It is the same relationship between the Philosopher's Stone and the Prima Materia. They are both made up of our essence, the truth of our being. The Prima Materia contains the elements of Essence, unchanging and whole unto itself. The painful and challenging situations we experience provide the intense heat and pressure necessary to forge the Philosopher's Stone. Separation allows us to sort through the pain of the experience to extract the gift. The purpose of the introspective sorting is not judgment and castigation of the self. The sword of separation is not intended to cut one to the quick. The purpose of separation is to gain clearer sight of the Philosopher's Stone by cutting away all that is not of Essence.

If our shadow were a storage closet into which we have thrown everything that we rejected in ourselves or felt to be rejected by others, calcination is the moment we inadvertently open the closet to have the entire contents fall down on our heads. What a shock! Dissolution is sitting on the floor in tears, holding our hurt head, overwhelmed by the sheer volume of stuff piled all around us. Separation begins the moment we take a deep breath, dry our tears, and start to open the boxes. It is a process that can require courage at times. Who knows what got stuffed into those boxes? But it is only through sorting through them all and deciding what is still of value to us and what has crumbled long ago that we can begin to attain a clearer sense of self. It is also important to keep in mind that there may be the odd box that contains a nesting mouse or centipede. We may have some moments that we really don't want to deal with that faces us. But not dealing with it does not make it go away. To coin a familiar and helpful axiom, "The only way out is through."

In separation we enter the process of determining who we are from who we are not. In childhood, out of reaction to our circumstances, we may have developed coping mechanisms (defenses and subpersonalities) to survive. But they are just that—mechanisms. They are not the whole of who we are. In childhood we may have marginalized aspects of ourselves that we still hold a great attachment to. This could be dreams we had, or activities we enjoyed, or aspects of our personality that we quite loved, even though others may have reacted against them. Unhealthy coping mechanisms need to be released. Aspects of self that continue to resonate with us need to be reclaimed. Separation is the process through which we begin to identify who we know ourselves to be, or who we choose to be. Knowing that, we can begin to anchor a new way of being in the world that reflects our inner truth.

Personal Alchemical Reflections

April 12: Reflect on a time when you experienced a "feedback loop" of destructive thoughts.

April 13: Reflect on whether you tend to see situations from another's perspective more than your own.

April 14: What are some inner messages that feel supportive to you?

April 15: In what ways do you choose to behave that do not feel like you?

April 16: To what extent are you able to be objective when looking at painful situations?

April 17: List five qualities about yourself that you think are wonderful.

April 18: List five qualities about yourself that you feel others may think are wonderful.

Eighteen

. . . .

Energetic Reflection on the Solar Plexus Chakra

SOLAR PLEXUS CHAKRA ASSOCIATIONS [7]

. . . .

Name: Manipura • **Location:** Around or just above the navel • **Color:** Yellow
Tone: E • **Gland:** Pancreas, Adrenals • **Body:** Abdomen, lower back, and digestive system
Yoga Path: Karma • **Symbol:** Ten-petalled lotus • **Stones:** Amber, Citrine,
Yellow Topaz, Golden Beryl, Cat's Eye, Golden Tiger's Eye

The solar plexus chakra is literally our "inner sun." It is the center of our identity and sense of self. It is the place from which our uniqueness shines forth, giving energy and vitality to our choices and expression in the world. When we are balanced in our solar plexus chakra, we know who we are, what is important to us, what we want, and all that we are capable of. We are able to value ourselves and operate from a place of healthy self-esteem. A healthy and balanced solar plexus chakra carries a message that is much needed in our culture: do unto yourself as you do unto others. More often than not, we treat others with far more empathy

. . . .

7 Solar plexus chakra associations adapted from *The Chakra Handbook: From Basic Understanding to Practical Application,* Shalila Sharamon and Bodo J. Baginski (Wilmot, WI: Lotus Light Publications, 1991).

and understanding than we allow ourselves. The solar plexus chakra helps us place ourselves in the center of our own story.

Many people operate from a place of unrelenting stress and anxiety, often fed by an inner belief that they are powerless to effect change in their lives and situations. Physically, this constant, internal pressure can lead to digestive problems and ulcers. It can also lead to exhausted adrenals—a physical symptom that is of near epidemic proportions in our society. Indicators of adrenal fatigue can include chronic fatigue, non-restorative sleep or insomnia, irritable bowel syndrome, craving salty or sweet foods, low immune system functioning, and allergies.

Psychologically, a blocked solar plexus chakra can be present in a tendency to be over-responsible for others, avoiding conflict, overextending by taking on more than one is able to handle, and giving our power away. There is an inability to set appropriate boundaries with others that often stems from confusion over what an appropriate boundary looks like. A boundary differentiates between your own self and the "other," helping you to discern what is your issue to address or own, as opposed to what is someone else's issue. For most people, boundaries have become blurred, which leads to taking on someone else's stuff. The truth is, boundaries are really very straightforward. These are mine: my feelings, my experiences, my beliefs, my choices, and my consequences. These are yours: your feelings, your experiences, your beliefs, your choices, and your consequences.

There is a wonderful emotion that communicates to us when a boundary has been crossed. That is anger. Anger is the emotion that tells us that we feel someone has crossed a line with us. Not listening to that message and neglecting to take appropriate steps to address the boundary violation can lead to anger issues and rage. Many people are afraid of anger, both experiencing it themselves and being on the receiving end. Often, it feels like anger is threatening and destructive, but that is because not many of us have had appropriate anger modeled for us. The true expression of anger is not loud, out-of-control, minimizing, and bullying; it is quiet, respectful, and firm. It is the message "This is not okay and I am making a different choice." It allows us to stand up for ourselves in a healthy way.

Being balanced in the solar plexus chakra allows us to discern what we have control over (ourselves), and what we do not (everybody else). We honor ourselves enough to put ourselves in the picture of our own lives and treat ourselves with acceptance, respect, and dignity.

Messages that help to balance the solar plexus chakra are:
I am comfortable saying no.
It is okay for me to feel angry.
I am responsible for my own feelings and experiences.
I am important and valuable.
I respect myself.

Personal Energetic Reflections

April 19: The color yellow makes me feel …

April 20: Reflect on a time when you felt anxiety in your torso and explore to what that may have been connected.

April 21: In what ways do you try to control situations?

April 22: What triggers anger in you and what might this be telling you?

April 23: In what ways do you communicate your anger to others?

April 24: What do you hold as dear and significant to you in your life?

April 25: What about yourself would you love for others to know?

Nineteen

Guidance Reflection on Bird Guides and Intuitive Reflection on Oracles

Bird Guides

Though there are those in the bird category that do not have the ability to fly, generally speaking, birds as guides offer messages of how to negotiate the space between earth below and sky above.

Air is the domain of higher energies, insight, and in days gone by, the realm of the gods. Birds, with their seemingly mystical ability to move freely in the air, are seen as the messengers of the Divine. They rise up to receive messages and come back down to us to offer the inspired communication. If aquatic guides connect us to our emotional energy and unconscious, the bird guides connect us to our superconscious, offering mental clarity and inspiration.

Humankind has always been fascinated with the realm of air. The desire to attain the heights offered by flight can be seen in the Greek myth of Daedalus and Icarus, the flying machine blueprints of Leonardo da Vinci, the invention of the airplane, and modern sports such as hang gliding, sky diving, and parasailing. We can learn to swim in water simply using our own muscles and coordination without the need for any equipment. But, without external support and mechanical devices, try as we might, we simply cannot fly. And yet, how we yearn.

We often find that the language around stepping into our full potential involves verbs like: to soar, to fly, or to attain the heights. The messages from our bird guides help us to discern how best to embrace our best and highest selves. As they soar, so do they inspire us to do the same.

Flightless birds, such as penguins and ostriches, still speak of the connection between heaven and earth, though they do not inhabit the space between these realms. These bird guides can be likened to *bodhisattvas*, compassionate, enlightened beings who choose to walk the earthly realm in order to serve as inspiration to others and to bring the energy of love and peace to the world. They carry the wisdom of the Divine within them and are dedicated to sharing that wisdom. An earth-bound bird guide reflects a similar message. As oft-quoted Teilhard de Chardin said, "We are not human beings having a spiritual experience. We are spiritual beings having a human experience." We need guidance on how to move through this earthly experience while remaining connected to our spiritual natures.

 Bird guides awaken our spiritual connection. They draw our eyes upward, and remind us of our innate Divine nature. It is up to us to determine how to translate this into our human experience.

Some Common Examples of Bird Guides

Blackbird	Bluebird	Blue Jay	Buzzard
Intuition, Psychic ability	Happiness, Contentment	Survival, Tenacity	Purification, Rebirth
Canary	**Cardinal**	**Chickadee**	**Condor**
Joy, Singing your own song	Manifestation, Balance	Power of small things	Nurturance through changes
Crane	**Crow**	**Dove**	**Duck**
Justice, Truth, Creation	Transformation on all levels	Peace, Love, Joy	Comfort, Protection, Loyalty
Eagle	**Falcon**	**Flamingo**	**Goose**
Wisdom, Insight	Discernment, Timing	Balance, Vivacity	Cooperation, Protection, Letting go
Hawk	**Heron**	**Hummingbird**	**Loon**
Vision, Patience, Spiritual guidance	Determination, Boundaries	Endurance, Accomplishing the impossible	Subtlety, Message to pay attention
Nightingale	**Owl**	**Peacock**	**Pelican**
Inspiration, Awakening	Mystery, Wisdom of the dark	Pride in endeavors, Watchfulness	Abundance, Responsibility
Penguin	**Pigeon**	**Raven**	**Robin**
Endurance, Navigating emotions	Home, Security, Family	Magic, Creation, Transformation	Renewal, Independence
Rooster	**Starling**	**Swan**	**Woodpecker**
Protection, Confidence, Poise	Relationships, Communication	Beauty, Empowerment, Grace	Rhythm, Harmony, Action

Oracles

In ancient times divination was the method for communicating with the gods, literally translating as "the power of supernatural foresight" or "the process of connecting with the Divine." Divination was tied to religious practice. As worship in ages past was focused on honoring or petitioning the gods, divination was about listening to what the gods had to say, and discerning whether any action was smiled upon or frowned upon by the Divine. The ancients saw the Divine as being part of all of nature. As such, all of nature provided a possible means through which this communication could take place. There are literally hundreds of different forms of divination, and almost anything can be approached from a symbolic perspective.

Divination through reading dust patterns is called *amanthomancy*, derived from the Greek words *amanthos*, meaning "sand or dirt," and *manteia*, meaning "prophecy." Divination by barley is *alphitomancy* (from the Greek *alphiton*, meaning "barley"). There is divination by flowers *(anthomancy)*, by frogs *(batraquomancy)*, by shells *(conchomancy)*, by beans *(favomancy)*, by birthdates *(genethlialogy)*, by sleep *(hypnomancy)*, by gems *(lithomancy)*, by clouds *(nephomancy)*, by lines in books *(stichomancy)*, by cheese *(tyromancy)*, and many, many more. Pick a format, add a "mancy," and you have a tool of divination.

The tool through which this Divine communication takes place is referred to as an oracle, which is literally "a speaking piece," and connected to the words orate and orator. For example, if working with alphitomancy, the barley would be the oracle. In some instances, the term oracle refers to a person through whom the messages come, or the place to which one would travel to seek the wisdom of said person. In ancient times it was usually a woman (a priestess) who stood as the voice of the gods, and it was up to the questioning individual to interpret the message sent through.

The most famous oracle was located in Delphi in ancient Greece. This oracle was dedicated to Apollo, who spoke through a priestess referred to as the Pythia. The earliest recorded oracle dates from the eighth century BCE, although there have been many famous ones from this oracle recorded and referred to in ancient writings. The oracle at the ancient healing center of Epidaurus (dedicated to Aesclepius, the great-grandfather of medicine) was particularly utilized to seek answers concerning medical questions. The temple at Karnak in Egypt was said to be the "mother of all oracles" from whence all other oracles stemmed.

Beautiful carved stone ovals known as *omphalos* were found at many oracle sites. Known as navel stones, the original meaning of these stones is lost. It is said that their location was determined by the meeting place of two eagles that Zeus sent out to fly in opposite directions around the world. How interesting that eagles (bird guides) and navels (solar plexus chakra) are both associated with famous oracles.

In ancient times individuals who had the talent for the interpretation of signs and symbols, but who were not enfolded into the religious structures as oracles or "mouthpieces of the Divine," were called *soothsayers*. It was a soothsayer who grabbed the hem of Julius Caesar's cloak and whispered the urgent, "Beware the Ides of March"—a message Caesar did not heed, and hence, he was killed by the entire Roman Senate, including his close friend, Brutus. The lot of the soothsayer shifted over time to become quite tenuous. By the time of the last days of the Roman Empire, with the political upheaval and unrest underlying the extreme suspicion of the emperors toward those trying to usurp their position (that could be anyone), there was a growing anxiety toward soothsayers, who were thought to be able to influence outcomes, as well as read messages.

The Mayan peoples of Yucatan called their oracular priests *chilanes*. It is said that the Books of the Chilam Balam (priests of the jaguar), dating from the seventeenth and eighteenth centuries, were written to preserve their ancient knowledge, part of which foretold the coming of the Spaniards. Tibet traditionally has a state oracle, called the "nechung oracle." Prior to the annexation of Tibet by China in 1950, the nechung oracle was the individual who acted as the head of the Nechung monastery. In Tibetan history, the oracle was an important element of religious ceremony and, at times, governmental decision-making.

In some cultures, oracles became more formalized, structured systems. An ancient Chinese tradition of casting bones is thought to have been the very ancient roots of the now familiar I Ching. The I Ching (which translates as "The Book of Changes") is said to have been around for about 4,000 years, although the oldest existing text dates back to about 1000 BCE. From the Norse we have the runes, and from the Celts we have the ogham. Perhaps the most well-known of the formalized divination systems is the tarot, which, out of them all, has the most mysterious of origins.

Nowadays there is a wealth of intuitive tools to choose from. There are many versions of particular systems (such as the tarot) and there is a plethora of wonderful oracle decks easily available. The importance of developing a relationship with oracles has nothing to do with the divination method itself. The method is a tool through which we open ourselves to communication with the Divine—or more specifically, with our Higher Self; that aspect of the Divine that relates to our own personal experience, growth, and healing. They acknowledge the importance of higher vibrational being. Each separate oracle or intuitive tool can be seen as different dialects of the same language and offer an amazing array of choice. There is most certainly an oracle to resonate with any individual's personal bent or preference, and it is through using them that we develop our intuition, the steady rudder that we use to steer our boats through the waters of our life's experience.

Basic Oracle Spread

Each different oracle deck generally comes with instructions for how to use that particular system. With many oracles a simple, single card pull at the beginning of each day is a wonderful way to set intention or gain particular messages about how to approach the day's activities and events. Alternatively, you can simply step out into the day and use the world itself as the tool for Divine communication, bringing your awareness to any special messages that may present through nature. The lines of communication are always open. We just need to listen.

For daily feedback on balancing your internal process with direction on how to proceed, pull two cards (or items) from your oracle of choice. You can use the technique called twittering birds to shuffle. Spread all the cards on a surface in front of you, and shuffle them every which way and direction on the flat.

First card: This position represents what is currently presenting for you. It may be something that you are already aware of (such as nervousness around a job interview), or it may be something that is still wavering beneath the surface. This card responds to questions such as: What is going on for me in this moment? What is bothering me? What am I trying to sort through? What am I anticipating today?

Second card: This position represents the Divine's recommendation on how best to approach whatever situation was presented in the first card. This card responds to questions such as: What strengths do I possess? What am I learning through this experience? What is the larger perspective of this situation? What support do I have around me?

Further Exploration on Oracles

Messages from Spirit: The Extraordinary Power of Oracles, Omens, and Signs by Colette Baron-Reid. Hay House, 2008.

The Oracle Within: Living the Intuitive Life by Jennifer Posada. Jennifer Posada, 2007.

The Way of the Oracle: Recovering the Practices of the Past to Find Answers for Today by Diana L. Paxson. Weiser Books, 2012.

Personal Guidance and Intuitive Reflections

April 26: Reflect on a time in your life when you felt your spirit was flying.

April 27: Do you respond differently to birds that can fly and those that cannot?

April 28: Have you ever had an unusual experience with a particular bird?

April 29: Reflect on a time when you felt you were receiving special messages.

April 30: What do you feel is the significant connection between the navel and Divine guidance?

May 1: What, for you, is the difference between Divine guidance and prophecy?

May 2: In what ways might you be more open and in tune to guidance?

The Centering Hynni of Esteem

When you find yourself in times of confusion. When you have lost a sense of your own self. When you feel out of control or overly concerned with what others think, this is the time to activate the Hynni of Esteem.

This Hynni symbol represents the appropriate boundaries that house and protect our innate value.

Preparation: Find a spot where you will not be disturbed. If possible, it would be beneficial to be outside or near an open window where you can experience a fresh breeze. You may choose to have a favorite oracle deck beside you. Get into a comfortable position. Place your hands in the center of your torso above your navel. Begin to breathe deeply and slowly, visualizing the breath moving in and out of your body as the color yellow.

Hynni: As you breathe, connect with the movement of air through your body. Be aware that each inhale and exhale moves out that you do not need in your body. Air moves into your body, clearing out the stagnant energy, filling you with freshness and clarity.

Gradually expand your awareness to encompass the space between the earth and the sky. Reach out with expansion to move through space as if you were the air itself. Rustle through trees. Swoop down over fields. Touch the highest mountains. Dance as delicately as a breeze and gust as mightily as a gale. Allow the experience of freedom and movement to be your guide.

Bring your awareness once more to the place in your body beneath your hands. What does it feel like in that space in your body? How much tension do you generally hold there? As you breathe, allow yourself to become aware of what the tension may be trying to tell you about what is going on in your life at this time. Or what it may be telling you about your feelings about yourself and your ability to maneuvre through life's challenges. Be aware of any shaming or critical messages and how those feel as they sit in your torso.

Begin to visualize the esteem symbol, visualizing a golden light that carries the intent of the symbol moving through your hands and into your torso. As you do, feel yourself fill with positive messages about your ability and competence. Connect to a strong sense of your own self—the delineation of who you are and all that is contained within that delineation. If there is anything that feels "not of you," visualize that as being blown outside the esteem symbol by a fresh gust of air, allowing a positive and affirming sense of self to pulse and reverberate on the inside of the symbol. As you become filled with this energy, you feel strong and empowered.

With an open heart and open mind, invite a bird guide to come to you. This guide may have a message for you in how it moves through the world physically, through its nature, or by what it symbolizes in different traditions. Know that whichever bird guide comes to you, it carries a perfect message for you in this moment.

When you have heard the message from your bird guide, bring your focus back to your breath once more, feeling centered in yourself and clear in your direction. Know that you are whole within yourself. Know that you have the capacity within to be able to move through whatever situations you may find yourself in. Know that you are worthy of respect and esteem, and that you are able to offer these supportive messages to yourself.

Take three deep, centering breaths, allowing each breath to bring you more fully back into the room. When you feel present once more, you may want to touch your feet to anchor yourself in conscious awareness. If you choose, use your oracle deck for guidance on what may be of most significance for you to remember at this time of your hynni meditation.

Part Five

Cycle Four
May 3–June 13

Union and Partnerships
"Honor Diversity"

PRESCRIPTIONS

Go through this section if you are experiencing any of the following:

- A lack of passion for activities and ventures
- Resentment toward others
- Unhealthy relationship dynamics
- Lack of compassion or empathy for others
- Burnout (particularly as relates to healthcare workers and healers)

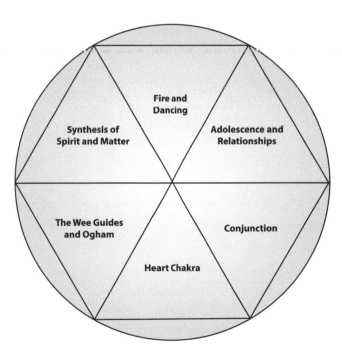

Twenty

·· · · · · · · · · · · · · · · · · · · ·

Mythological Reflection on the Synthesis of Spirit and Matter

The arrival of May is a joyful time. A time to feel the passion and life-force arising in us once again, rejoicing in creative ecstasy of union, and anticipating the bounty that results.

In ancient times, this was the time of reigniting the fires of the community. For the ancient Celts, it was one of the great Fire Festival celebrations. In Ireland, the bonfire lit by the Ard Ri (High King) at Tara signaled the lighting of bonfires across the land from which the family hearth fires would be lit. This practice, representing the interconnection of all in the community, stopped in 433 CE, when St. Patrick lit a fire at Slane Hill (ten miles from Tara) before the High King (by some accounts, Lóegaire mac Néill) was able to light his. This action by St. Patrick, symbolically eclipsing the power of the High King, arguably turned the tide in cementing Christianity in Ireland.

If the Spring Equinox symbolized the celebration of life through resurrection, the beginning of May was a celebration of life through the interconnections with others. With an ability to travel once more, tribes and clans came together, forging bonds and negotiating contracts. Important economic and personal relationships were formed with the hope that they too would bear the fruit of success in the future.

One tradition that has come down through the ages, granted in a much-shifted form, is that of the Maypole. If there is one aspect that is absolutely necessary for life to come forth, it is the union of the masculine and feminine energies. Without the two together, there is no life. With the need for the fertile earth to accept the seed that carried the anticipation of the harvest to come, rituals and ceremonies were enacted to embody this mystery. The Maypole represents the directed force of the masculine (tree pole) in connection with the receptive attributes of the earth. The dance in which ribbons were woven around the pole rejoiced in the union of the two, celebrating the abundance that would surely result.

Unsurprisingly, there were overtly sexual overtones to the festivities of this time. A tradition of greenwood marriages allowed for an attitude of "what happens in the woods, stays in the woods." The children born around the beginning of January tended to be looked upon as having special blessings, as they were likely conceived during this most auspicious time. Perhaps it was this sexual energy that prompted St. Patrick to take his stand at this particular festival rather than one of the other three Fire Festivals. Certainly, though traditions like the Maypole dance have survived the centuries, the sexual implications of those traditions have been long lost.

The themes at this time honor the balance of masculine and feminine, highlighting that both must be present for any new creation to spring forth. There is an earthy joy in the pleasures of life, and an acknowledgment that passion creates a force of energy that opens us to extraordinary wonder.

Main Themes for Cycle 4:
Union
Passion
Synthesis

Ancient Cultural Archetypes of The Lovers

Inanna (*Sumerian*) is a goddess of fertility and sexuality. She is turned to a corpse during a visit to the underworld, and her lover, **Damuzi,** a vegetation god, takes her place, spending half the year in the underworld and half the year on earth.

Ishtar *(Babylonian)* is a goddess of fertility and sexuality. One version of her myth presents that she undergoes trials in the underworld to bring her lover, **Tammuz,** a vegetation god, back to earth.

Cybele *(Phrygian)* is a mother goddess who was adopted by the Greeks, known as **Magna Mater** to the Romans. Her lover is **Attis,** a vegetation god.

Isis *(Egyptian)* is the great Queen of the Heavens whose worship spread from Egypt through the Mediterranean. Isis evidenced her love for **Osiris** by searching the world for his body after he was killed and dismembered by his brother, **Set.** From his reconstructed form she became pregnant and gave birth to their son, **Horus.**

Ares *(Greek)*, known as **Mars** to the Romans, is the fiery god of war, and one of **Aphrodite's** many lovers. They had five children: **Deimos** (Fear), **Phobos** (Panic), **Anteros** (Requited Love), **Eros** (Erotic Love), **Himeros** (Desire), and **Harmonia** (Harmony).

Personal Mythological Reflections

May 3: What in you comes alive at this time of year?

May 4: What does passion mean to you?

May 5: In what ways do you honor both vision and manifestation?

May 6: Reflect on a time of great love in your life.

May 7: What sacrifices have you made in order to bring your dreams to life?

May 8: In what ways do you feel connected to your greater community?

May 9: Reflect on what you choose to harvest in the coming months.

Twenty-One

Elemental Reflection on Fire and Active Reflection on Dancing

Fire: The Activation of Passion

In Celtic culture fire was not considered one of the prime elements. They looked upon the elements of earth, water, and air as connected to land, sea, and sky—the great triune. Fire was special unto itself. With its ability to meld disparate components together, it is the great transformer and the motivator for acts of creation. When one had the presence of land, sea, and sky in perfect union and balance, one could experience *awen*: the Fire of Inspiration or Spiritual Illumination. Awen allows the light of truth to be received.

It is through the spark of fire that new light and life is ignited. At the very dawn of humankind, it was mastery over this element that moved our history in a completely different direction. Fire keeps us warm. It cooks our food. It forges our tools. It changes what is raw into that which is of use and benefit to our survival, growth, and expansion. There have been many areas that the evolution of humankind took gigantic leaps. Arguably, the knowledge of the ability to create fire was one of the biggest.

The other elements have the power to douse fire. However, fire does not douse; it enhances. It melts earth. It boils water. It agitates air. When we add fire, we contribute to the intensification of whatever it is that we are undertaking. We speak of "fiery individuals" as being those who are passionate and intense, who are motivated and unstoppable, and who seem to burn with an inner energy that can move mountains.

Fire is the passion that brings meaning to our endeavors. Passion can be expressed in many forms—not just sexually. However, if there is going to be a challenge in expressing passion, it is in the sexual arena that the discomfort tends to fall. We can have no problem expressing passion as it relates to our work, our hobbies, our relationships, or our passionate commitment to the earth, and experience a hesitation or shyness around sexual passion. An ability to express ourselves sexually is as vital to our holistic health as physical, emotional, or spiritual concerns. Sexual passion is a flaming urge toward the peak experience of union.

Passion is the energy of fire that propels us toward that which activates our Spirit. In order to create any new thing, there needs to be a spark—something that leaps across the gap between the material and the ethereal, bringing the two together and transforming them both in the process. Fire is that motivator, both the soft flame that gently guides and the blinding conflagration that changes all in an instant.

Messages that help to connect us to the element of fire are:
I activate change in my life.
I am inspired and inspiring.
I bring passion to my ventures and endeavors.
I shine with an inner glow.

Dancing

Dance is a time-honored way of lifting our spirits and joining with others in celebration. Many ancient creation myths include movement and dance as part of what brought the world into being—the interplay of masculine and feminine dancing life into being. The cosmic dance of Shakti and Shiva illustrates this. As Rumi said, "We come spinning out of nothingness, scattering stars…the stars form a circle and in the center, we dance." The rhythm of the body provides a reflection of the rhythm of the universe.

Isis was said to have brought dance to the Egyptians. Bast (the gentle, joyful cat goddess) was celebrated through dance, as was Artemis. Dancing to the goddess Tara was said to clarify obstacles.

When we dance, we are expressing the Divine through our bodies. It is a means through which spirit rejoices. Dance has certainly been a part of our spiritual expression for millennia. Evidence of dance in ancient art has been traced back to around 7000 BCE. Illustrative examples in written history abound. In spiritual tradition, dance can be either expressive or formalized. Certain cultures performed set, traditional dances to enact particular myths and stories, bringing those teachings and/or prayers into physical form: preparation for battle, the planting of crops, influencing weather conditions, acknowledging rites of passage, and recognizing change in leadership. The Morris dancers of England wear bells on their legs and wave sticks or handkerchiefs to reawaken the earth after the cold months of winter. The Whirling Dervishes of the Sufi tradition represent the moon, and they spin around the Sheik, who represents the sun. Many of these dances have been reclaimed as part of a cultural tradition and even show similarities across cultures. Step dance focuses on the footwork while the rest of the body remains somewhat restricted. Irish dance is a form of step dance that has become popularized due to the success of *Riverdance*. However, similar movements can be seen in Scottish or Highland dance, tap dance, flamenco, or clog dance. The essence of the expression remains the same, although different areas express in slightly different manners.

The fact that dance, or certain forms of it, have been forbidden or outlawed is a testament to the recognition of its potential to ignite passion—sexually, culturally, or politically. In most instances, certain dances that are well-known in contemporary times were banned by the religious authority of past times. The Maypole dance, with its long tradition in Britain, tended to be accepted when the ruling religion was Roman Catholic, and banned when it was Protestant. Queen Elizabeth I banned the dance, while Queen Mary reinstated it. American Protestant missionaries who arrived in Hawaii in the early 1800s opposed the Hula dance as heathen, and public performances were banned in 1830 by the newly converted Queen Ka'ahumanu. The Charleston, loved by carefree flappers, was banned in America in the 1920s for encouraging women to dance in a manner that was deemed unbecoming and in skirts that were far too short. Other famous dances that have had their moments of authoritative disapproval include the belly dance, the tango, and the waltz.

A beautiful contemporary dance movement is Sacred Circle dance. Circle dance has long been a part of ancient culture. Circle dance can still be found, in large part, in Greek and Israeli folk dance. The aforementioned Maypole dance is another example of the community brought together through the weaving of circular dance. Bernard Wosien is said to have brought many traditional European dances to the Scottish Findhorn community in the 1970s, prompting the resurgence in the popularity of these dances for inspiring spiritual and community connection. There are now hundreds of choreographed circle dances and many communities host Sacred Circle dance evenings.

Even more recently, pole dance, which has traditionally been associated with strip clubs, has garnered more mainstream acceptance. Many are recognizing it as an excellent way to build strength and flexibility, and some have taken this dance form to extraordinary levels of performance art that leave the audience breathless with its beauty.

In a more freeform approach, dance has been recognized as a powerful way to raise energy, opening us to altered states of consciousness. Expressive dance allows us to translate the emotions that flow within into physical form. Trance dance becomes a moving meditation through which one experiences union with the Divine.

Dancing brings us into alignment with our own bodies. Regardless of whether we are performing a memorized dance or allowing our bodies to move in intuitive, creative ways, dancing brings the energy of spirit into physical form. It opens our hearts to joy. Connecting with fire opens us elementally to activation and change. It provides the inspiration and impetus to move us into transformation.

 Further Exploration on Dance

Circle Dancing: Celebrating the Sacred in Dance by June Watts. Green Magic, 2006.

Dance–The Sacred Art: The Joy of Movement as a Spiritual Practice by Cynthia Winton-Henry. SkyLight Paths, 2009.

Dancing on the Earth: Women's Stories of Healing and Dance edited by Johanna Leseho and Sandra McMaster. Findhorn Press, 2011.

Maps to Ecstasy: The Healing Power of Movement by Gabrielle Roth and John Loudon. New World Library, 1998.

Personal Elemental and Active Reflections

May 10: What motivates you on a daily basis and in the greater scheme of your life?

May 11: What douses your fire?

May 12: In what ways do you fuel yourself?

May 13: What spark within do you tend to as precious?

May 14: In what ways do you use movement to shift your energy?

May 15: Reflect on a time when you danced in a group or community and how it made you feel.

May 16: How comfortable are you dancing to your own internal rhythm?

Twenty-Two

Developmental Reflection on Adolescence and Psychological Reflection on Relationships

Thirteen Years of Age to Early Adulthood

One element that is a little complicated when referring to adolescence is that the parameters of the age range keep changing. For the bulk of history, there is no reference point to adolescence. It did not exist. You were a child. Then you were an adult. When girls crossed the threshold of menarche, they were ready to bear children and become mothers. In ancient cultures, boys underwent rites of passage that created a similar marked threshold into manhood, taking on the responsibilities of adults. It was the facing of death, either in childbirth or in battle, that marked the shift from childhood to adulthood. The concept of the teenager is said to have been born out of post–World War II America. Rock and roll, in combination with the recognition of teen buying power, created a demographic that had not previously been noted. The teenager was the one who still lived at home, but who had the means with which to spend—on records, movies, clothes, and other pop culture offerings. The end of the teen years was marked as the age that one moved out of the family home, becoming independent, and requiring funds previously delegated toward entertainment for necessities such as shelter, food, or raising a family.

The past number of decades has seen a shift in what is labeled as "the teen years." This range is getting longer and longer. Children seem to be growing up faster. Parents are noticing teen behaviors in children far younger than thirteen. On the other end of the spectrum, with a high cost of living and increasing post-secondary education expenses, children are dependent on parents longer. In the late 1990s the end of adolescence was placed at around age twenty-six. Currently, the age thirty-five tends to be bandied around. An individual who lives at home, who depends on parents to provide a certain level of basic needs, and who is not able to take full financial responsibility for him or herself is still operating within the realm of the adolescence sphere. There is simply not the level of autonomy and self-determination that constitutes having entered adulthood.

That being said, financial dependence is a different fish than emotional and mental maturity. When looking at what inner development occurs during the adolescent years, one must take the whole range of development up to this point into consideration. The adolescent years are, unquestionably, some of the most challenging years. There is a major transition that is occurring, on all levels of being. Physically, the child is flooded with hormones that morph their body into adult form. Emotionally and psychologically, this stage is the regeneration of all the childhood stages. In essence, it is the opportunity to address what has not been developed in childhood. What is truly occurring is the solidification of identity through the unconscious revisiting of the earlier stages of development.

Erik Erikson's Psychosocial Development Stages[8]

Stage	Task Polarity	Method	Ego Strength
Infant	Trust vs. Mistrust	Trust is developed when caregivers provide reliable care, meet needs, and offer affection.	Hope
Toddler	Autonomy vs. Shame and Doubt	Autonomy is developed when children are able to experience a sense of personal control over physical skills.	Will
Preschool	Initiative vs. Guilt	Initiative is developed when children begin to recognize a level of control over their environment.	Purpose
School Age	Industry vs. Inferiority	Industry is developed when children integrate new social and academic demands.	Competence
Adolescence	Identity vs. Role Confusion	Identity is developed through exploration of sense of self.	Fidelity

The ability to navigate adolescence is dependent on previously developed ego strengths. If these have not been previously integrated due to issues or traumas in earlier stages of development, these will present in adolescence. Through conflict and challenge an opportunity is given once again to successfully integrate before embarking on adulthood. The neediness of infancy, the oppositional challenge of the toddler, the struggle with competence—parents will likely recognize these familiar themes appearing once again in the teen. On a physical level, the adolescent years are confusing and chaotic; bodies ache with bone growth and emotions flare with hormonal influx. Add in what is occurring on a psychological level and it is no wonder these years are often a rocky roller-coaster.

The development of identity and a sense of self in adolescence transpire through the exploration of different paths of possibility. It is through the taking on and rejection of various "ways of being" that we begin to develop a true sense of what fits and what does not. You

....

8 Adapted from *Identity and the Life Cycle: Selected Papers,* Erick H. Erickson
(New York: International Universities Press, 1959).

might have a teen who is jeans and T-shirt one week, full goth the next week, and steampunk the next. This is all part of the process of testing out various, disparate avenues for internal resonance.

The teen years are also a time of experimentation with different ideas and concepts, all within the context of "What does this mean to me? How is this important to me? How does this impact on my world?" There is a wonderful passion that can develop at this stage—an energy of focus and commitment. Liking music can become a passion with all available hours spent listening, practicing, and jamming. Having a connection to the earth can become a passion for environmental issues and joining groups that are dedicated to activism, promoting awareness, and supporting change. The commitment to a cause or activity contributes to the development of fidelity, loyalty, and dedication.

Adolescence is a time for exploring what it means to be an adult, and there can be a great deal of ambivalence in this. Especially in the early teen years, there can be major fluctuations between acting from the perspective of the child and taking on the mantle of the adult, ill-fitting though it may feel. It can be a confusing flip-flop for parents to experience when they are faced with an individual who wants to curl up for a snuggle one day and wants nothing to do with the parents the next. The child's need for parental comfort and the burgeoning adult's need for distance and autonomy, all contained within this one transitioning individual, is a necessary polarity that, ideally, leads to internal reconciliation. Both ends of the spectrum need to be validated. They are both true, in their moments.

There is also an extreme polarization during these years between the need for connection and communication, and the feeling of isolation and loneliness. Similarly to the infant and toddler stages, which operate from a position of egocentricity ("It is all about me"), the adolescent feels not only under the microscope, but that no one is able to understand the particular problems, issues, and conflicts being experienced. Certainly not any adult or parent. This contributes to ultra-sensitivity to perceived responses and hyper-attention to personal presentation. At the same time there is a high need for communication that tends to manifest in peer relationships. The adolescent who spends hours on Facebook or texting is responding to the inner unconscious need to feel connected, and to explore his or her sense of identity and belonging in the context of peers.

Adolescents need presence and guidance. They need supportive encouragement in their experimentation of roles and ideas. This includes constructive feedback. The narcissistic tendencies of this period need to be understood, but not indulged. More than anything, teens need to take in the message that regardless of how confusing this time is, their core Essence is seen and validated, and that their identity does and will reflect their inherent worth and value.

Relationships

Another key aspect of adolescence is entering into significant relationships with the "other": dating, first loves, broken hearts. This is another trend that seems to be happening at younger and younger ages, to the detriment of individual and personal development. Healthy relationships are formed when each individual in the relationship has a solid sense of self, including their own strengths and limitations. When we do not have a sense of personal identity, it is impossible to form a true partnership, which is why the relationships of the very young tend to be experienced as hurtful and traumatic. The dissolution of the relationship becomes a rejection of the self and can lead to a devastated self-esteem. But the unfortunate truth is that this is not exclusive to the relationships of the very young. Many adults experience pain in relationships due to these very same causes.

The question becomes "What is the basis of a healthy relationship?" The answer lies in all that was explored in the previous chapters. When we are conscious—knowing our needs and how to get them met, knowing our issues and the tools for working through them ourselves, knowing our boundaries and how to be firm or flexible as the situation requires, knowing that we are responsible for our own feelings and happiness—then we are able to meet another from a place of autonomy. We do not look to another to fulfill us. We are whole within, but we can choose to meet another to experience the joy of walking through a life side-by-side.

Many relationships are formed out of an unconscious pull to resolve old issues and heal old wounds. Unnerving as it may be, we tend to attract the person who will best help us to work through old patterns so that we might gain insight and find healthier ways to be in our lives. To paraphrase Carl Jung, that which we shove to the darkest corner of our inner closet will find a way of making itself known. And the deeper it is repressed, the more problematic and destructive it will present. What we store in our unconscious shadow (never to see the light of day, we hope) becomes projected onto and acted out upon the other person in the relationship. And it becomes even more complicated when what the other person has stored in their shadow is projected and acted out upon us. If I am over-responsible, I will be drawn to another's relaxed sense of fun. If I am under-responsible, I will be drawn to another's stability.

Relationships tend to follow a predictable pattern—all in response to these unconscious influences.

The Romantic stage is what we, as a culture, have tended to define as what a relationship is supposed to look like—always. It is the wonderful sense of having lost ourself in another. Falling in love. Being in love. This is the time when everything about the other person fills us with joy. We feel we have found the perfect person. We have found the one who completes us. But this is not the truth of the human journey, because it is never another's role to complete us. To turn responsibility for our choices and happiness over to another, placing our sense of self outside of ourselves, is actually referred to as *codependency*. It becomes a problematic relationship dynamic that inevitably leads to the next relationship stage.

The Power Struggle stage is an important stage in personal healing and self-actualization, but it is very hard on relationships. Many relationships do not survive. This stage is often marked by the first disagreement or argument. The blush comes off the rose. Very often the cry of "You've changed!" is heard. But it is our perception that has changed. The relaxed sense of fun we so loved now appears to us as irresponsibility, and our own over-responsible tendencies kick in. Or the stability that gave us comfort now feels like a concrete weight hindering our ability to fulfill the desire to go where the wind blows. The Power Struggle stage is imperative in order for the individual to take stock of what may be repressed within. What we fight so hard against outside of us is actually what we are battling within. We fight what we see as irresponsibility in the other at the same time as we yearn for that release and freedom within. More often than not, we are also battling the internalization of what we have seen in our parents' relationship, and the dynamic that contributed to the environment of our developmental years. Asking the questions "Who am I most like in this relationship—Mom or Dad? And who is my partner most like?" can lead to phenomenal insights about the dynamics that we have created in our own adult relationships. Deep-rooted fears and issues, such as fear of abandonment, fear of engulf-ment, fear of intimacy, or fear of commitment come to light at this stage.

Though the Romantic stage tends to last around six months or so, the Power Struggle stage can drag out for months or years. It can be an exhausting, confusing, and painful stage. Out of this, there are two possible outcomes.

Independence can be achieved by the actual ending of the relationship, or it can manifest as emotional independence within the context of the relationship—two beings coexisting and cohabiting, but not having any truly intimate exchanges and few points of contact. For some relationships, flirting with independence becomes the exhausting merry-go-round of on-again, off-again, engaging, and rejecting. In unconscious relationships, the pull of re-turning to the Romantic stage versus the challenge of the Power Struggle stage causes a pain-ful dynamic referred to as "the dance of intimacy," which can continue until the individuals are able to stop the movement of the dance and address their own inner issues, or they give up and end the relationship, cementing the Independent stage.

Interdependence represents the other possible outcome to the Power Struggle stage and consists of developing a conscious and healthy relationship. Interdependence recognizes that each individual in the relationship is whole and complete within themselves. Each in-dividual is responsible for his or her own feelings, perceptions, beliefs, actions, and choices. Both individuals in the relationships are responsible for their own needs and happiness. Each individual is aware of his or her own issues and is committed to doing the work to understand and resolve those issues. But, within the context of that, each person in the rela-tionship knows that the other is there as a support, an ear, and a cheerleader.

Interdependence is the healthy interweaving of dependence and independence, of in-timacy and solitude, of autonomy and partnership. It is the inner message "I am capable of being on my own, but I choose to be with you." It is in this dynamic that the possibility of true love can flourish. There is no fear. There is no expectation that it is up to another to soothe or alleviate our own inner issues or dragons. Each in the relationship recognizes his or her own strengths and weaknesses, and recognizes the other's strengths and weaknesses. And each in the relationship takes ownership for his or her own weaknesses, doing their best to sort through and resolve while supporting and encouraging the other to do the same.

In a conscious relationship it is understood that the first relationship is always to the self. When the importance of self is acknowledged, there is room to honor the importance of the relationship. I need to be my first priority to myself, and I understand that you need to be your first priority to yourself. Then, for each of us, we are able to come fully into the relationship. In a disagreement, this may look like "This is my perspective on the situation. It is valid. I hear your perspective on the situation. It is valid. Now how can we approach these differing perspectives to come to a sense of collaboration, synthesis, and resolution?" This is not necessarily an easy task. It requires time, patience, understanding, communication, and energy, but it is always worth the effort.

It is only through a conscious relationship that true intimacy can be achieved. Intimacy means we allow ourselves the vulnerability to allow our true feelings, perceptions, and beliefs to be seen by another. And we honor another's vulnerability to us—not judging, belittling, or trying to control if what we see makes us uncomfortable, remembering that our discomfort is our issue, not our partner's issue. Seeing my partner being challenged or in pain means we empathize. It does not mean we have to fix it. Hearing another's needs means we reflect that those needs are important. It does not mean we have to meet our partner's needs, although we can certainly choose to do so. More often than not, we do choose to do so, but that is very different than feeling that we have to meet our partner's needs in order for them to either understand that we do care or to ensure that they do not leave or reject us.

When the trust that is established in an interdependent relationship is the basis of a dynamic between two people, intimacy can be experienced on all levels, including sexually. Intimacy as expressed through sexuality becomes a sacred union. It is two wholes coming together in openness and vulnerability to become something that is greater than them both. It has as much to do with spirituality as with physicality. It is about the sharing of our true inner self, our Essence, and our being through the expression of the body.

There has been a long tradition in our culture of denying the needs of the body, particularly identifying sexual needs and impulses as bad or shameful. Sacred union includes the concept that there is an inner union—the body and the spirit. As Sam Keen states, "The underground spring that waters our spirituality, sexuality, and sensuality are connected."

In relationships, sexuality is about dissolving the boundaries that separate us, experiencing connection through surrendering ourselves to another. There is an element of it that reflects the dynamic of the Romantic stage, the loss of the self in the experience of the other. When we come together with another, having first established a solid foundation of knowing and accepting the whole of who we are, the melding union with another is an exquisite experience. It becomes a true and powerful dance of intimacy. If instead we carry deep shame about who we are along with fear of rejection, the vulnerability that sexual connection exposes can feel very threatening. The challenges that are connected to sexuality in our culture are merely signals that there is still much inner work to be done to address the shame that many carry within.

Healthy relationships, romantic or otherwise, are anchored in a positive self image. They reflect the acceptance of opposites and celebration of diversity. They allow for acknowledgment of our human needs and spiritual expression. They give us both the stability and the freedom to share our inner truth with courage and passion.

Further Exploration on Relationships

Boundaries and Relationships: Knowing, Protecting and Enjoying the Self by Charles Whitfield. Health Communications, Inc., 1994.

Codependent No More: How to Stop Controlling Others and Start Caring for Yourself by Melody Beattie. Hazelden, 1992.

Conscious Loving: The Journey to Co-Commitment by Gay and Kathlyn Hendricks. Bantam, 1992.

Creating Love: A New Way of Understanding Our Most Important Relationships by John Bradshaw. Bantam, 1994.

The Art of Sexual Ecstacy: The Path of Sacred Sexuality for Western Lovers by Margo Anand and M. E. Naslednikov. Tarcher, 1990.

The Dance of Intimacy: A Woman's Guide to Courageous Acts of Change in Key Relationships by Harriet Lerner. Harper Perennial, 1997.

The New Codependency: Help and Guidance for Today's Generation by Melody Beattie. Simon & Schuster, 2009.

Personal Developmental and Psychological Reflections

May 17: Did you experience your teen years as exciting or painful?

May 18: How were you supported in the physical and emotional changes you experienced during adolescence?

May 19: Were you passionate about an activity or cause as a teenager?

May 20: What messages about yourself did you take away from your first significant relationship?

May 21: To what extent do you take on Mom or Dad character traits in relationships?

May 22: What fears do you have in a current relationship (or have had in a previous one)?

May 23: Reflect on your comfort level with the vulnerability of sexual intimacy.

Twenty-Three

Alchemical Reflection on Conjunction

"Its nurse is the Earth."

FROM *THE EMERALD TABLET*

CONJUNCTION ASSOCIATIONS [9] "THE WHITE PHASE"

Element: Earth • **Metal:** Copper • **Planet:** Venus (sometimes Earth)
Symbols: Hermaphrodite, King and Queen, Child, Rooster, The
Intelligence of the Heart • **Dream Imagery:** Weddings, sexual activity

Conjunction is the bringing together of the various elements that have been previously explored in order to create cohesion. It literally means "to join with." The imagery connected with the stage of conjunction is that of the king (calcination) and the queen (dissolution) coming together in relationship. The ancient imagery appears to have sexual implications, but the true symbolism is that of opposites finding a means of reconciliation to form a new dynamic.

---

9 Conjunction associations adapted from *The Emerald Tablet: Alchemy for Personal Transformation,* Dennis William Hauck (New York: Penguin/Arkana 1999).

Alchemy has always had an air of mystery around it. Many ancient alchemists purposefully shifted the order of the stages so that only those who had some knowledge and understanding would be able to understand. This is one of the stages that presents much confusion. It is often interchanged with coagulation, which is generally felt to be the seventh alchemical stage. The reason for this could be that the fourth stage is a natural plateau. Here, a certain level of self-insight has been attained. There have been new beliefs put into place and new choices explored out of the new self-concept. An acknowledgment of both the rational and the emotional sides of self has been accepted, and from this a level of peace carries forth. No longer held in the dark by the shadow of the past and no longer directed by societal convention, a person who has arrived at the fourth alchemical stage is not under the thrall of an unhealthy ego. The individual has an understanding of his or her inner psyche, including strengths and limitations.

However, this is not the end of the journey. Empowerment has been achieved, but not enlightenment. The road ahead is about to get dicey, but it is through the challenges to come that true wisdom is attained. Ultimately, the truth does not rest in duality and opposites: King and Queen, Hermes and Aphrodite, reason and emotion. In conjunction we honor both aspects of self, but, if one chooses to pursue further, one will discover that beneath the duality there lies once again the unity of "the One."

This stage is sometimes known as the *Lesser Marriage* and its gift the *Lesser Stone.* From a psychological perspective, a great deal of growth has occurred and many stop the journey to self-actualization at this stage. One of the symbols of this stage is a crown, and certainly there is a high degree of self-esteem and empowerment, which marks a crowning achievement. To rest at conjunction means that we have learned a great deal about ourselves and have let go of the influence of our painful past. For many, this is a triumph in and of itself. There is no need to continue to journey. From an alchemical perspective, the true purpose of the journey is to experience ourselves as fused with the Divine and to see ourselves as the expression of the Divine in the earthly realm. It is the movement through transformation into transcendence. This requires more than creating peace between all aspects of our selves. It requires the further work of integrating those disparate aspects into the experience of oneness that can never be destroyed. For the journey to be completed, there are more stages to endure. But the crown that awaits is the Triple Crown and the achievement of the Philosopher's Stone.

Personal Alchemical Reflections

May 24: Reflect on how you bring both intellect and emotion to the task of your life.

May 25: What peace has releasing baggage from the past brought to your life?

May 26: What, if anything, is stopping you from feeling perfectly fine in this moment?

May 27: In what ways do you listen to your feelings and your intuition?

May 28: In times of happiness what within you propels you to explore further?

May 29: What new ways of being have you embraced that are serving you well?

May 30: List five personal achievements of which you are proud.

Twenty-Four

Energetic Reflection on the Heart Chakra

Heart Chakra Associations [10]

Name: Anahata • **Location:** Center of the chest • **Color:** Green (healing) or Pink (love) • **Tone:** F • **Gland:** Thymus • **Body:** Chest, ribs, back, and circulatory system • **Yoga Path:** Tantra • **Symbol:** Twelve-petalled lotus
Stones: Emerald, Jade, Rose Quartz, Pink Tourmaline

The heart chakra is the center of love and healing. In the endocrine system, it is associated with the thymus gland, which may have been named for the Greek *thumos*, meaning "heart, soul, desire, or life." The heart chakra is the meeting place of our human and spiritual selves—a center of connection, union, and synthesis.

Carrying the pain of old wounds can block the heart chakra, leading one to feel that they have a "heart of stone." A blocked heart chakra can result in heart problems, high blood pressure, difficulty breathing, and panic attacks. When we have not experienced love and support from our childhood caregivers, it is a challenge to know how to give this love to ourselves. The message of not being lovable creates a heartache that does not go away until we learn how to accept ourselves and recognize that we are indeed lovable,

10 Heart chakra associations adapted from *The Chakra Handbook: From Basic Understanding to Practical Application,* Shalila Sharamon and Bodo J. Baginski (Wilmot, WI: Lotus Light Publications, 1991).

even with our human failings and foibles. When we are able to love ourselves, we are able to forgive others for the ways they may have hurt us. We are able to see that they too are human and carry pain of their own, releasing the pain they may have caused us, and freeing ourselves from carrying the emotional weight of the past.

Grief is a pain we carry in our hearts and can be very challenging. It is a strong and natural impulse to want to push the grief away so that we don't have to take in the fact that we have lost something dear to our hearts. But the message of grief is that we have loved. It is our capacity to feel a strong, open connection to another that is so painful when life circumstances take that person from us. Rather than tell us how much we hurt, the pain of grief can be a reminder to us of how deeply we loved.

The heart chakra guides us to love ourselves, in all the ways we can, to take care of our bodies, to allow ourselves to explore our dreams, to provide security for ourselves, to allow safe and supportive people into our lives. This love that emanates from a healthy heart chakra is unconditional love, a term that can sometimes cause confusion. Unconditional love does not mean that all my choices are okay. It does not mean that I have to love everything about you at all times. It does not mean that I cannot say anything about my feelings or my responses. Unconditional love allows us to see that each person, including ourselves, carries the spark of the Divine within, recognizing that sometimes we make choices that move us away from that Divine spark. Whether directed toward ourselves or others, unconditional love acknowledges the highest vibration of Spirit at the same time as challenging perceived limitations. When we love ourselves unconditionally, we are truly able to reach out to others—both in encouraging support and in loving confrontation.

Unconditional love is a great healer, and the heart chakra directs healing energy. To be effective healers, we must have compassion and empathy for what ails another. We must also have understanding and presence for those clients who continue to engage in self-destructive patterns. This does not mean we believe those choices are okay, but that we understand the struggle to shift into healthier patterns. Unconditional love in a healing context means that the healer is able to meet the client exactly where the client is at, offering feedback for change, but allowing the client to shift at his or her own pace. A challenge for many healers is how to embrace an attitude of presence and compassion without losing themselves in the process. So many practitioners come to the healing services because of their caring hearts and their honest desire to help others. However, the codependency that can be found in romantic relationships is a potential danger in the healing dynamic as well. Healers with blocked heart chakras run the risk of being caretakers, approval-seekers, or rescuers, all of which can lead to burnout.

Being balanced in our other chakras, particularly the solar plexus chakra, supports a healthy heart chakra, allowing us to connect with others without running the risk of losing our own sense of self in the process. The heart chakra encourages love and compassion for all, including ourselves.

Messages that help to balance the heart chakra are:
I embrace my human nature and my Spirit.
I treat myself with care and respect.
I am open to love.

 Personal Energetic Reflections
May 31: The color green and the color pink make me feel…

June 1: Reflect on how you have been hurt in the past and how you have released the old hurt.

June 2: In what ways do you accept and love your human limitations?

June 3: What does unconditional love mean to you?

June 4: What challenges you in loving others?

June 5: What has been most helpful to you in a healing process?

June 6: How do you feel in your heart when you are helping or guiding others?

Twenty-Five

. . . .

Guidance Reflection on the Wee Guides and Intuitive Reflection on the Ogham

The Wee Guides

The lengthening days and the warming sun bring these tiny guides that have not been with us to a great degree during the winter months. The insects start to awaken and get busy with their work, which continues through the heat of the summer. We have a tendency to see the wee guides as pests, and often try to get rid of them with a myriad of techniques from creams slathered on a body to electric zappers in the backyard. Certainly, we do not want to be overrun by these little creatures that often bite and sting, but if we allow ourselves to be open to their messages, they teach much of the power that comes in very small things.

The wee guides, as a whole, are agents of great change. If the aquatic guides connect us to our emotional life, and the bird guides bring us messages from higher levels of consciousness, it is these wee guides that propel us to activate that knowledge into new directions and new ways of being. More so than any other guide, these tend to elicit very strong reactions. Some of them we connect with openly and enthusiastically, while others we react against strongly and negatively. People respond very differently to a butterfly than to a spider. In looking at our reactions to them, the wee guides encourage us to look at what is core to our movement into wholeness. What inspiration gives us the hope to continue to shift? And what resistance would we benefit from addressing? Guides that we respond to with great positivity are light aspect guides. They teach us what is the best in ourselves, reflecting our strengths and gifts. Guides that we react against or carry fears toward are shadow aspect guides. They teach us what still lies within our potential, waiting to be embraced and accepted. They show us what we still need to reclaim in order to be whole and complete within ourselves.

The gift of the wee guides is the teaching that, though the movement may appear to be miniscule, it makes a huge difference. As the saying goes, a butterfly flapping its wings in Japan can cause a storm in America. What may seem inconsequential can actually have great impact. Something may seem to be a small shift, but the energy of the intention behind the small, outward shift has the power to create enormous transformation.

Wee guides also teach that there are huge miracles contained in the very small. Some ants can carry objects five times their own weight. To translate that into human measurement is unfathomable. Science claims that it should be aerodynamically impossible for a bumblebee to fly, and yet it does. A midge can beat its wings 1,046 times per second. A flea can jump 150 times its own body length. These tiny guides carry the message to never underestimate the potential that lies at the heart of the wee.

Most insects live in colonies and have much to share about living in community. They offer lessons in teamwork and collaboration. They show us what incredible feats can be accomplished when we work in the context of a whole with dedication and commitment.

If a wee guide comes to you, even if your initial impulse is to swat or run, try to take a moment to observe. Some of the greatest feats of nature come through these tiny creatures, and they have much to teach us about strength, determination, perseverance, and beauty.

Some Common Examples of Wee Guides

Ant	Beetle	Bee	Butterfly
Industry, Community	Resurrection, Rebirth	Productivity, Sweetness of life	Transformation, Joy in change
Caterpillar	Cockroach	Cricket	Firefly
Patience, Preparation	Survival, Adaptability	Intuition, Communication	Illumination, Wonder
Fly	Grasshopper	Ladybug	Mosquito
Responsiveness, Prosperity	Leap of faith	Manifestation, Protection	Energy depletion, Sacrifice
Moth	Scorpion	Spider	Wasp
Sensitivity, Awareness	Vigilance, Intensity	Creativity, Connection, Centered	Construction, Taking a stand

The Ogham

The ogham comes from Celtic tradition, though its origins are shrouded in mystery. It is well known that the druids worked with an oral tradition. Teachings were not written down, but memorized. Druids underwent years and years of intensive training so that they could carry the traditions within them. That being said, archeology reveals remains of this cryptic script dating back to the fifth century CE, around the time that the Romans pulled back from the British Isles. It seems possible that the script was invented several centuries earlier to be used in opposition to the power of Rome, but was not brought into written, tangible form until it was safe to do so.

The ogham seems to have been primarily inscribed on wooden staves. However, there are many beautiful stone remains, particularly in Ireland and Wales. This is interesting as the ancient Celtic language had two main branches that were phonetically different—Goedelic and Brythonic. Irish (along with Scottish Gaelic and the extinct Manx) was Goedelic. Welsh (along with Breton and the newly revived Cornish) was Brythonic. The ogham seems to make no distinction between the two languages, although the ancient words that have come to us to name the individual letters are Welsh.

Indicative of the close relationship the ancient Celts had with nature in general and trees in particular, the ogham is reflective of the indigenous trees to be found in the ancient Celtic lands. Many of these trees were used in creating items both practical and spiritual in purpose, the efficacy of which would be enhanced by the energy of the wood itself.

The earliest ogham seems to have consisted of twenty letters arranged in four sets *(aicme)* of five letters each. The first three aicme consist of consonants, and the last aicme contains vowels. An additional five symbols, referred to as *the forfeda*, seems to have been a later contribution, allowing for the complexity of *diphthongs* (vowel combinations). The visual impact of the forfeda is considerably different than the main core of the ogham, and many choose not to include them when working with this system symbolically.

In written form, the letters are placed along a central vertical line flowing from the bottom to the top of the stave or stone, allowing for a small gap between words. It also had the added benefit of having the capacity to be used as a secret sign language. For those that could read the signals, using fingers to indicate the numbers of letter lines, and the bridge of the nose or the arm as the central column could allow for communication untranslatable by those not in the know.

The ogham is a beautiful system that carries the energy of the trees, with their roots deep in the earth and their branches reaching to the heavens. Each tree in the ogham reflects that we are both of the earth and of the stars and that, at our very center, we hold the potential to synthesize those two very different energies. The center of the tree draws up water from the roots and brings in light through photosynthesis, transforming both into that which nourishes and supports its growth. So too do we pull from above and below to support our own growth, through the strength of our hearts. The ogham allows us to gain insight into our own tools so that we can utilize them to bridge our inner worlds and meet any situation with love.

Basic Ogham Spread

Take some time to center yourself, using breath to connect to the deep support of earth energy and the expansiveness of the cosmos. Hold the intention that you will be guided to receive the message that you most need to hear in this moment. The Celts had a teaching tradition of the triads, which presented history, laws, and moral guidance in triplets. These triads can be seen as reflected in the three rays of the modern druidic awen symbol, representing the "fire in the head," which alights with inspiration. For this reading, the following Welsh triad offers a structure for working with three trees of the ogham.

Three teachers of humankind:
One is event, that is from seeing and hearing;
The second is intelligence, and that comes from reflection and meditation;
And the third is genius, individual, a gift from the Mighty Ones

Choose three ogham staves or cards for guidance on where you are at in this moment in relation to these three teachers. Place the first to the far left, the second to the far right, and the third in the center.

First position: This position represents the event. It is what we know of what is currently facing us. It may be the past situation that has led to where we are right now. It may be that of which we are consciously aware: the problem, the issue, the concern. With this tree, ask yourself *how am I feeling about what is going on in my life at this time? What is the root cause of the current situation?*

Second position: This position represents the intelligence. It is the undercurrent energy of the situation. It is what is really at the heart of the issue, rather than what we may first believe is the issue. With this tree, ask yourself *what is most challenging to me about this situation? In what ways does it require me to grow?*

Third position: This position represents the gift from the mighty ones, the message from the Divine. It may offer guidance on how this situation will unfold in the future. It may reflect an aspect of our own Essence, or the strength of our True Self. With this tree, ask yourself *what is the gift or blessing in this event? How does this situation fit with the larger pattern of my life?*

The Ogham[11]

⊢	⊨	⊨	⊨	⊨
Beth (B) **Birch** Beginning Renewal	**Luis (L)** **Rowan** Protection	**Fearn (F)** **Alder** Oracular powers Strength	**Saille (S)** **Willow** Flexibility Imagination	**Nuin (N)** **Ash** Linking inner and outer worlds
⊣	⊣	≡	≡	≡
Huath (H) **Hawthorn** Relationships Sexuality	**Duir (D)** **Oak** Strength Stability	**Tinne (T)** **Holly** Action Assertion	**Coll (C)** **Hazel** Creativity Intuition	**Quert (Q)** **Apple** Beauty Love
⼂	⼂	⫽	⫽	⫽
Muin (M) **Vine** Introspection Planning	**Gort (G)** **Ivy** Determination Patience	**Ngetal (NG)** **Reed** Memory Communication	**Straif (ST)** **Blackthorn** Hardship Perspective	**Ruis (R)** **Elder** Transformation Wisdom
＋	＋	≢	≢	≢
Ailm (A) **Elm** Clarity Higher perspective	**Ohn (O)** **Gorse** Action Resourcefulness	**Ur (U)** **Heather** Freshness Prosperity	**Eadha (E)** **Aspen** Victory Vision	**Iodo (I)** **Yew** Optimism Passage
✳	◇	◚	⼁	▦
Koad (EA) **Grove** Wisdom gained past illusion	**Oir (OI)** **Spindle** Finish obligations	**Uilleand (UI)** **Honeysuckle** Secret desires Sweetness	**Phagos (IO)** **Beech** New information	**Mor (AE)** **Sea** Sacred or inner journey

....
11 Adapted from *Magical Alphabets,* Nigel Pennick (York Beach: Red Wheel Weiser, 1992).

Further Exploration on the Ogham

Celtic Tree Magic: Ogham Lore and Druid Mysteries by Danu Forest. Llewellyn Publications, 2014.

Ogam: The Celtic Oracle of the Trees by Paul Rhys Mountfort. Destiny Books, 2002.

Ogam: Weaving Word Wisdom by Erynn Rowan Laurie. Megalithica Books, 2007.

The Healing Power of Trees: Spiritual Journeys Through the Celtic Tree Calendar by Sharlyn Hidalgo. Llewellyn Publications, 2010.

Personal Guidance and Intuitive Reflections

June 7: Is there an insect that you have a strong aversion toward?

June 8: Which insects do you consider to be pests or parasites?

June 9: To what extent do you pay attention to small things?

June 10: Reflect on a time of great dedication or sacrifice in your life.

June 11: Is there a certain tree that you have an affinity toward?

June 12: In what ways does connecting with nature help you to experience Spirit?

June 13: Reflect on a time in your life that the presence of a tree played a significant role.

The Bridging Hynni of Synthesis

When you find yourself in times of relationship conflict. When you feel pulled in two directions. When it feels impossible to balance your inner and outer worlds or yourself with others, this is the time to activate the Hynni of Synthesis.

This Hynni symbol represents the meeting place of our human experience and spiritual insight.

Preparation: Find a spot where you know you will not be disturbed. If possible, it would be wonderful to find an embracing tree to rest against. You may choose to have an ogham set beside you, either in card form or stick (stave) form. Begin to breathe deeply, visualizing the breath moving in and out of your body as the color green or pink. Release any tension you may be holding in your body, breathing into that space and bringing yourself to center.

Hynni: Bring your awareness to your upper torso, placing your hands over the center of your chest. Feel your hands resting there gently as a soothing, loving hug. Holding your hands over the heart chakra reminds you that you are important and loved. You are truly the center of your own universe. Be aware of the energy of your body—not of any particular aspect of your physicality, but of the current that runs through each and every part of you. Connect to the spark that animates you. It is this spark that brought you into physical being, and it is contained in every single cell in your body. Explore the particular energy and nuances of your own spark.

Begin to connect your spark with that of all that surrounds you. Expand your awareness to reach out across space and across time, bringing yourself to the very first spark of all—the big bang. Feel the force of creation and the beautiful unfolding of all that has come into being out of that moment. And breathe.

Breathing into your heart center, allow yourself to expand so that you are aware of the ground beneath you and the sky above you. Begin to focus on the synthesis symbol, visualizing a golden light that carries the intent of the symbol moving through your hands and into your heart. Taking a moment to focus particularly on the bottom triangle of the Hynni symbol, pull earth energy up into your heart. Feel yourself as connected with all that supports your foundation with the energy that pulses through the earth feeding and nourishing you. Taking a moment to focus particularly on the top triangle of the Hynni symbol, draw in energy of the cosmos. Feel yourself as connected with the vibrancy and potency of All inspiring and uplifting you.

You are human and you are spirit. You are your feelings and you are your intellect. You are the force of pure emotion and the cool gaze of reason. You walk your path alone but in the company of others. The interplay of opposing poles comes together in the heart. Not at odds, but each validating the other, making them both greater than they are separately. Focus on the meeting point of the two arrows of the Hynni symbol and become awash in the experience of union.

With an open heart and open mind, invite a wee guide to come to you. This guide may have a message for you in how it moves through the world physically, through its nature, or by what it symbolizes in different traditions. Know that whichever wee guide comes to you, it carries a perfect message for you in this moment.

When you have heard the message from your wee guide and feel filled with support and insight, begin to bring your focus back to your breath, and send the energy of connection and synthesis through your body. Pay attention to any areas that you feel may be in need of healing, intentionally sending the energy to those places. Allow strength, vitality, and health to fill your whole being and know that you are truly loved. Take three deep, centering breaths, allowing each breath to bring you more fully back into the room. When you feel present once more, you may want to touch your feet to anchor yourself in conscious awareness. If you choose, pick a single ogham tree that can give guidance on what may be of most significance for you to remember at this time of your hynni meditation.

Part Six

Process Phase Two
June 14–20

Full Moon:
Fullness and Fruition
"Celebrate Accomplishments"

PRESCRIPTIONS

Go through this section during any Full Moon,
or if you are experiencing any of the following:

- Inability to acknowledge your successes
- An urge to jump from one goal to the next
- Perfectionism
- Ineffectiveness
- Emptiness

Twenty-Six

Full Moon Phase of Fullness and Fruition

The full moon has long enthralled us. There is an exquisite beauty in the sight of a full moon sitting lushly in a dark sky. In the days before electricity, the light cast by the moon's round glow must have been welcome indeed. There was no need to fear the dark when the moon provided light as bright as a delicate dawn.

With its dependable cycle, far briefer than the annual cycle of the sun, full moons were often used by ancient cultures to mark gathering times. Calendars were the domain of the elite and the educated. For the ordinary folk, it was far better to agree to "meet when the moon is full again."

There is a tension that is relieved when the moon reaches its peak of fullness; a sense of coming to completion, and that what needs to be done has been done, for the time being. If the waxing moon brings new elements into being, the full moon sees those elements coming to fruition. In this, the full moon is associated with The Mother—the full pregnant womb ready to bring forth what has been gestating.

At this time of the full moon, it is important to take a moment to pause in the glory of our achievement. There may have been lessons that were hard-won, and most certainly, the journey has already seen challenge and sacrifice. The mother gives no less than her whole being to the child growing within her. It is a truth that underlies the requirement of pregnant women to pay particular attention to caring for their own health. The body will provide for the growing infant, first and foremost, before providing for the mother, taking energy, nutrients, and calcium as required. The sacrifice is generally so unquestioned by the mother that it is not even perceived as one. Whatever needs to be done to bring life to fruition is the only thought. It is this impulse that is recognized at the full moon: that we have done whatever needed to be done to bring our task or dream to fruition.

With the full moon we honor the flow of the cycle that brings us to fullness, a certain level of accomplishment and understanding, a degree of success and mastery. We appreciate the richness of our lives and take stock of the abundance that surrounds us. The journey is about to continue—moving into the darkness of release and endings. But for now, we can sit in the joy of fruition before continuing the journey.

Main Themes for Process Phase 2:
Nurturing
Growth
Completion

Ancient Cultural Archetypes of Fruition

Nut *(Egyptian)* was considered to be one of the oldest goddesses of the Egyptian pantheon. She is the goddess of the sky, arching over the earth, and mother of Osiris, Isis, Set, and Nephthys.

Gaia *(Greek)* or **Terra** *(Roman)* is the great mother goddess. She gave birth to the Titans and Giants.

Rhea *(Greek)* is the daughter of Gaia. She was considered the "mother of the gods" and gave birth to the Olympians.

Demeter *(Greek)* or **Ceres** *(Roman)* is a goddess of the grains and mother of Persephone. She was associated with **Terra Mater** *(Roman)*, originally known as **Tellus.**

Modron *(Celtic)* or **Matrona** *(Roman)* is the mother of the Divine son **Mabon.**

Danu *(Celtic)* is the mother of the gods and of the ancestral Irish tribe, the Tuatha De Danann.

Frigg *(Norse)* was called "foremost amongst the goddesses." She was the wife of Odin and mother of Baldur.

Erda *(Norse)* is an earth goddess who lived in a cave next to the roots of the world tree, Yggdrasil.

Personal Full Moon Phase Reflections

June 14: What have you nurtured into being?

June 15: Reflect on a period of great effort in your life and how you felt when it was over.

June 16: To what degree do you allow yourself to experience success?

June 17: What have you brought to fruition that you are proud of?

June 18: To what extent are you aware of your various accomplishments and how each builds upon the other?

June 19: Do you allow yourself to experience something as done, complete, finished, and final?

June 20: What gifts or qualities do you possess that contribute to your ability to manifest?

The Settled Hynni of Fullness

At the completion of a project. When you are acknowledging an accomplishment. When you have come to a certain level of achievement or attainment of a goal, this is the time to activate the Hynni of Fullness.

This Hynni symbol represents the fulfillment of potential.

Preparation: Find a spot where you will not be disturbed and eliminate all possibility for distraction. Get into a comfortable position. Begin to breathe deeply and slowly, focusing on the breath moving in and out of your body. Allow the tension to fade from your body. Be aware of nothing but your breath.

Hynni: As you breathe, take some time to connect with where you are at in this moment in your life. Reflect on all that has brought you to the place where you are right now. Take some time to flow through the different times in your life and all the different goals you set for yourself.

- What goals did you bring to fruition?

- What contributed to your ability to do so?

- What goals fell by the wayside or shifted significantly
  as you set out to accomplishment other goals?

Pay attention to whether it was an internal or external circumstance that caused the shift in direction, decision, and outcome.

As you journey through the experiences of your past, visualize the completion of each goal as a hilltop. See yourself setting out to climb the hill, reach the summit, or take a turn toward a different hill. How do you feel as you approach each hill? How do you feel as you change course? How do you feel as you crest the top? Allow yourself to explore this journey and all the emotions and energy you have brought to each venture.

Focusing on your breath, bring yourself back to this moment of your life. See yourself at this point sitting at the top of the plateau. The whole of the journey thus far stretches out behind you and you can see, spread out before you, more hills and hillocks of the adventures and goals yet to be broached. But for this moment, in this time, simply sit at the top of the plateau and appreciate what you have accomplished on your journey, as you look up to see a gorgeous full moon casting her lovely glow upon you.

Place your hands on your heart and begin to focus on the fullness symbol, visualizing a golden light that carries the intent of the symbol moving through your hands and into your heart. As you do, feel yourself fill with the remembrance of your effort and the ease that comes with knowing you did all you could to bring yourself to this place in the movement from vision to achievement and from planning to fulfillment. Feel the light of the full moon fill your every cell with celebration.

When you are ready, take three deep, centering breaths and open your eyes, feeling nurtured and full.

Part Seven

Cycle Five
June 21–August 1

Shining Our Truth and Creativity
"Walk Your Talk"

PRESCRIPTIONS

Go through this section if you are experiencing any of the following:

- Difficulty sharing your thoughts and beliefs
- Repressed creativity
- A sense that what you say doesn't matter
- An excessive need to communicate
- A depleted sense of will or belief in the efficacy of your choices

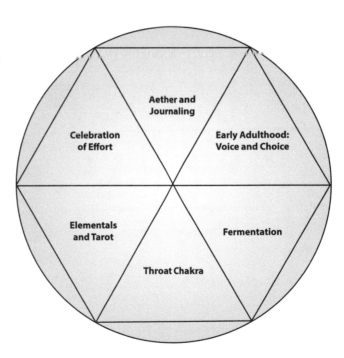

Twenty-Seven

Mythological Reflection on Celebration of Effort

If the Winter Solstice is the celebration of the birth of the sun, the Summer Solstice sees the sun coming to full strength. It is the longest day of the year and the shortest night. In ancient times this was considered midsummer, the culmination of work and effort. The wonder child, who was born at the darkest point of the year, has now grown into a strapping adult full of vigor and drive.

The ancients were aware of the "turning of the wheel" and that each festival held an echo of what was "across the wheel." These long, hot days of summer were fully embraced, knowing that the movement from this point on was toward the dark. If the Winter Solstice holds the echo of the fullness of life, born out of the dark, the Summer Solstice holds the echo of decrease, of death in life. When we see life linearly, everything is a movement from the least to the most until we attain the pinnacle, or the height, of perfection. The ancients saw life as a cycle, which is most acutely appreciated when one is aware of the cyclic dance of increase and decrease and increase once again—of life, death, and rebirth.

At midsummer when the heat of the sun is felt most vigorously, there is celebration for the work that has been done. The crops have all been planted. For the most part there is nothing to be done except pray that the balance of rain with the energy drawn from the sun's strength will nourish those crops into full bounty. The young of the livestock have all been born and nurtured through their early months. What can be done has been done—at least for the time being.

The festivals of old were joyful. The work of the harvest is yet to come. It is just around the corner. But this moment allows the sense of accomplishment to fill us with pride. We have lost the ancient traditions for this festival, many that include fiery activities that reflect the sun's power. In the past huge summer bonfires would be built. In parts of Britain, wheels of straw were lit on fire and rolled down hills. Nowadays, we celebrate with long weekends and vacations. The "dog days of summer" have an energy of relaxation as we rest in the knowledge that we have put in good effort. We are now able to sit for a moment, allowing the work of our accomplishments to take hold. We relish the heat of the sun, sipping icy drinks, and losing ourselves in summer blockbusters and beach-worthy novels. We slip away from city bustle to spend days or weeks camping in the wilderness, being mesmerized late into the night by the dance of the campfire flames. The muscle-gripping tensions of winter's blast is a far-off memory as we feel our muscles soak up the warming rays. For many, it feels as though these days are a reward for all the hard work we have done and they are to be thoroughly enjoyed.

For *The Great Work*, the celebration of the Summer Solstice marks the attainment of the plateau. We have put in the great effort of achieving a high level of self-awareness. As we celebrate this accomplishment, we allow the light of our inner truth to shine bright.

Main Themes for Cycle 5:
Accomplishment
Acknowledgment
Gathering strength

Ancient Cultural Archetypes of Light's Attainment

Aten *(Egyptian)* is a reflection of the sun god, **Ra** *(Egyptian)*. Aten, usually depicted as a sun disk with emanating rays, was introduced by the pharaoh Akhenaten and removed very quickly by the subsequent pharaoh, Tutenkhamen.

Sekhmet *(Egyptian)* is the lion-headed sun goddess who offers strength and power.

Helios *(Greek)* is a Titan who drove his chariot across the sky bringing the sun every day. He was eventually replaced by the Olympian, **Apollo.**

Hyperion *(Greek)* is sometimes confused with Helios through the name "Helios Hyperion." Hyperion was distinguished as the god of watchfulness, wisdom, and light, whereas Helios was considered the incarnation of the sun.

Apollon *(Greek)* or **Apollo** *(Roman)* is the son of Zeus and the mortal, Leto. He is the twin of Artemis—the sun to her moon. Replacing Helios as a god of the sun, Apollo is also known as the god of medicine and healing, the god of music and poetry, the patron of flocks and herds, and the patron of oracles and prophecy.

Aine *(Celtic)* is the goddess of the sun, wealth, and sovereignty.

Arianrhod *(Celtic)* is a goddess of celestial rhythms and cycles who guides us to empowerment.

Bel *(Celtic)* is a sun god whose name means "The Shining One." He was also known as **Belenos** *(Celtic),* and may be associated with **Baal** *(Hebrew).*

Lugh *(Celtic)* is a hero-god much loved for his success at all endeavors. He was associated with **Lleu Llaw Gyffes** *(Celtic)*, his Welsh counterpart, whose name means "fair-haired one with the skillful hand."

Thor *(Norse)* is the hammer-wielding hero-god known for his strength and virility. He is associated with thunder, lightning, and oak trees.

Sol *(Norse)* is a sun goddess and twin to **Mani**—the sun to his moon. Both twins are chased by wolves, Skroll and Hati respectively, that close in on them during eclipses.

 Personal Mythological Reflections

June 21: In what ways do you restore your energy?

June 22: What things do you do just for fun, enjoyment, and play?

June 23: Reflect on a time in your life when you got away and left all regular cares behind.

June 24: What do you consider your greatest triumph?

June 25: To what extent are you able to let things percolate in their own time?

June 26: Does celebrating others' accomplishments fill you with joy, or make you think about what you need to do?

June 27: Reflect on your own shining light and what that may bring to others.

Twenty-Eight

Elemental Reflection on Aether and Active Reflection on Journaling

Aether: The Ephemeral Wisp

Aether (also spelled ether) is an intangible, almost conceptual element that is notoriously difficult to understand. The ancient Greeks believed aether to be that pure essence that filled the space between the earth and the sky, though it was not air as we know it. It was of a purer form and was the element breathed by the gods. The elements of earth, water, air, and fire are translatable to those actual, physical substances that we find in the material world. Aether starts to take us out of that realm and into the immaterial. To a certain degree, aether has been associated with energy itself.

In alchemical teachings, aether is referred to as *quintessence*, which literally translates as "the fifth element." Aristotle included it in his system of classical elements, stating that the other four elements are subject to change; whereas the fifth element (aether), relating to the element contained in the cosmos, did not appear to change. Just as the celestial bodies always moved in set, predictable ways, so was aether immutable and constant. This quintessence became a cornerstone of later alchemical teachings. Where you have the four elements of earth, water, air, and fire in perfect balance, you create the fifth element. It is akin to what occurs in music. John Phillips of The Mamas and the Papas spoke of the magical "fifth singer" who would be heard when the four voices of the group melted in perfect unison. He attributed much of the group's success to this fifth-singer phenomenon.

There is a gestalt to the concept of aether. A sense that when elements combine in perfect harmony, what is created is greater than the sum of those elements. Aether takes us to another level completely, where we approach an ability to touch pure form.

Messages that help to connect us to the element of aether are:
I am more than the sum of my different aspects.
My choices are informed by my Essence.
My core self is pure and unchanging.
I am balanced in all areas of my life.

Journaling

Journaling is the process of placing your inner life in an external medium. A journal can be a friend and confidante—a listening ear that will quietly accept all thoughts, ponderings, and feelings without judgment. Traditionally, a diary is a record of external events that tends to place the author in the context of history and historical circumstances, whereas a journal is a record of internal events. A journal offers the validation of expression, ownership of your inner reality (even if you recognize that reality consists of shifting sands and changing perceptions), and the possibility of witnessing the progression of your own growth.

We have learned much of history through the writing of those men and women who have kept diaries through the centuries. Samuel Pepys kept a diary from 1660 to 1669, which is a wealth of information of London and the English Restoration, providing firsthand accounts of the Plague and the Great Fire of London. Sir Walter Scott kept a diary between 1825 and 1832, recording his personal financial troubles and the steps he took to overcome them. Contemporarily, almost everyone is familiar with the inspiring and tragic diary of Anne Frank, which chronicles her family's two years of hiding from the Nazis in the Netherlands. Anne died of typhus in a concentration camp and the diary, found by one of the individuals who hid the family, was given to Anne's father, who decided to publish it. It was published in English under the title *The Diary of a Young Girl*, and is arguably one of the most important books of the twentieth century.

Diaries may or may not be written with the intent of providing historical context for posterity. Regardless of the original intent, they do help us to understand humanity's past as seen through the eyes of an individual. Journals, on the other hand, do not tend to be written with a larger context in mind. They are intimate and personal explorations. As such, they offer a freedom of expression not necessarily afforded through other means. Whatever is experienced within can be confidently placed in its pages. Taking the time to slow down and put your thoughts into words, recording the images and symbols of your dreams and meditations, or simply conveying a message of the value of your journey through the act of writing itself allows a strong relationship with the self to develop.

There are many types of journals. Some journals are focused on keeping track of specific areas and can be purchased in an established format. Exercise journals, food intake journals, project journals, or gardening journals are all examples of ways to record what you may want to accomplish and how you are faring in the journey to attain a certain goal. These types of journals are helpful for seeing your progress and keeping you in alignment with the ultimate vision. Tracking journals of a more introspective nature include gratitude journals, anger journals, and dream journals.

Gratitude journals have the purpose of allowing time each day to focus on events or circumstances, both seemingly inconsequential and those of enormous import, that we can connect to with a sense of thankfulness and appreciation. We go through much in life that challenges us, and it can seem an aspect of human nature that we focus first on what upsets us. A gratitude journal actively shifts the direction of our intention to that which supports us, connecting us to the energy of expansion and attraction. If we want more of the good stuff in our lives, then we must take the time to acknowledge the good stuff that is already present. Gratitude journals are a perfect tool for those who have a tendency to be discouraged or cynical about life.

Anger journals are a very effective tool for those who struggle with expressing anger appropriately, whether that presents as anger management issues or as anxiety around conflict and confrontation. Keeping track of when anger is triggered can provide insight into how anger operates in your life. Writing about a situation or exchange that has caused anger within can clarify how you feel a boundary has been crossed, and open the way to insight on how to establish firmer boundaries in the future. For those who avoid conflict at all costs, an anger journal allows feelings to be expressed in a manner that feels safe, and can often provide the confidence to address the situation more directly.

Dreams are the method our psyche uses to express our inner hopes and fears when our conscious mind does not have as much pull. Dream journals are our way of telling our psyche we are listening. They are best written in the morning when the dream is still fresh in the mind. Because dreams are symbolic in nature and have a language and structure all their own, keeping a dream journal over time allows for deeper connections to be made, deciphering one's own inner language. As you continue to add dreams to your journal, creating your own personal dream dictionary of recurrent themes and objects is an extremely handy additional tool.

The most common journal is the personal journal, which may be a combination of all of the above. It may contain facts about situations that are occurring in your life, as well as the feelings you are experiencing in response to those events. It may contain plans and vision for the future, as well as challenges and victories you are experiencing in the process of manifesting the vision. It may contain words, images, and inspiring quotes. The most important feature of a personal journal is that it is private. It is not a blog, nor Twitter, nor Facebook. Those are wonderful methods through which to share with others, but a personal journal is just that—personal. It is the one place where we can absolutely release all the roles we take on in order to explore who we truly are. It is the place we can explore who we know we can become, without fear of judgment or need for approval. It is a place for us to come to know and accept ourselves in all our aspects.

Regardless of which type of journal you may choose to create, the act of journaling is like choosing to become your own best friend. When we journal, we set aside the time to be with ourselves, listening to our own stories, and encouraging our visions for the future.

Further Exploration on Journaling

One to One: Self-Understanding Through Journal Writing by Christina Baldwin. M. Evans & Company, 1991.

The Artist's Way by Julia Cameron. Tarcher/Putnam, 2002.

Writing and Being: Embracing Your Life Through Creative Journaling by G. Lynn Nelson. New World Library, 2004.

Personal Elemental and Active Reflections

June 28: Reflect on a time in your life when you felt completely in balance.

June 29: What, to you, is a transcendent moment?

June 30: What cycles are you aware of in your life?

July 1: What connects you to each and every moment in your life?

July 2: What is your comfort level with expressing yourself through writing?

July 3: Reflect on a time when writing something out helped clarify your thoughts and feelings.

July 4: Is there any aspect of your life you would hesitate to put in writing?

Twenty-Nine

··

Developmental Reflection on Early Adulthood and Psychological Reflection on Voice and Choice

Thirties and Forties

We move now into years that are less determined by age and more determined by what is transpiring at this stage of life. There are certain milestones that we all encounter in the journey of our lives. These are not the external milestones of getting a job, a car, or a house, although these external events can be a reflection of the internal shifts.

Early adulthood is marked as the time after we have completed our education and have begun to create a life of our own choosing, using all the tools and teachings we have gathered to date. If you have gone on to further education after high school, this would be the period that you begin to develop a career. If you have not gone on to higher education, this stage will occur far earlier, in your twenties, rather than in your thirties.

There are many decisions to be made at this time; decisions about how to go about putting your hard work to best effect. It may involve decisions around where to start to put your roots down, moving geographically because of work opportunities. It may involve decisions around work specializations, and how to fine-tune the range of what you have been learning into a specific area of expertise.

Times have changed. In past generations, often the decisions made during this period would create a concrete foundation that would be the basis for the rest of life. A career entered into in the thirties would often see thirty-five years of service until retirement age of sixty-five. In contemporary times there is more flexibility, which sometimes leads to more uncertainty. There is a current trend that sees the average career spanning about ten years. It is more common now that we will have at least two major careers in life, often seeing a major life shift in our forties.

Regardless of what changes in life choices may occur down the line, this time is key for beginning to put into practice those elements that have been guiding factors for years. Relationships solidify into long-term unions or marriages. Children are born and families started. Home locations are settled or houses purchased, allowing for a sense of stability and rootedness.

These early adulthood years are the ones when we start to plant our identity in the world. What we have spent years developing on the inside begins to be reflected in the outer world. Who we are is expressed in our work, our relationships, and the little corner of the world we are creating for ourselves. With each passing year a sense of comfort and mastery in our ability develops. What was learned and undertaken professionally, with at first perhaps some nervous and tentative steps, begins to become second nature as we become more adept. This is the time to move out into the world and express what we know ourselves to be capable of.

Voice and Choice

Voice is about more than the words we say to others. Voice is the expression of ourselves in the world. It is in our choices and our actions, as well as words. We activate our voice in a thousand different ways on a daily basis. But are we aware of what we are activating and what we are communicating about ourselves?

We use our voice when we vote, when we choose certain items at a grocery store (or decide to shop at a local market instead), in the hobbies and activities we engage in, and in how we connect with others. We use our voice in the clothes we wear (and what businesses we support in purchasing them), in what we spend our money on, in what we put into our homes, and how we choose to spend our non-working hours.

The world is communicating to us all the time. One shift that the world has seen with the advancements of technology and its extreme presence in our lives, is that there are even more avenues through which we take in messages. It can, at times, feel like an onslaught of information. Do this. Buy this. Sign up for this. Support this. Telemarketing, apps, computer pop-ups—they are all urging us to choose in a certain way and put our voice behind a certain something. On this front, two things are certain.

The first is that what we choose makes a difference. Even if we cannot immediately see the impact that our choice may have made in our lives or in the world, it does have an impact. Sometimes the difference is internal. We may see no difference at all in the world, but feel clear within, knowing that we operated with authenticity. Sometimes the difference is cumulative. Over time, as we continue to make the same choice, we begin to see tiny shifts becoming significant changes.

The second is that we decide by choice or by default. To think that we can avoid outcomes by not choosing in any direction is faulty thinking. If you can't decide whether to take a certain job or not, it is guaranteed that at some point, life will decide for you, most probably by giving the job to someone else while you wavered. When you have spent the time to become really clear on what is important to you, the choices become very clear. If you know what you value, what you envision for yourself and the world, and what your own strengths and gifts are, it is far easier to discern what is in alignment with that and what is not. The choice then is between "my life" and "no longer an option"—an expression of your voice. When we live from this place, we are voicing our truth and operating in the world with integrity. This supports our positive sense of self, contributing to self-esteem and self-respect.

We may not always make the best choice for ourselves. We may not always operate from our truth. That is part of the human experience. These experiences also become opportunities for us to learn more about ourselves, and to commit to making a different choice in the future when the opportunity arises again. The best thing you can do is become aware of your choices and accept that you are wholly responsible for them. Coffee or tea? Milk or cream? Collaboration or conflict? Expression or silence? The choice is yours.

Personal Developmental and Psychological Reflections

July 5: Reflect on the decision-making process that led to your first job in adulthood.

July 6: What shifts have you experienced in your work or career experience?

July 7: What patterns can you discern in major adult choices?

July 8: How do you respond to information overload?

July 9: In what ways do you choose to spend your non-working time?

July 10: List three elements of life that are of unquestionable value to you.

July 11: To what extent do you take in the message that what you choose matters?

Thirty

Alchemical Reflection on Fermentation

"Separate the earth from the fire,
the subtle from the gross."

FROM *THE EMERALD TABLET*

FERMENTATION ASSOCIATIONS [12] "THE RED PHASE"

Element: Quintessence, Sulfur • **Metal:** Mercury
Planet: Mercury • **Symbols:** The Peacock's Tail
Dream Imagery: Death, poison, vultures, worms, thunder, lightning

With the completion of the first four stages of alchemical healing, a certain level of self-understanding and mastery has been achieved. There is recognition that the past is part of our story, much of which has been resolved through inner work and insight. We no longer use the persona or false self as a protective armor. There is an acceptance of our emotional life as relevant and informative. There is more awareness of synchronicity and higher guidance, an appreciation of higher vibrations and the perspective of patterns in our lives. This

....

12 Fermentation associations adapted from *The Emerald Tablet: Alchemy for
Personal Transformation,* Dennis William Hauck (New York/Arkana, 1999).

is a great place to be, but it is not the end of the journey. The fourth alchemical stage sees us arriving at the Lesser Marriage and attaining the Lesser Stone. Further along the path, the Great Marriage and the Philosopher's Stone await.

The first four stages operate on expanding and integrating our human experiences, allowing us to see ourselves as much more than what we project into the world. We have moved from a two-dimensional experience of self (what you see is what you get) to a multi-dimensional experience of self. We can acknowledge the complex layers that all contribute to what others see, knowing that at any moment others are just seeing a small part of the picture. We may not share all our feelings with others, but they are there. We may not share all of our dreams with others, but they are there. Others may see the particular role we choose to take on at any given time, but we know we carry the depth of all the experiences in our unconscious and we thrill to all the heights of the potential we carry in our superconscious.

In a psychological approach to alchemy, the next three stages operate on a higher level, delving into the collective unconscious and the realm of the transpersonal. To achieve the Philosopher's Stone we must rid ourselves of any last vestiges of the ego, morphing the multi-dimensional self into one unified whole. *Fermentation* starts the next part of the journey. The hard work is about to begin.

Fermentation actually consists of two stages that may seem indistinguishable: putrefaction and fermentation. In the creation of alcohol (spirits), the initial substance is literally allowed to rot. Left to sit in heat initializes the process of fermentation, in which the mash seems to come alive once more with an influx of live culture, like bacteria or yeast. In alchemy, this stage that seems to be the most disturbing is actually signaled by the display of the "Peacock's Tail"—a gorgeous array of colors that indicates that something wondrous is occurring.

Psychologically, putrefaction is the realization that, with all the work we have done, we are still so very human. It is the acknowledgment of the clingy nature of our core issues that follow us throughout life. It is the despairing thought that the more things change, the more they stay the same. It is the experience of coming face to face with another facet of an issue that had been dealt with many times before and that we thought was well put to rest. It can precipitate another dark night of the soul, or mid-life crisis. It can feel that, even in spite of all our hard work, life is still a challenge and contains pain. At its worst, it can present as the niggling destructive thought *oh, what's the point?*

Fermentation is the glimmer of new life, allowing for the thought that there is hope. That if "this mortal coil" does indeed contain pain, there is something of a higher nature that will prevail. It is the message that "things happen for a reason," but rather than take that message as a call to passivity, it is an invitation to explore what that reason may be. Moving through these higher alchemical stages propels us toward the rebirth of ourselves as spiritually directed humans with a Higher Purpose to fulfill during our time here. This stage begins to provide some clues to the purpose.

Differing from the intense fire of calcination, fermentation heats with gentle warmth that allows the soul to come forth to be nurtured and encouraged in the next stages.

Personal Alchemical Reflections

July 12: What patterns do you see come up for you again and again?

July 13: What still has the power to knock you off center?

July 14: What thoughts or experiences still bring up shame for you?

July 15: Reflect on a time of despair in your life, and what brought you to that point.

July 16: What is your motivation to get out of bed each morning?

July 17: What hope fills your life with meaning?

July 18: If there was one word to describe your experience of your soul, what would it be?

Thirty-One

. . . .

Energetic Reflection on the Throat Chakra

THROAT CHAKRA ASSOCIATIONS [13]

. . . .

Name: Vishuddha • **Location:** Throat • **Color:** Light blue • **Tone:** G
Gland: Thyroid • **Body:** Lungs, throat, vocal chords, jaw, and neck
Yoga Path: Mantra • **Symbol:** Sixteen-petalled lotus
Stones: Aquamarine, Turquoise, Chaldecony, Kyanite

Along with the solar plexus chakra, the throat chakra is the one most often blocked in individuals. The two are intimately connected. If we do not know who we are (solar plexus chakra), how can we express who we are to the world (throat chakra)?

The throat chakra is about communication and all the different ways we share with others and the world at large. It is partly about the words we say, but it also encompasses all forms of expressive communication, regardless of whether they are verbal or not. Writing, painting, and dancing can all be emanations from the throat chakra in that we delve into our own inner selves to draw forth that which we express outside of ourselves.

A blocked throat chakra can manifest as physical disease through colds, bronchitis, sore throats, and tonsillitis. Breathing issues such as asthma can also be indicators of a blocked

. . . .

13 Throat chakra associations adapted from *The Chakra Handbook: From Basic Understanding to Practical Application*, Shalila Sharamon and Bodo J. Baginski (Wilmot, WI: Lotus Light Publications, 1991).

throat chakra, as well as thyroid conditions such as hypothyroidism (an under-active thyroid) and hyperthyroidism (an overactive thyroid).

If we have taken in a message that what we have to say does not matter, it will affect this area. We need to believe that our voice matters, even if the other person is not able to hear or does not agree with what we have to say. It is the claiming of our own voice that is important. But attention needs to be paid to how something is communicated. Choosing our words with care and realizing that words have significance is part of encouraging a healthy throat chakra. When our words reflect our truth, in connection with our Essence, then we are truly expressing ourselves. If you are angry you can communicate the crux of that anger with facts ("When you did this . . .") and feelings ("I felt this . . ."). Hostility, swearing, and put-downs are not part of the equation. They are reflective of a wounded ego, not the True Self.

Often it is not just how we communicate that reveals to us how our throat chakra is functioning; it is also how much we are communicating that serves as a signal. Words can be used to facilitate understanding, or they can be used to baffle and confound. When communicating, it can make a significant difference to take the time to choose our words precisely, and use only as many words as is necessary to share what needs to be shared. Filling airspace with a stream of words that do nothing to illuminate perspective or clarify issues is not communication; it is distraction.

When we speak our truth we are coming from a place of integrity. There is an old saying that all a man has is his word. When we lie, we are acting out of sync with our highest and best selves. Energetically this shuts us down, starting with the throat chakra. Our truth may shift as we become privy to more information, but to be honest with ourselves and others from a heart-filled, compassionate place will keep our throat chakra vibrant and do much to honor and validate our own selves.

Messages that help to balance the throat chakra are:
I communicate clearly and effectively.
What I say matters.
I express openly and safely.

Personal Energetic Reflections

July 19: The color light blue makes me feel…

July 20: Reflect on how sharing your stories and adventures was responded to as a child.

July 21: In what ways do you communicate what excites you to others?

July 22: Reflect on a time when you may have had a frog or a lump in your throat.

July 23: If you have ever lied, what were you afraid to say?

July 24: What emotions are the hardest for you to express?

July 25: What message do you want to share with the world?

Thirty-Two

· · · · · · · · · · · · · · · · · · · ·

Guidance Reflection on Elementals and Intuitive Reflection on Tarot

Elementals

Ancient cultures were full of stories about creatures that could be seen in this world but were not of this world. These beings lived in the realm of the otherworld but could impact the human world. There are literally hundreds of names for these beings, and each of them has a slightly different sense, or "flavor." Each one connects to a specific aspect of the world and has its own stories, both of intrigue and of caution. Sidhe, elf, brownie, pixie, selkie, kelpie, goblin, sprite, leprechaun. These are just some of the names that come down to us through stories. The aspect that connects all these beings together is the sense that there is another realm that still connects to the world of nature, but that is of a higher and finer vibration.

Elementals are nature spirits that interact with the natural world but connect to this otherworldly realm. They give us entrance into a magical, yet still earthy, experience of our lives. Though there are many of these creatures, Paracelsus seems to have been the first to attribute elementals to certain alchemical elements, giving us insight into how to work more directly and effectively with these energies.

Gnomes are connected with the element of the earth and are sometimes referred to as dwarves. There is a similar energy between the two, and the difference in names seems to be a language difference. The term gnome, coined by Paracelsus, comes from the Latin *gnomi* meaning "earth dweller." The term dwarf comes to us from Norse, and seems rooted in the old Norse word *dvegr*. A dvegr is a small creature who lives in the mountains, is very wise, and is involved in mining and smithcraft. Gnomes and dwarves help us connect to the solid physicality and beauty of the earth. They are the keepers and protectors of earth's treasures and are useful to work with in matters of money, abundance, work, and honing a craft.

Undines are water spirits connected with the element of water. Undines were also written of quite extensively by Paracelsus. More commonly, we attribute the term mermaid to those elemental creatures of water. The ancient Greeks called them *naiads*. Undines are said to be found in streams, springs, ponds, and lakes. They are sensual and graceful, connecting us to emotions such as love. They are useful to work with in matters of love, friendship, and desire.

According to Paracelsus, the elementals associated with air are *sylphs*, although there is no known mythology for them. They have tended to be interchanged with fairies, which appear in the folktales and stories of many cultures. Being of light, aetheric material they are often confused with angelic energy, although angels have a completely different resonance. Sylphs are active, energetic, and subtle. They can help us in matters of the intellect and in the development of ideas. Fairies tend to have a particular energy which connects them to plants, flowers, and trees.

The elemental that Paracelsus attributed to the element of fire is the most challenging to access. Salamanders as fire spirits are not the wee lizard that comes to mind. Though similar in feature to the natural salamander, the elemental is often pictured in alchemy as coming forth from the flames or having the ability to put out fire, withstanding any amount of heat. Salamanders are explosive and forceful, helping us in matters requiring courage and will. But they are notoriously unpredictable, and one is urged to use caution when working with salamander energy.

To access elementals you can use the element (earth, water, air, or fire) as a connection point. There are also a number of wonderful oracle decks that can provide much insight. Most of these decks focus on fairy energy. Pay attention to unusual plays of light or movement caught out of the corner of your eye when out in nature. This can be an indication that one of the wee folk are by your side. Unusual, natural formations such as a flattened ring in a field of grass can also indicate evidence that there have been otherworldly beings about.

There are some who caution around interacting with the wee folk. Many old stories are cautionary tales of what one should or should not do in the case of an encounter. Rip van Winkle fell asleep on a fairy mound and woke up a hundred years later. Changelings were fairy children exchanged with human ones. It was well known that after October 31, anything left in the fields was for the wee folk and woe betide anyone who tried to harvest after that date. A mermaid's beautiful song served to entice sailors overboard to their doom.

Rather than see these messages as promoting anxiety around interacting with these elemental guides, it can be helpful to see that there has always been a respect for the interaction between humans and elementals, and yet the nature of our realms are very different. Stories present that, in the otherworld, things look sharper and brighter. Food is tastier and drink is like nectar. Time moves differently. In many ways, the otherworld begins to sound like the idealization of ours. But what we cannot forget is that our human aspect is just as beautifully significant as our spiritual aspect.

The elementals and their otherworld can teach us much, but we are still living with our feet in the human realm. The tales of warning are not so much about not being open to the teachings of these wonderful creatures, but to take care not to get lost in their realm. If we do stumble upon a fairy mound, the true beauty lies in bringing the transformative experience back to apply to our own lives.

Further Exploration on Elementals

A Field Guide to the Little People by Nancy Arrowsmith with George Moorse. Farrar, Straus and Giroux, 1977.

Enchantment of the Faerie Realm: Communicate with Nature Spirits & Elementals by Ted Andrews. Llewellyn Publications, 2002.

Fairies: Real Encounters with Little People by Janet Bord. Dell, 1997.

The Healing Power of Faery: Working with Elementals and Nature Spirits to Soothe the Body and Soul by Edain Mccoy. Provenance Press, 2008.

Tarot

Tarot is an eloquent, intuitive tool that speaks of the multiple layers and aspects of life and self. A true tarot deck consists of seventy-eight cards made up of two distinct sections: the major arcana and the minor arcana. The minor arcana, similar to a regular deck of playing cards, is made up of four suits. Each suit has ten numbered cards (from Ace to ten), generally referred to as the *pips*, and four court cards consisting of a Page, Knight, Queen, and King (or equivalent). The four tarot suits of pentacles, cups, swords, and wands are associated with diamonds, hearts, spades, and clubs found in regular playing card decks. Some tarot decks name the suits differently, but the area of focus remains consistent. What makes the tarot a completely different kettle of fish are the twenty-two cards of the major arcana. These cards are sometimes referred to as the *trumps,* and have been the cause of fascination for centuries.

No one is really certain of tarot's origins, though there has been much speculation about when it first truly made an appearance and from where it originated. Some theories place its origins in Egypt and link it to Egyptian esoterica. Other theories have its origins in Italy, presenting that the cards were representations of the Triomphi floats that reminded people of the vices and virtues. Although there is some meager historical evidence for the cards dating back to the fifteenth century, what we do know for certain is that in the late eighteenth century, the cards came to the notice of Eugene Court de Gebelin. An essay written by Gebelin in 1781 presented the Egyptian origin theory connected the tarot to the twenty-two letters of the Hebrew alphabet and suggested meanings for the cards. This essay influenced a French fortuneteller, named Etteilla, who popularized reading tarot to a wider audience, creating the foundation for contemporary approaches to tarot.

For *The Great Work,* and as the intuitive tool of this cycle, the tarot is ideal for addressing the interplay between our inner and outer worlds. The major arcana reflects the grand patterns that shape our lives, and the minor arcana reflects four aspects through which we experience our lives. This may be seen as akin to the difference between a career and a job. A career is an overarching pattern (major arcana) that may filter through many different jobs (minor arcana). Whereas the cards of the minor arcana reflect innumerable situations, events, emotions, and responses, the cards of the major arcana represent archetypal energy.

An archetype is defined as a "ruling energy." In and of themselves, archetypes are nothing but empty vessels. Carl Jung presented that archetypes exist in the collective unconscious and are common to each and every person. We all contain the empty vessel of each archetype, but it is not until we encounter an archetype in our own personal life that it begins to take shape. The particular shape it takes informs us about our own experiences. For example, we all carry the archetype for "mother," but what mother means to me will be different from everyone else because my experience is specific to me. Additionally, each archetype has a light and shadow aspect. Each archetype has the side that inspires and encourages (light) and the side that represses and diminishes (dark). I may have had experiences of the nurturing mother or the smothering mother. They are very different, but both reflect the archetype. Working with archetypes allows us to reveal how we have filled the empty vessel, releasing the negative hold of any dark attributes and integrating the positive influence of the light aspects. This shift from dark to light is what the healing journey is all about.

In this approach, the major arcana can be divided into three sections of seven cards, with one card, The Fool, standing alone. The Fool is the card that represents the soul embracing the journey from folly to wisdom.

The first seven cards can be viewed as the "archetypes of character" who shape our journey through childhood to adulthood. In the Magician, High Priestess, Empress, and Emperor we see the guiding energies of the spiritual masculine and feminine followed by the earthly parents. The Hierophant takes us into school-age years as the societal guide that can represent an institution (including educational or religious). The Lovers opens us to experience of the other in relationship, which often occurs in adolescence. The Chariot sees the youth setting out for the world as a young adult, having taken in the teachings from all he or she has encountered up until this point.

The middle seven cards are "archetypes of quality," which act as tools we can draw upon to help us through the challeng-

The Fool (0).

ing times. In reflecting concepts like "levels of consciousness," they balance each other beautifully. There are the three guides offering insight into our unconscious, conscious, and superconscious. Strength represents our instinctive side, connecting to the Inner Child, the unconscious, and our feelings. Justice represents our discernment, connecting to our True Self, the conscious, and our reason. Temperance represents higher guidance, connecting to our Higher Self, the superconscious, and wisdom. The Wheel of Fortune and the Hanged Man teach of balance and moderation. The Wheel of Fortune shows us that the truth is in the center of the wheel—not in the ups and downs. The Hanged Man reminds us that the truth is in the middle—not in the polarization of extremes. Both the Hermit and Death hint that, ultimately, the sacrifice of the material world is necessary. Whereas the Hermit transcends the material world by removing himself from it, Death transforms it by engaging with those elements that may limit us.

The final seven cards present the challenging journey from unhealthy ego (or false self) to individuation (or true self). The Devil represents attachment to the material world expressed through the unhealthy ego. The healing journey begins with the Tower, which generally indicates calcination or entering a period of the "dark night of the soul." The Star (superconscious), Moon (unconscious), and Sun (conscious) offer the opportunity to explore different aspects of self as multi-dimensional beings. But, as was mentioned in fermentation, this is not the end of the journey. Judgment opens us to truly release any last vestiges of an unhealthy ego so that we can experience ourselves as a wondrous, whole, and integrated self in the world.

The sheer beauty of the tarot is that in twenty-two cards, the entire of the potential of the human experience in the journey from unconsciousness to consciousness, and indeed superconsciousness, is illuminated.

So what, then, are the remaining fifty-six cards? Why do we need the minor arcana? If the cards in the major arcana represent the archetypes, the cards in the minor arcana represent the different aspects of day-to-day life. The suits of the minor arcana are associated with the various levels of self—physical, emotional, mental, and spiritual—allowing for information on the different areas in our life that may need focus and attention. Within the minor arcana are the court cards that are notoriously challenging to access. When using the cards for self-insight, these cards also represent some aspect of self, rather than another individual in your life. They are associated with various levels of personal growth within the domain of the suit: learning, testing, integrating, and mastery.

Pentacles are associated all those aspects that provide a firm foundation in our lives: work, money, our home, our bodies, and physical health. Pentacles give us information about how we are taking care of the material aspects of our lives. They resonate with earth and the root chakra.

Cups show how we embrace emotions as an integral part of our lives and how we process the challenging emotions. Cups give us information on how we move through the stages of grief and allow joy in our lives. They also reflect how we are in relation to others and our memories of the past. They resonate with water and the sacral, solar plexus, and heart chakras.

Swords are associated with our mental process and beliefs. They challenge us to look at the thoughts that distance us from our emotional life, serving only to criticize, attack, and delude us. They resonate with air, and the throat and brow chakras.

Wands are associated with vision and inspiration. They inform us of our ability to envision our futures, what we want to create in our lives, how we work in collaboration with the Divine, and how we manage to overcome obstacles. They resonate with fire and the crown chakra.

There are many different spreads or layouts that can be used in different circumstances to gain insight. For an overview on all aspects of self and current lessons, The Alchemist Spread is recommended. It is a five-card journal spread that can be done on a daily basis.

The Tarot Alchemist Spread

This spread is best done in the morning to give a sense of what energies are at play within that may unfold throughout the day. If you are just starting to work with the tarot, it can be helpful to revisit the spread in the evening, making note of what the day held. Correlations can be made between what cards appeared in the morning and what events, feelings, or thoughts occurred during the day.

Take some time to center yourself and shuffle the cards. The twittering birds technique of shuffling works well to allow for some cards to be reversed. Major arcana reversals tend to indicate that you are working with a dark aspect of the archetype. Reversals in the minor arcana can indicate your own resistance to the situation or emotion. Reversals show us where we are blocked and what, in particular, needs our attention.

Pull five cards, placing them in order from left to right. This spread adds a level of complexity to reading, requiring the interpretation of the card in the context of the position. Pulling a pentacle for the first position could indicate the status of your financial situation. Pulling a cup for the first position could indicate your feelings about your financial situation. Pulling a sword for the first position could indicate your beliefs about money. Pulling a wand for the first position could indicate brilliant new ideas for changing your financial situation. Pulling a major arcana for the first position indicates that there are deep archetypal influences or shifts occurring around your relationship with money. Pay attention to both the card itself and how it relates to the areas of focus indicated by the card position.

First position—Earth: This position gives us information about our physical health, work, or finances. How we are feeling in our bodies or how stable we feel in our lives.

Second position—Water: This position reveals where we are at emotionally or in relation to others. What may be contributing to joy or what we still need to grieve.

Third position—Air: This position illuminates the thoughts or beliefs are prevalent in the current situation. What negative messages limit us or how we can release them.

Fourth position—Fire: This position reflects what new ideas, plans, or dreams may be percolating. What visions inspire us and how we may change the current situation.

Fifth position—Aether: This position informs us on lessons or higher insights we can benefit from knowing at this time. It shows us how spirit is guiding us to shift into our highest potential.

The Major Arcana

The Magician (I)

- the act of changing consciousness at will
- spirit in nature
- knowledge of interrelation of things

The High Priestess (II)

- intuition
- wisdom through teachings
- higher truths through inner knowing

The Empress (III)

- "Mother"
- nurturing
- encouragement of growth and emotional life

The Emperor (IV)

- "Father"
- protection
- establishment of boundaries and order

The Hierophant (V)

- "Society"
- rules and guidelines
- teaches how to live in context of others
- authority

The Lovers (VI)

- "Partnership"
- union
- synthesis of opposites
- communication

The Major Arcana

The Chariot (VII)

- "Ability"
- establishing one's place in the world
- expression of self through work

Strength (VIII)

- "Guide of unconscious self"
- instinct
- reaction vs. response

Hermit (IX)

- "Transcendence"
- solitude
- distance from material world to attain higher insight

Wheel of Fortune (X)

- "Centeredness"
- not being swayed by life's ups and downs
- being the hub rather than the wheel

Justice (XI)

- "Guide of conscious self"
- discernment
- seeing truth as opposed to illusion

The Hanged Man (XII)

- "Balance"
- moderation between extremes
- releasing attachment to rigid roles

The Major Arcana

Death (XIII)

- "Transformation"
- letting go of that which no longer serves
- release of old patterns

Temperance (XIV)

- "Guide of superconscious self"
- messages from our Higher Self about larger perspective

Devil (XV)

- "Materialism"
- false self or persona
- attachment to material world
- addiction

The Tower (XVI)

- "Crisis" or "Dark night of the soul"
- loss
- sudden change
- shock

The Star (XVII)

- "Superconscious"
- hope and optimism
- nourishing both body and soul

The Moon (XVIII)

- "Unconscious"
- feelings
- our past, including old wounds and unresolved issues

The Major Arcana

The Sun (XIX)

- "Conscious"
- reclaiming the Inner Child in True Self
- health ego
- energy and vitality

Judgement (XX)

- "Final Release"
- making amends for past hurts or mistakes
- moving into forgiveness

The World (XXI)

- "Being whole"
- balance of all aspects of self
- attainment of Philosopher's Stone

The Suit of Pentacles

Ace
New
foundation

Two
Balance (i.e.,
work and play)

Three
Advancement
through skill

Four
Attachment to
wealth, miser

Five
Physical or
material crisis

Six
Charity,
generosity

Seven
Hard
work and
enterprise

Eight
Honing
one's
craft

Nine
Prosperity,
affluence

Ten
Achievement,
balance of work
and home

Page
Learning new
approaches
to health
or finance

Knight
Cautious
application

Queen
Resourceful and
generous
application
(see Empress)

King
Practical and
pragmatic
application
(see Emperor)

The Suit of Cups

Ace
New relationship
or aspect of
emotional life

Two
Support,
healing, love
(see Lovers)

Three
Joy,
celebration

Four
Contemplation,
boredom, taking
for granted

Five
Emotional
crisis,
grief

Six
Nostalgia, happy
memories,
"rose-colored
glasses"

Seven
Choices,
dreams,
temptation,
illusion

Eight
The work
of the heart,
reevaluation
(see Hermit)

Nine
Achievement,
happiness but
emotional
isolation

Ten
Fulfillment,
harmony,
connection

Page
Learning new
approaches to
feelings and
relationships

Knight
Sensitive
and
gentle
application

Queen
Nurturing
and
loving
application

King
Compassionate
yet
firm
application

The Suit of Swords

Ace
New
thought
processes

Two
Compromise,
emotions in
decisions

Three
Anger,
resentment,
hurtful words

Four
Introspection,
meditation

Five
Crisis of beliefs,
victory at
any cost

Six
Distance
from
confrontation

Seven
Deception,
denial

Eight
Trapped,
circular
thinking

Nine
Negativity,
depression,
Inner Critic

Ten
Despair, overcome,
turning point
for new dawn

Page
Learning new ways
to approach self
and situations,
psychology

Knight
Enthusiastic
and
vigorous
application

Queen
Tempered,
sometimes stern
application
(see Justice)

King
Strict,
principled
application

The Suit of Wands

Ace
New
projects

Two
Contemplation
of leaving the
familiar

Three
Visioning
new
possibilities

Four
Harvest
and
celebrations

Five
Crisis of
commitment,
defending vision

Six
Victory,
recognition

Seven
Perseverance,
rededication

Eight
Inspiration,
increased
activity

Nine
Pause,
exhaustion,
reevaluation

Ten
Weariness,
exploring how to
carry one's load

Page
Open to new
avenues of expression
and vision

Knight
Passionate and
spontaneous
application

Queen
Creative and
energetic
application

King
Courageous
and charismatic
application

Further Exploration on the Tarot

Around the Tarot in 78 Days: A Personal Journey Through the Cards by Marcus Katz and Tali Goodwin. Llewellyn Publications, 2012.

Jung and Tarot: An Archetypal Journey by Sallie Nichols. Weiser Books, 1980.

Rachel Pollack's Tarot Wisdom: Spiritual Teachings and Deeper Meanings by Rachel Pollack. Llewellyn Publications, 2008.

The Tarot: History, Mystery and Lore by Cynthia Giles. Touchstone, 1994.

Tarot for Your Self: A Workbook for Personal Transformation by Mary K. Greer. New Pages Books, 2002.

Personal Guidance and Intuitive Reflections

July 26: What stories of the wee folk do you remember from childhood?

July 27: To which elemental (gnome, undine, fairy, or salamander) do you feel drawn?

July 28: Reflect upon a time in your life that you had a magical encounter in nature.

July 29: To which major arcana card do you respond most strongly?

July 30: To which minor arcana card do you respond most strongly?

July 31: How might you see a single event through the lens of each minor arcana suit?

August 1: How does exploring the connection between archetypal energy and day-to-day life enhance your self-awareness?

The Clear Hynni of Expression

*When you find yourself silenced. When you feel that what you say has no signifi-
cance or your expression in the world has no value. When it feels impossible to put
your choices into action, to communicate with others or honor your truth, this is the time to
activate the Hynni of Expression.*

*This Hynni symbol represents the amplification of voice through all means of
communication.*

Preparation: Find a spot where you know you will not be disturbed and eliminate
any possible sources of distraction. You may choose to have a tarot deck beside you. Begin
to breathe deeply, visualizing the breath moving in and out of your body as the color light
blue. Release any tension you may be holding in your body, breathing into that space, and
bringing yourself to center. Focus on the breath moving in and out of your body, through
your nose or mouth, and moving down your windpipe into your lungs.

Hynni: As you breathe, allow yourself to become aware of your body and all the physiological systems that support it. Feel the density of your skeletal system and the structure
it provides. Feel the flow of your circulatory system, transporting nutrients through your
blood. Feel the current of your respiratory system, delivering oxygen to your blood. Feel the
charge of your nervous system, processing information throughout your body. These and
other systems within your body all work together, each operating differently, and yet contributing to the same purpose. Working together they create something greater than each of
them operating separately.

Bring your awareness to your throat. If it feels comfortable, place your hands gently
over your throat center. Take care not to apply any pressure. Just rest your hands lightly in
place. If this feels too constricting, place your hands on your chest, holding the intention
of focusing on your throat as you move through the hynni mediation. Begin to sense what
the energy feels like in your throat—if it feels like it is moving and flowing or if it is blocked
and stuck. Be aware of this energy as carrying that which is deep within you to the external
world. It can either act as a megaphone, amplifying and expanding your message for all to
hear, or it can act as a clamp, shutting down the flow of all your expressions and actions.

Begin to focus on the expression symbol, visualizing a golden light that carries the intent of the symbol moving through your hands and into your throat. As you do, feel your voice becoming clear. You are the soft nudge of a whisper. You are the joyful shout from the rooftops. You are the monologue heard by many ears, the dance of dialogue, and the melody of vibrant discussion. You are filled with messages that support the integrity and importance of your voice. You are seen and heard. Whether others agree and acknowledge or not, your voice is significant.

If you choose, begin to shuffle your tarot deck. Hold in your mind a question or situation for which you need guidance or insight. It may be a choice or decision that may need to be made. It may be regarding a conversation or confrontation that may need to be made. It may be regarding a conversation or confrontation that may need to occur. Allow one card to come away from the others, taking that card as the guiding message and putting the other cards aside. As you look at the card, begin to visualize it as an environment to explore with all your senses. See all the elements in the card surround you in living color, immersing yourself in the experience and allowing your hearing and sense of smell engage in the process. If there are people in the environment, approach them. Talk to them about what messages or insights they may have. How does the energy of this space hold a key to the situation or question you have? Explore until it feels you have a clear answer and thank any people you may have consulted in this place for their guidance. Slowly allow the inner vision of the tarot environment to fade away and focus once more on your breath.

With an open heart and open mind, invite an elemental to come to you. This elemental may speak to you in relation to its element, or have a further message with respect to the tarot card. Know that whichever elemental comes to you, it carries a perfect message for you in this moment.

When you have heard the message from the elemental, and feel filled with enlivened and creative energy, begin to bring your focus back once more to the room. Take three deep, centering breaths, allowing each breath to bring you more fully back into the room, knowing that you are the vessel for a special message to the world that is yours alone to share. When you feel present once more, you may want to touch your feet to anchor yourself in conscious awareness.

Part Eight

Cycle Six
August 2–September 12

Visioning Self
"Gaze Upon the Earth with Clarity of Light"

PRESCRIPTIONS

Go through this section if you are experiencing any of the following:

- Confused or racing thoughts
- Difficulty in "turning off the brain"
- Critical or harsh inner dialogue
- Difficulty envisioning or planning the future
- Under- or overactive imagination

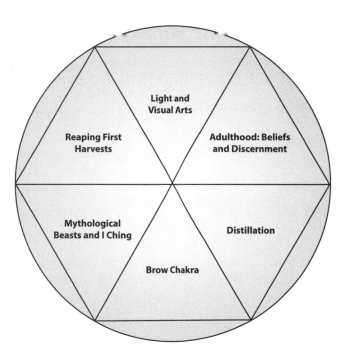

Thirty-Three

· · · · · · · · · · · · · · · · · · ·

Mythological Reflection on Reaping First Harvests

In ancient cultures the beginning of August brought festivity, as well as refocused work and effort. The growing period was at an end, and there was limited time to bring in the harvest. The period between this festival and the next was a time of busy preparation, integral to planning for the survival of the tribe through the dark winter months that were inching closer and closer. At this time of the first reaping the culmination of abundance was at hand. Some traditions hold that this is the time for the baking of the first bread: a special loaf that holds the promise of all the loaves that will come forth out of the harvest.

This celebration is a reflection of the pre-spring purification, preparing for a time of activity and laying plans for the future. There is the gathering of harvest, but also the gathering of seeds that will be necessary for future harvests. What is to come in the cycles ahead needs to be kept in mind with conscious awareness at this time. No seeds for the future means no harvest in the future. With this in mind, as the crops were stored for use in the winter months, so were the seeds stored for use in the spring ahead. Abundance comes, not just through hard work and effort in the present days, but through good planning and preparation for the future.

This was a time of pride and the sharing of accomplishment—recognition for the abundance waiting to be collected. The work of the harvest required the hands of many. The gathering of the tribes began, and it was a playful time to put forth pride in ability through games and competition. As the days grow shorter this is a celebration of life and effort, of hard work and sacrifice. The games provided both an enthusiastic outlet and an honoring of the strengths developed and mastered.

One name for the ancient games associated with this time of year was *Lughnasadh*, named for the Celtic god Lugh, who was particularly skilled and fond of games involving shows of strength. Myth presents that he was fostered by the goddess Tailtiu, who undertook the great task of clearing a great forest in her love for the people at the cost of her life. In his great love for his foster mother, Lugh instituted games to be held in her honor, known as the Tailteann games. Some records show these games to date as far back as 2000 BCE, traditionally held in the place cleared by Tailtiu, the modern Irish town of Telltown (i.e., Tailtiu's town).

Many fall fairs have their roots in this celebration with feats of strength, tractor pulls, baking competitions, and livestock judging. The gathering of the community to celebrate hearkens back to the ancient celebration held in honor of the goddess who sacrificed her life to prepare the land for her people. In ancient times the strength displayed at the games would be truly put to the test in the coming days with the effort to harvest the fields. There is no time to waste when the time is ripe. But, for a moment, at least, there can be a pause to engage in community and revelry. In this moment there is the opportunity to celebrate the triumph of human activity and ability, and of human victory over the challenges presented by life and nature.

Main Themes for Cycle 6:

Pride

Ability

Strength

Ancient Cultural Archetypes of Wealth and Prosperity

Bahet *(Egyptian)* is a goddess of wealth and abundance.

Euthenia *(Greek)* is one of the Graces, connected to prosperity. Her sisters are **Eukleia** (good repute), **Philophrosyne** (welcome), and **Eupheme** (acclaim). Her opposite is **Penia** (poverty).

Hades *(Greek)* or **Pluto** *(Roman)* is the god of the underworld, with access to the wealth buried deep in the earth.

Abundantia *(Roman)* is a goddess of abundance whose name gives us the word abundant.

Copia *(Roman)* is a goddess of abundance whose name gives us the word copious. The abundance connected with her also implies wealth of resources and opportunity.

Fortuna *(Roman)* is a goddess of good fortune whose name gives us the word fortune. She also presides over good luck and the positive implications of fate.

Ana *(Celtic)* is a goddess of fertility, wealth, and abundance. She is often interchanged with **Danu** *(Celtic)*, the ancestral mother goddess connected with the land.

Dagda *(Celtic)* is a jovial father god of abundance who fed the world from his cauldron of plenty.

Epona *(Celtic)* is a goddess of horses, fertility, and abundance. She is sometimes interchanged with **Rhiannon** *(Celtic)*, a goddess associated with horses and whose birds could awaken the dead.

Maeve *(Celtic)* is a goddess of the land, particularly revered in Ireland.

Fulla *(Norse)* is a goddess of abundance and one of Frigga's handmaidens.

Freyr *(Norse)* is a god of virility, fertility, and prosperity.

 Personal Mythological Reflections

August 2: What are your greatest strengths?

August 3: What do you do for enjoyment in the company of others?

August 4: What have you sacrificed to accomplish a sought-after goal or to benefit your community?

August 5: Reflect on a time of competition in your life and how comfortable you felt in that dynamic.

August 6: How do you reflect the best in yourself to others?

August 7: Reflect on a time you were celebrated.

August 8: How do you celebrate the successes of others or support their efforts?

Thirty-Four

Energetic Reflection on Light and Active Reflection on Visual Arts

Light: The Play of Perspective

From a technical perspective light is electromagnetic radiation. Light that is visible to the human eye falls in a range from infrared to ultraviolet, depending on its wavelength—the color spectrum that we see so beautifully evidenced in the rainbow.

Light plays an integral role in classical physics in that the speed of light (in a vacuum) is a constant. Though intensity, wavelength, and direction are variables that change, the speed of light is consistent at 186,282 miles per second. It is used to measure distance (i.e., light years) and is the constant variable in the equation to measure energy. In the famous equation $E=mc^2$, the speed of light is represented by the symbol "c." The equation literally reads that "energy is equal to mass times the speed of light squared." The only consistent element in the equation is the speed of light.

Light has long fascinated scientists and artists. The first attempts to measure light were by Galileo. The Impressionist artists of the nineteenth century created an entire style of art based upon attempts to capture the changing quality of light, utilizing visible brush strokes to highlight light play.

With light we begin to enter into the mutable character of the elements. Quantum physics has been instrumental in illuminating that the structure of light itself can change even if its speed does not. Light is not a thing in itself. The question that has been a key point of debate in the physical sciences for hundreds of years is, "Is light a particle or a wave?" This was answered in the twentieth century by the potentially befuddling response of "both." Modern technical innovations allowed for experiments that were previously impossible, contributing to the acceptance of the concept of wave-particle duality. We now know that, depending on a number of factors including environment (i.e., the experiment process) and intensity (i.e., how bright or dim), light has the potential to present as either a wave or as a particle. In many ways, it is the expectation that creates the outcome. The resulting reality we see is dependent on initial factors that impact on the process of determining that reality itself.

Connecting with light as an element allows us to begin to see ourselves within that same context. Our reality depends not only on the external factors around us, but the factors we bring to that experience. We are able to see the impact that our own perspective has on how we experience the world around us. Additionally, we are able to accept that we too have a paradoxical nature. We are both body and spirit. We are both the unchanging core of Essence and the shifting responses we exhibit in different situations. Connecting to the element of light opens us to an experience of self that is both constant and changing. Through this we begin to embody the true paradox of a human experience.

Messages that help to connect us to the element of light are:
My vision reflects my highest potential.
I embrace the paradox of my human-spirit nature.
I see clearly from the highest perspective.

Visual Arts

The activity of drawing or painting tends to bring up resistance in many who hold high standards for themselves as to what a piece of art is supposed to look like and what criteria needs to be applied to make such work valid. Granted, there are great works of art and other not-so-great works of art. There have been centuries of debates of what constitutes great art. To a large degree, the problem with deciding what is great is that the judgment is entirely subjective. What constitutes a great work of art? Truly, it is that which you feel is a great work of art, and that will be completely different from what someone else feels.

There is one purpose to art, and that is to express. Each artistic method offers a different mode of expression. Visual artists share their vision of how they see the world. There have been many visionary artists of the past whose work seems to carry a precognition of what scientists later deduce through research and experimentation. Time and time again there have been those artists who "see" the truth before we can actually "prove" the truth. A work of art will move us. It evokes an emotional response, sometimes even a negative emotional response. Art always invites us to see the world from a different perspective. We don't have to hold to that perspective, but to even entertain it for a moment always serves to expand our consciousness.

To open yourself to exploring the gifts of this cycle through the visual arts, you need only reconnect to the energy of that Inner Child who sees a box of crayons as the wonder of discovery and joy! Tapping into that openness allows you to enter the experience of creating for the sheer joy of creating, rather than being guided by an attachment to what the end result may be. If three forceful purple squiggles is a dragon picking daisies in a forest, who is anyone to say differently? The beauty of picking up the crayon without a preconceived idea of what the image is supposed to look like, is that the imagination becomes engaged and we learn the process of allowing our creativity to unfold.

For those who truly have reservations about picking up the pencil, crayon, or marker, a collage is a wonderful method of visual artistry. Gathering photos or cutting images from magazines for your own personal use can provide a whole other palette to work with. Intentional collages, otherwise known as a *vision board*, have become a popular technique that helps you to gain clarity on the direction of your future-building, and to maintain a focus of commitment to that vision. In the creation of a vision board you activate an emotional connection to the images being used, and create a "future memory" of your goal. In the mechanics of a brain's function, imagination and memory touch upon the very same areas. In other words, whether we are remembering the past or imagining the future, we are using the same parts of our brain. Using imagination to envision what we want to attract into our lives starts a resonance within us that helps in manifesting it into reality. This is an important first step in the process that includes the emotional energy of desiring the outcome, and the belief system that supports us in the steps we must take to actualize the outcome. Taking the time to put inner vision into outer visuals helps to clarify where we may be out of alignment with what we must do or where adjustments need to be made.

Scrapbooking is another visual technique that can used to support the healing journey. Traditionally, scrapbooks have been approached as "memory keepers," and there are many resources available that can help one create stunningly beautiful, evocative keepsakes. It is a small shift of intention to make a scrapbook into a work of reclaiming rather than remembering. An Inner Child scrapbook can reconnect you to the optimism and enthusiasm you had for life as a child. One approach to an Inner Child scrapbook is to create a page per stage, focusing on your experiences during that stage, the qualities and strengths you expressed at that stage, what you remember as being important to you, or the dreams you had. Giving visual expression to these years validates the experience, allowing for self-acceptance and incorporating those qualities that may have been repressed for years.

Art, like music, circumvents our intellectual side and opens us to a visceral, felt experience. We remember what we feel in our bodies far longer than facts in our heads. Allowing expression through the visual arts is a powerful way to activate change in our lives.

Further Exploration on the Visual Arts

Art and Healing: Using Expressive Art to Heal Your Body, Mind, and Spirit by Barbara Ganim. Echo Point Books & Media, 2013.

Art & Physics: Parallel Visions in Space, Time, and Light by Leonard Shlain. William Morrow Paperbacks, 2007.

Einstein's Space and Van Gogh's Sky: Physical Reality and Beyond by Lawrence LeShan and Henry Margenau. Macmillan, 1983.

The Complete Vision Board Kit: Using the Power of Intention and Visualization to Achieve Your Dreams by John Assaraf. Atria Books, 2008.

The Soul's Palette: Drawing on Art's Transformative Powers for Health and Well-Being by Cathy A. Malchiodi. Shambhala, 2002.

Personal Elemental and Active Reflections

August 9: Do you prefer being in bright light or a dark, subdued setting?

August 10: How aware are you of your impact or effect on events?

August 11: What about yourself do you know to be a constant?

August 12: Have you ever found yourself mesmerized by the play of light?

August 13: Reflect on an image or painting that impacted you greatly.

August 14: What is your comfort level around drawing or painting?

August 15: How might an image or picture help you to focus on a goal or vision?

Thirty-Five

Developmental Reflection on Adulthood and Psychological Reflection on Beliefs and Discernment

Fifties and Sixties

As we move through our adult lives, much of the angst and consternation of the earlier years fades into a level of acceptance. This is part of what contributes to the generation gap. Adults, with the perspective of time, don't tend to get as worked up about issues as the young. The young often feel that the older generations have given up or sold out. In many cases, it is not that as we get older we care less about issues, situations, and circumstances. It is that we gain more of an understanding of how things tend to unfold. We understand that urgency is not the same as significance, and that considered use of effort has far greater effect than reactive use of effort.

Often by our fifties and sixties we have come to a sense of equilibrium and peace about life. The forties often see another reevaluation, the infamous mid-life crisis with the questions of "What have I done with my life? Was the sacrifice worth it?" or, "How did I make such a wrong turn?" The fifties and sixties see more of a coming to resolution. This may not have been the life I originally envisioned, but it is the life I have, and it is up to me to do what I can with the time I have left to feel satisfied and fulfilled.

By this stage in life the areas of challenge have often been alleviated. Children have been raised and are self-responsible. Perhaps there are now grandchildren in the picture, and there is a far different dynamic between grandparent and grandchild than there is between parent and child. There is more possibility for the expression of pure love, joy, and acceptance than the day-to-day guidance and worry that tend to be associated with raising one's own children. Often, work concerns have lessened. For many, the drive and attention associated with building a career has settled as we move into the twilight of our work years. Many also experience more financial ease at this time if expenses connected with raising children and paying mortgages have been lifted.

According to Erikson, this time is focused on the development of "generativity," as opposed to stagnation. We need to feel that we are useful, that what we put our energy into has meaning, and that what we do has a positive effect on others. We need to feel that we make a difference and that our strengths are a benefit to the world. At this stage of life it is important to look at our life and take stock. Celebrate the successes. Gather the seeds for what still may need to be done or for what we choose to continue to explore. Make sure we have prepared for the years to come, for retirement, and the shifted focus that accompanies that change of life. There is a sense of mastery that can be experienced in these years—of knowledge hard-won through experience. It is to be enjoyed.

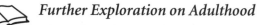 *Further Exploration on Adulthood*
The Life Cycle Completed by Erik Erikson. W.W. Norton & Company, 1998.

Beliefs and Discernment

There is a well-known saying that "you are what you eat," which can be expanded to say "you are what you take in." What we incorporate into our beings and accept as a part of us on all levels can absolutely be experienced as "who we are." It is not just what we eat, but what we hear, what we see, and what we experience that contributes to what we believe to be true about ourselves and the world around us.

We create our realities. What we carry inside of us, in our beliefs and perceptions, has the ability to color how we see and experience the world. If I believe the world is a cold and uncaring place, that is exactly what I will experience, and that experience will reinforce my belief in an unending circle. To change our lives and our experience of the world, we have to look at our beliefs. And this is far easier said than done.

We come into the world as mostly blank slates. If this is true, then how do we come to believe the things we believe? There are some philosophies that present that we are not absolute *tabulae rasae*. Immanuel Kant, for example, presented that there are certain concepts that we know to be true without having had to experience them in the world. In philosophy there are two types of knowledge. *A posteriori* is that which needs proof or experience in order for us to know its truth. That which does not need life experience in order to verify its truth and can be deduced from reason alone is called *A priori*. In addition, there are two ways through which to process information. *Analytic* statements are logical statements that the information contained in the statement itself determines its truth. For example, we know that all bachelors are unmarried. Bachelor and unmarried are states dependent on each other, and so we don't need to check with every bachelor in the world to make sure this is indeed true. *Synthetic* statements require a level of experience. You can say that "all bachelors are unhappy," but you don't really know this to be true unless you interview every bachelor in the world. Kant was trying to unravel how we know what we know about the world, and in this he made a distinction between what is true and what is what we believe to be true. He differentiated between objects as they appear to us (phenomena) and objects as they really are (noumena). Where Kant really went out on a limb was to suggest that we come into the world with certain synthetic a priori knowledge. What this means is that Kant believed that each one of us carries within us certain presuppositions that relate to our own perception of the world that are not based in logic, nor arrived at through experience. We do carry truths, but what we need to realize is that they are truths about ourselves.

Kant's approach, called *Transcendental Idealism*, is reflected in Jung's theory of archetypes. The Collective Unconscious carries certain forms that we bring into the world when we are born. These archetypes are innate within us. However, that being said, once we arrive in this world, we start to gather experiences that coalesce within us to create certain ideas and beliefs around these archetypes. The archetypes are noumena—they just are. We each experience them, but for each individual they are phenomena—they appear to us differently than they do to someone else. However, as is human nature, we cement our experiences into our beliefs and concepts, and then we become very attached to those beliefs and concepts.

If you have had many experiences of feeling rejected as a child, you will develop a negative self-concept and see the world as rejecting. From a subjective and personal perspective the world is a lonely, terrible place. That becomes the belief. But you do not see that perception as subjective (synthetic a posteriori). We all tend to slant our beliefs as objective, seeing them as the truth (analytic a priori). We do not see the belief as "my experience of the world is rejecting" (phenomena). We interpret the belief as the non-negotiable fact that "the world is rejecting" (noumena). The more we become aware of our beliefs, and see them as reflections of the world as we interpret it as a result of our life experiences, the more we are able to arrive at what is true for us and have respect for what is true for others.

If you do not know what you believe, simply look at your life. Your feelings, your responses, and your choices are all fed by your beliefs. Discernment is the ability to differentiate what is truth from what is illusion; to separate fact from fiction, and to recognize whether our beliefs are coming from a healthy or an unhealthy place. Discernment is about having the clarity of vision to see the patterns underlying what is presenting, and being able to reconcile our inner and outer worlds. It is about being able to enter the space where we recognize the difference between "the world as it is" and "the world as we experience it."

Some of the most damaging beliefs we can carry are "I am unlovable. The world is a threatening place. I am not supported. No one understands me or cares about me. I am worthless. What I do doesn't matter." These beliefs are intensely toxic. They are devastating to the spirit. And the sad fact is that so many carry these beliefs on such a core level that they are not aware that they are there pulsing their poisonous message into all facets of life.

The truth is that we all matter. We are all worthy and we are all lovable. Our existence is validated purely through the fact of our existence. Everything else stems from that place. This does not mean that we can't have our preferences. We may be more drawn to friendship with one person than another, and that is a valid preference. It does not mean there is something inherently wrong with the person to whom we are not drawn. Someone else may have a preference in that direction instead of toward us. That is fine as well. When we become aware of our beliefs, we can apply discernment to our choices and preferences. We can continue to see the world as threatening, or we can recognize that is an unhealthy belief that does nothing to support an engaged relationship with the world and others. Entertaining the possibility that the world is actually a dynamic, complex place that has both supportive and challenging opportunities and circumstances allows one to develop a responsive approach.

Using our feelings as a guide and applying discernment allows for choice, empowerment, and an expansive response to life. Rather than setting an armed fortress against the world, we can decide when to raise the drawbridge, staying comfortably behind the gates, and when to lower the drawbridge, venturing out to an exciting world of possibilities. To know we have choice about what we believe to be true opens us up to a life of wonder.

Personal Developmental and Psychological Reflections

August 16: Reflect on what you love of what you have created in your life.

August 17: In what areas in your life do you feel settled and satisfied?

August 18: What do you feel is a great contribution you have made in your life, to others, or to community?

August 19: What work do you feel still needs to be done?

August 20: What belief has supported you through challenging times?

August 21: What belief has contributed to making a time more challenging for you?

August 22: To what extent do you pause to explore discernment before acting?

Thirty-Six

· · · · · · · · · · · · · · · · ·

Alchemical Reflection on Distillation

"It rises from the earth to heaven and descends again to earth,
thereby combining within itself the power of both the above and the below."

FROM *THE EMERALD TABLET*

DISTILLATION ASSOCIATIONS [14] "THE RED PHASE"

Element: Mercury • **Metal:** Silver • **Planet:** Moon • **Symbols:** Pelican, Owl
Dream Imagery: Flowers in bloom, fountains, dew

Distillation is the same process that gives us essential oils and alcohol. It is the careful and repeated boiling and condensation of a solution to reduce it to its very essence. It is the intentional application of gentle heat and gradual cooling to increase the concentration, potency, and purity of the initial substance. If a flower smells lovely, the essential oil of a flower contains all that loveliness in a drop. It is said it takes 1,000 rose petals to create a drop of pure rose essential oil. That is the power of the process of distillation. It is a process of refinement and purification. Medieval alchemists used a popular distillation device called

· ·

14 Distillation associations adapted from *The Emerald Tablet: Alchemy for Personal Transformation*, Dennis William Hauck (New York/Arkana, 1999).

a pelican, which was like a simplified still, having two tubes connecting the neck with the lower portion. This design allowed for a circulatory process that refined the condensed matter each time the process was applied.

From a psychological perspective, distillation is often experienced as a continuance of situations, sometimes in very rapid succession, that break down old, outmoded beliefs and allow for new perceptions and higher perspectives to come into view. With the degree of conscious awareness that has already been attained through the first four stages of alchemical healing, there is openness toward self-reflection that is a necessary aspect of the distillation stage. Often, the fluctuation is between the inner and outer worlds, recognizing our inner thought processes and how they may be out of sync with our experiences. Applying discernment in the observation of the gap between our inner and outer realities allows for the possibility of recognizing the inherent truth that connects the two together. You may find yourself resentful of work, thinking "I am going to quit" when days are hard and frustrating, but feeling grateful at the end of the day for the paycheck and the security it affords. Bouncing between frustration and gratitude with conscious attention can lead to a balanced sense of resolution that acknowledges the truth of both. Often, out of the synthesis of the opposites comes a higher perspective that transcends both.

Distillation can be experienced as very unbalancing. Moving so quickly between beliefs and experiences often creates a sense of disequilibrium. The truth of life is that nothing is static and we are constantly shifting between states. It is the constant shifting that is required for movement and growth. For example, it is impossible to ride a bicycle or run a race by keeping ourselves absolutely, unerringly centered. Forward movement is actually created from the rhythmic flow from side to side. The movements we make need to be the same on both sides in order for the maximum forward motion to occur. We pedal on the left the same as we pedal on the right, and we need to practice with both the left and right sides to master the movement.

Distillation affords us the opportunity through life experiences to practice with both our human and our spiritual selves. The more rapidly we cycle through these experiences, the more aware we become that they are actually two opposite reflections of exactly the same movement. Each experience offers the opportunity for us to fine-tune our approach, moving us closer to the experience of the essence of our own truth that is the connection between the two extremes. We are moving from "I am my experiences in the here and now, including my feelings and responses. And I am my dreams for the future, including my hopes and expectations," into the exquisitely simple statement that "I am."

Distillation is the doorway to the experience of self as integrated and whole. It is the entrance to the Philosopher's Stone.

Personal Alchemical Reflections

August 23: Reflect on a time that you felt pulled in two contrary directions.

August 24: Do you experience a gap between your inner world and your outer experience?

August 25: Have you ever experienced a time when it felt situations were happening faster than you could assimilate?

August 26: What is your sense of your own purest Essence?

August 27: What guides you through chaotic times?

August 28: If you ever feel like giving up, what keeps you going?

August 29: Reflect on a time you could see the absolute truth in two contrary conditions.

Thirty-Seven

Energetic Reflection on the Brow Chakra

BROW CHAKRA ASSOCIATIONS [15]

Name: Ajna • **Location:** Center of forehead above eyebrows
Color: Indigo blue • **Tone:** A • **Gland:** Pineal • **Body:** Face, nose, eyes, ears,
and sinuses • **Yoga Path:** Yantra • **Symbol:** Ninety-six-petalled lotus
Stones: Lapis Lazuli, Sodalite, Blue Moonstone, Sapphire

The brow chakra, sometimes referred to as the third eye chakra, is the center of our vision: inner and outer, human and spiritual. Physically, we may experience a blocked brow chakra as headaches, migraines, sinus issues, blurred vision, or tinnitus.

Psychologically, when our brow chakra is open and clear we are able to see things as they truly are without being clouded by misperception and illusion. We have a greater ability to see situations in our lives from an objective perspective, rather than attachment to our own personal, and somewhat limited, view. Internally, we are able to utilize our imagination and the power of fantasy to activate a vision of what we would like to create in our outer worlds. There is awareness of the joy that comes from daydreaming, allowing certain visions to come and go just for the pure experience of enjoyment. But there is also awareness of the

15 Brow chakra associations adapted from *The Chakra Handbook: From Basic Understanding to Practical Application,* Shalila Sharamon and Bodo J. Baginski (Wilmot, WI: Lotus Light Publications, 1991).

power of vision as an active process of manifestation, serving a purpose that is farther reaching than a transitory daydream moment.

The brow chakra is the center of our psychic and intuitive abilities, which acknowledges a different way of seeing. This aspect is more connected with the higher spiritual realms than the more human realm of vision-building. *Clairvoyance* is a psychic ability that literally translates as "clear seeing." Clairvoyance is the ability to see past the material world to the subtler energies of higher vibration. With psychic ability, we look with the inner eye to discern information about another person that is inaccessible through more grounded levels of consciousness. Intuition uses the same focus, but is directed toward information about our own situation.

Discernment is absolutely key when working with the brow chakra for intuitive or psychic purposes. For intuition, we need discernment to know whether information is coming from a healthy or unhealthy place. Is this intuition or is the message attached to my hopes or fears? For psychic readings, we need discernment to recognize what is our own stuff and what is truly a message about the other person. I will see all messages through the lens of my own unresolved issues, so the clearer I am on my own stuff, the more I can trust that the messages I receive are objective. We need discernment to know what to share. A message that warns of impending crisis may have come to us in order that we may approach the other with kindness and compassion, not that we need to share the details of the vision. We also need discernment to know when to share. It is a negation of our human choice and a boundary violation if we share psychic messages without the other person's express permission to do so. Just because I receive a message about you does not mean that I have your permission to share it with you. Certain situations carry implicit permission. If I go to a psychic for a reading, I don't have to say, "I give you permission." However, if I am in a conversation with someone and I receive a message for that person, I need to ask if the person wants to hear what came to me before sharing. If that person says they don't want to hear, that needs to be respected. The ability to see what others do not carries with it the responsibility of ensuring we are coming from a centered and clear perspective with no attachment to the outcome, and without the muddying effects of an unhealthy ego. Never worry that if you don't share the message, it is lost forever. I always maintain that the Divine is much smarter than me, and will find a way to convey any message that needs to be shared. If not through me, then through some other means.

The brow chakra serves to illuminate our path with clarity and integrity of intention. If we have done the work of balancing our lower chakras, the brow chakra is the unwavering light of supportive beliefs that shines through any darkness.

Messages that help to balance the brow chakra are:
My vision for my life is valid.
I am open to receive higher guidance.
My beliefs are supportive and encouraging.
I recognize that my perceptions may differ from others' perceptions.

 Personal Energetic Reflections
August 30: The color indigo makes me feel...

August 31: Do you follow the messages and nudges you receive from your inner voice?

September 1: Have you ever had what you might describe as a psychic experience?

September 2: Do you remember using your imagination as a child?

September 3: Reflect on what might be a perfect day for you. Allow your imagination to soar.

September 4: What situations cause your vision to become cloudy?

September 5: In what ways do you support your vision for your life?

Thirty-Eight

Guidance Reflection on Mythological Beasts and Intuitive Reflection on I Ching

Mythological Beasts

Throughout the ages humankind has not only connected with the animals seen in the natural world, but with those creatures that have arisen from the imagination and that appear in myths and stories passed down through the centuries. These creatures differ from the energy of the elementals. Fact or fiction, there are many stories of actual interaction between humans and the beings of the otherworld. This is not the case with the mythological beasts. They live purely in the realm of human fantasy and serve a very important function.

Most mythological beasts are composite creatures. Within their beings, they carry complex energies that connect us to varied elements at once. A centaur is part human, part horse. A chimera is a lion with the head of a goat on its back and a snake's head as a tail. The sphinx, immortalized in the great stone monument in Egypt, has the head of a woman, the body of a lion, and the wings of a great bird. As guides, mythological beasts offer us an opportunity for insight into many perspectives at the same time. If we try to access the message of the sphinx by focusing on the female aspect, we will have missed the strength and pride of the lion, and the transcendent quality of the wings. Each of those aspects contributes to creating a message that allows for several, sometimes contradictory, perspectives to coexist.

Mythological beasts guide us in our quest to find the synthesis between our inner and outer worlds. They are of this world, in some form recognizable, but transformed. Many of them have been used in heraldry to represent the essential qualities of a family lineage that maintains its integrity over time, serving as a connection to both the heritage of the past and the legacy of the future. With a mythological beast by our side, we are guided to integrate the past with the present, the present with the future, and the inner world of imagination with the outer world of material substance to find the commonality of elements that link all factors together.

If you find you have been drawn to a certain mythological beast, it is helpful to get a sense of the different elements that combine within that one creature. If it is a beast of several components, what is your sense of the particular guidance for each of the disparate parts? Once you have a sense of the elements on their own, begin to play with them in combination. If with the centaur, you connect with the discernment and wisdom from a human perspective, and the loyalty of partnership and journey's aid from a horse perspective, what is the transformative message that arises out of both of those messages when enfolded into each other as one cohesive whole? And how does the message of the mythological beast serve to light your journey into the embracing of your best and highest self? Sometimes the light aspect of this guide's message reveals some dark, cobwebbed corners of our past yet to be resolved, but this revelation is always the opportunity for us to move more consciously into our truth.

Mythological beasts invite us to enter the world of wonder and magic.

Some Common Examples of Mythological Beasts

Centaur	Chimera	Dragon	Gryphon
(Horse & Human)	*(Lion, Goat, & Snake)*	Treasure,	*(Lion & Eagle)*
Virility, Courage	Bridging cycles	Expansion	Valor, Enlightenment
Harpy	**Hippogriff**	**Hydra**	**Kraken**
(Bird & Human)	*(Gryphon*	Conquest,	Unconscious
Boundaries,	*& Horse)*	Challenge	fears
Consequence	Nobility		
Minotaur	**Pegasus**	**Phoenix**	**Satyr**
(Bull & Human)	*(Horse & Bird)*	Rebirth	*(Goat & Human)*
Confusion,	Inspiration,		Sensuality,
Feeling trapped	Creativity		Earthiness
Sphinx	**Thunderbird**	**Unicorn**	**Wyvern**
(Lion, Bird, & Human)	Messenger	Purity,	Protective
Knowledge, Vigilance		Realizing dreams	barriers

Further Exploration on Mythological Beasts

The Element Encyclopedia of Magical Creatures: The Ultimate A–Z of Fantastic Beings from Myth and Magic by John Matthews and Caitlin Matthews. Harper Element, 2010.

The Magical Personality: Identify Strengths and Weaknesses to Improve Your Magic by Mike Leslie. Llewellyn Publications, 2002.

The Mythical Creatures Bible: The Definitive Guide to Legendary Beings by Brenda Rosen. Sterling, 2009.

I Ching

The I Ching (literally translated as "The Book of Changes") is said to be the oldest-known formalized oracle system. By some accounts it is around 5,000 years old. Historical records show that the first written version of the I Ching appeared around 1143 BCE, and Confucius stated that if he had another fifty years to live, he would devote it to studying the I Ching.

Carl Jung presented a similar sentiment, except he suggested he would spend a whole other lifetime studying the I Ching.

> The changes, what do they do? The changes disclose things,
> complete affairs and encompass all ways on earth. This and
> nothing else. For this reason, the holy sages used them to penetrate
> all wills on earth and to determine all fields of action on earth and
> to settle all doubts on earth.   —Confucius, *Ta Chuan*

The I Ching is a binary code made up of solid (yang) and broken (yin) lines. Three lines of solid and broken line combinations make up eight trigrams, which relate to eight significant guiding energies.

The Eight Trigrams[16]

Heaven	Thunder	Water	Mountain
Awareness	Stimulating	Dissolving	Grounding
Challenging	Spirit	Soul	Body
Creative	Energetic	Instinctual	Stable
Earth	**Wind**	**Fire**	**Lake**
Nurturing	Sensing	Thinking	Feeling
Will	Breath	Joining	Tolerance
Receptive	Insightful	Illumination	Malleable

16 Adapted from *I Ching: A New Interpretation for Modern Times,* Sam Reifler (New York: Bantam Books, 1974).

Combining two trigrams together (placing one above and one below) gives a possible sixty-four combinations consisting of six lines each. These are referred to as hexagrams, or gua, and it is these that make up I Ching. In the hexagrams, the upper trigram represents the outer world, and the lower trigram represents the inner world. How these two realms come together carries a special dynamic and message that is illuminated through the text of the I Ching.

There are several different methods for determining the lines that make up the trigrams and hexagrams. One of the oldest is using yarrow sticks. This tends to be a long process that is wonderful for creating a contemplative space if one has the time. A more common method is that of using three coins, either special I Ching coins or regular ones. For this method (regardless of what type of coin you use), the heads side carries a value of three, and the tails side carries a value of two. Tossing the three coins at once and totaling the combination of values (threes and twos) gives one of four possible outcomes. This is done six times, creating the lines that will make up a hexagram, starting with the bottom line first and ending with the top line.

I Ching Coin Values

3 heads	9	Solid line	Changes to broken line
2 heads, 1 tail	8	Broken line	No change
1 head, 2 tails	7	Solid line	No change
3 tails	6	Broken line	Changes to solid line

What becomes wonderfully complex about the I Ching is that, not only do you arrive at a hexagram of six lines (the message that you then turn to the I Ching text for clarification and insight), tossing either three heads or three tails creates what is referred to as a changing line. After gaining insight on the initial hexagram, further elaboration can be explored by reading the specific messages in the text regarding the changing lines. They also create a new hexagram that adds yet another perspective and opportunity for guidance.

For example, hexagram 64 (Fire over Water) has been created. The first three coin tosses create the trigram for water through the values: 8 (2 heads, 1 tail), 7 (2 tails, 1 head), and 8 (2 heads, 1 tail). The second three coin tosses create the trigram for fire through the values: 7 (2 heads, 1 tail), 8 (2 heads, 1 tail), and 9 (3 heads). This last line is a changing line. First, read the I Ching for hexagram 64 (Completion) along with the special note on the changing line. Then, create a new hexagram by turning the top solid line into a broken line. This turns fire over water into thunder over water, which creates hexagram 40 (Relief).

Sitting with the beautiful and evocative text of the I Ching offers an incredible depth. It requires time and patience, but such complexity is reflective of the nuances of life.

Basic I Ching Reading

To do a reading, you will need to have access to an I Ching text. There are several recommendations listed below. After taking some time to center yourself, hold an intention that you will be guided to receive the message that you most need to hear in this moment.

Using the three coin method, toss three coins together a total of six times. Note the lines indicated by the coin value totals of each toss, having the first toss indicate the first line (at the bottom), and working upward to the sixth line (at the very top). Make note of any changing lines—any tosses with a value of either 9 or 6. The first three lines create your bottom trigram. The following three lines create your top trigram.

Take a moment to sit with the sense of these two trigrams and how they relate to each other. For example, if you create earth over fire, how to you connect to the sense of earth and all that represents for you? How to you connect with fire and all that represents for you? How does it feel for you when you have the dynamic of earth over fire? How does that change the sense of each and the relationship between them?

Use the I Ching chart to determine which hexagram is created by your two trigrams. In the example of earth over fire, it is hexagram 36 (Darkening of the Light). It can be illuminating to meditate on your sense of the hexagram before reading the text. How does "Darkening of the Light" reflect your sense of the earth over fire dynamic? After you have read the text, address any changing lines that may have occurred. Create the new hexagram from the changed lines, and approach the new hexagram in the same way as the initial hexagram.

The Sixty-Four Hexagrams[17]

(top trigram ↓ / bottom trigram →)	Heaven	Thunder	Water	Mountain	Earth	Wind	Fire	Lake
Lake	43 Break-through	17 Following	47 Oppression	31 Influence	45 Gathering Together	28 Great Exceeding	49 Revolution	58 Joyful
Fire	14 Great Harvest	21 Eradicating	64 Before Completion	56 Traveling	35 Progress	50 Establishing the Now	30 Brightness	38 Diversity
Wind	9 Little Accumu-lation	42 Increase	59 Dispersing	53 Develop-ment	20 Contempla-tion	57 Proceeding Humbly	37 The Family	61 Inner Truth
Earth	11 Peace	24 Return	7 Multitude	15 Modesty	2 Responding	46 Pushing Upward	36 Darkening of the Light	19 Approach
Mountain	26 Accumu-lation	27 Nourishing	4 Childhood	52 Keeping Still	23 Splitting Apart	18 Remedying	22 Grace	41 Increase
Water	5 Waiting	3 Beginning	29 Darkness	39 Hardship	8 Union	48 Replen-ishing	63 After Completion	60 Limitation
Thunder	34 Strength	51 Action	40 Relief	62 Little Exceeding	16 Enthusiasm	32 Duration	55 Abundance	54 Marrying Maiden
Heaven	1 Initiative	25 Innocence	6 Conflict	33 Retreat	12 Hindrance	44 Encoun-tering	13 Harmony	10 Fulfillment

Read across for top trigram. Read down for bottom trigram.

17 Adapted from *I Ching: A New Interpretation for Modern Times*, Sam Reifler (New York: Bantam Books, 1974).

Further Exploration on the I Ching

I Ching: A New Interpretation for Modern Times by Sam Reifler. Bantam, 1994.

The Complete I Ching: The Definitive Translation by Taoist Master Alfred Huang. Inner Traditions, 2010.

The I Ching, or Book of Changes by Richard Wilhelm and Cary F. Baynes. Princeton University Press, 1967.

The I Ching Plain and Simple: A Guide to Working with the Oracle of Change by Stephen Karcher. Harper Element, 2004.

Total I Ching: Myths for Change by Stephen Karcher. Piatkus Books, 2009.

Personal Guidance and Intuitive Reflections

September 6: What mystical creatures did you know of as a child?

September 7: Reflect on any creature stories that may have been told to scare you.

September 8: Does it feel different for you to connect to composite beasts with several different elements to them?

September 9: Use your imagination to create a composite mythical beast that speaks to you.

September 10: Which trigram do you find yourself most drawn to?

September 11: What is your sense of how the upper and lower trigrams impact on each other?

September 12: Reflect on the force of change in your life and the changes you have experienced.

The Illumined Hynni of Vision

When you can't see past your own self perceptions. When your vision of your life is muddied or confused. When it feels impossible to see potential or possibility, won-der and joy, or when it feels like you only see yourself through others' judgments, this is the time to activate the Hynni of Vision.

This Hynni symbol represents the expansion of the inner eye toward multiple per-spectives.

Preparation: Find a spot where you know you will not be disturbed and elimi-nate any possible sources of distraction. You may want to have your I Ching coins and text close by. Begin to breathe deeply, visualizing the color indigo. Release any tension you may be holding in your body, breathing into that space and bringing yourself to center. Focus on the breath moving in and out of your body, connecting to the sensation of light.

Hynni: Bring your awareness to the space in the center of your forehead just above your brows. If you choose, place your dominant hand over your brow. Begin to sense what the energy feels like in this place. Be very gentle as you focus on this area. If it begins to ache or if you feel pressure, focus on moving your breath down to your feet, allowing the energy to be diffused.

With each breath, feel yourself getting lighter and lighter. You move from experiencing yourself in the density of your physical body to feeling yourself made of finer stuff, vibrating at a high frequency. Allow an inner vision of this higher vibration to unfold. Become aware of your light body, expanding into the ethereal glow. Imagine yourself as this light body moving through the world, touching a leaf with a dapple, highlighting a wave upon the water, revealing what is hidden in a shadow or bouncing something dim into glory.

Allow yourself to connect to both constancy and mutability. There is that in you that never changes. It has been with you since before you began this human adventure. It has been present through each and every experience. Sometimes it shines more brightly than the sun. Sometimes it is a dim flicker. But it is always there. Yet there is also that within you that shifts depending on the circumstances. There are aspects of yourself that change with the stages of your life in response to the people around you or situations that you find yourself involved in. The part that is constant and the aspects that change do not contradict each other. They are both true. Breathe into this, your dual nature, and open yourself to the power of this vision.

Begin to focus on the vision symbol, visualizing a golden light that carries the intent of the symbol moving through your hands, and glowing lightly over your third eye. As you do, see its light emanate from you out into the world and the cosmos. Allow your perception to expand, casting light in dark areas and reaching the furthest corners. From this place, you may choose to focus on a particular situation that has been challenging for you. With your mind's eye, allow the situation to play out in its familiar way. The way you have been seeing it. The way that is causing the challenge. Then, shift your focus and allow the glow of the Hynni symbol to emanate on the scene. You may find this brings a different perspective, that you are able to penetrate another's perception on the situation, or that it allows the vision of an alternate choice, path, or outcome to unfold. Allow your imagination to flow, as silly or unreasonable as it may seem. It does no harm to explore what the hynni has to offer.

With an open heart and open mind, invite a mythological beast to come to you. For this guide, take some time to explore its composite aspects (if it has any), getting a sense of how each element contributes its own particular guidance. Know that whichever mythological beast comes to you, it carries a perfect message for you in this moment.

When you have heard the message from your mythological beast, knowing that you are a visionary with enormous capacity to cocreate a life of your choosing, begin to bring your focus back to the room. Take three centering breaths, allowing each breath to bring you more fully back to the room. When you feel present once more, you may want to touch your feet to anchor yourself in conscious awareness.

If you choose, from this place, bring in the wisdom of the I Ching. Know that life is always in flow. Change is the natural state. Stasis leads to stagnation, decay, and death. Whatever is before you is changing. The power of your imagination can facilitate how that change transpires. Your inner vision can guide your every step along the way, if you open yourself to the guidance.

Part Nine

Process Phase Three
September 13–19

Waning Moon:
Experience and Community
"Be Cloaked in Wisdom"

PRESCRIPTIONS

Go through this section during any Waning Moon
Phase or if you are experiencing any of the following:

- Bitterness
- Attachment
- Feeling discarded
- Lack of appreciation for your gifts and talents
- Resigned

Thirty-Nine

·····················

Waning Phase of Experience and Community

The waning moon is a time of release. As the moon moves toward being a sliver once more, the focus is on decrease and letting go. The reflection of the crescent moon in this phase of the journey is called the balsamic moon. It represents the latter stages of journey, or the recognition of what is extraneous and burdensome.

The waning moon, embodied in the Crone archetype, gives us the exact opposite reflection of the Maiden's waxing moon. It is the energy of wisdom gained through experience. Whereas the Maiden is autonomous and self-centered in a positive, excited, and necessary way, the Crone is autonomous, yet with an eye to the community at large. Like the Maiden, the Crone answers to no one and yet she has much to share. This is the village wise woman, the midwife, the healer, the elder, and the grandmother. She is the keeper of stories, the protector of the younger, the keen eye, the piercing mind, and sharp tongue. In many ways, she is the glue that holds the community together. The Maiden experiences, but with naiveté. The Mother nurtures, but often only her own young or those close to her. The Crone enfolds the whole.

The presentation of these archetypal energies in a three-fold system of Maiden, Mother, and Crone presents the Crone as the one who transitions us through the mysteries of death and dying. In this four-fold system, the midwifing of souls through death is the task of the Dark Mother, and so the waning moon Crone becomes elder. In current jargon, she would be a "junior senior," rather than a "senior senior." Still energetic and vibrant. Still with much guidance and purpose in life. Her focus is on conveying that there are certain battles that we can walk away from. There are certain truths that we should never give up on. And above all, it is the whole that is greater than any of its individual parts.

Often we find with this archetype that there is a lightness and humor. This does not take away from the significance of life events, but helps to put it in the context of balance. Life happens, so one may as well "wear purple." If challenges and difficulties have not been processed and understood from a higher perspective, we may find the Crone sharp-edged with bitterness. But that same experience filtered through a sense of Higher Purpose allows for the sharp wit of humor instead.

At this time of the balsamic moon we are surer of the pulse of our own rhythms with a reawakened confidence that allows us to let go of all that creates drag upon the waters of our journey. The boundless energy of the Maiden has become contained in the precisely focused energy of the Crone. We know what is important and what can be released. The Crone as elder holds the wisdom of the community gained through years of experience. And that is an awesome power indeed.

Main Themes for Process Phase 3:

Assessment

Guidance

Release

Ancient Cultural Archetypes of Experience

Hera *(Greek)* or **Juno** (Roman), **Zeus's** wife, is the goddess of marriage, community, and sovereignty.

Hygeia *(Greek)* is the goddess of health whose wisdom encourages preventative care.

Hestia *(Greek)* or **Vesta** *(Roman)* is the goddess of hearth and home. Her important temple in Rome held an eternal flame tended to by the Vestal Virgins.

Ceridwen *(Celtic)* is a goddess of transformation, magic, and
herbal knowledge.

Personal Waning Phase Reflections

September 13: In what ways do you find yourself a
role model for others?

September 14: What feelings come up in you around pondering
a life's twilight?

September 15: What special gifts do you feel you have to offer
your community?

September 16: In what areas do you feel you could still grow and learn?

September 17: What within you do you feel requires release?

September 18: Reflect on a relationship with an elder that taught you
something significant in your life.

September 19: What still holds excitement for you, but tempered
through the lens of experience?

The Balanced Hynni of Experience

As you move into another level of mastery. When you are simplifying and reordering your life and environment. When you feel you have wisdom to share and a desire to be of service to others, this is the time to activate the Hynni of Experience.

This Hynni symbol represents the many sides of life's experience and the multiple ways to touch the lives of others.

Preparation: Find a spot where you will not be disturbed and eliminate all possibility for distraction. Get into a comfortable position. Begin to breathe deeply and slowly, visualizing the breath moving in and out of your body. Allow the tension to fade from your body. Be aware of nothing but your breath.

Hynni: As you breathe, take some time to connect with where you are at in this moment in your life. Reflect on all that has brought you to the place you are right now. Take some time to flow through the different times in your life and all the different experiences you had over the years.

- How did challenges add to your knowledge and skills?

- What have you come to appreciate about yourself?

See yourself sitting beneath a massive tree, resting your back against its firm, supportive trunk as you gaze up at a dark sky bright with stars and the most beautiful sliver of a waning moon. In the distance you can hear the quiet, sleepy, winding-down bustle of a community you know to be yours. It is familiar and the sound of it expands your heart. You feel yourself as solid as the trunk of the tree that you lean against. As you take stock of all that has brought you to this place, you feel your experiences, both the triumphs and the challenges, as tangible parts of yourself. Like the rings that make up the inner map of the tree, all you have gone through in your life has formed your own inner map of rings, each one contributing to your inner strength, wisdom, and peace.

Allow yourself to become aware of any element that still feels unresolved, baggage that feels irrelevant, or negative perceptions that weigh you down. Take some time to explore what has been keeping these in place, and what part in you is ready to finally release them. Know that as the moon itself becomes encompassed by the dark, so these unhelpful and heavy burdens can also be given up to the dark. To do so frees your energy to attract and expand all the positivity that you already contain within you.

Place your hands on your heart and begin to focus on the experience symbol, visualizing a golden light that carries the intent of the symbol moving through your hands and into your heart. As you do, allow yourself to appreciate all that has come your way in your life. Rejoice in your successes. Rejoice in your lowest moments. Rejoice in the spectrum of the tapestry you have woven, and know that others benefit from this tapestry as well. Know that within the vision of your story, there is the potential for others to be inspired by your successes and learn from your challenges. The greatest gift you have to share with the world is the gift of your experience. With this in your heart, you are truly wise.

When you are ready, take three deep, centering breaths and open your eyes, appreciating your experience and wisdom.

Part Ten

Cycle Seven
September 20–October 31

Effects of Gratitude on Life Purpose
"Practice Gratitude and Acts of Thankful Appreciation"

PRESCRIPTIONS

Go through this section if you are experiencing any of the following:

- Lack of trust that all will work out
- Resistance to life's lessons
- Attachment to proof
- Having one's "head in the clouds"
- Avoidance of physical or emotional needs

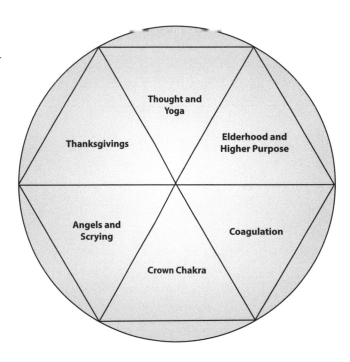

Thought and Yoga

Thanksgivings

Elderhood and Higher Purpose

Angels and Scrying

Coagulation

Crown Chakra

Forty

Mythological Reflection on Thanksgivings

Here at the Fall Equinox, we find familiar traditional themes of harvest celebration and thanksgiving. The bulk of the work of bringing in the crops has been done. Recognition that the success of the harvest is due to the work of many hands underlies the swell of gratitude that is at the heart of the celebrations.

In reflection of the Spring Equinox, this is another time of balance. Once again, light and dark stand in equal measure, but this time the movement is tilted toward the dark. The light has seen the end of its days of strength and is on the path of its slow demise for the year. For ancient cultures, these were seen as the last days of the dying god. If the earth was the feminine energy that supported and nurtured the harvest, the crop itself was the masculine. The cutting of the harvest was the death of the masculine principle—for the time being. It is no coincidence that traditional depictions of death show him holding a scythe, the ancient harvest tool. Certainly though, it is a time to be thankful for all the earth has provided through the sweat and perseverance of all the work done over the past months.

It was not just the final clearing of the fields that required attention at this time. There was also attention paid to what needed to be cleared out in order to make room for storage and preparation. Spring cleaning is about making room to bring in the new. Fall cleaning is about releasing what is no longer useful. It is taking stock of what is absolutely necessary and letting go of anything else. A sense of justice, balance, and even karma is contained in this—the sense of reaping what we have sown.

One name for the festival associated with this time of year is Mabon, in reference to *Mabon ap Modron* (Welsh for "Mabon, son of Modron," or literally "son of the mother"). The tale of Mabon's disappearance as a child is central to the story of the hero, Culhwch (cul-hooch). Culhwch must undertake impossible tasks to win the hand of the beautiful Olwen, including finding Mabon. Since Mabon's location is a mystery, with the help of companions including Arthur (as in King Arthur), Culhwch turns to the oldest animals for information: the Blackbird, the Stag, the Owl, and the Eagle. None of them have the information he seeks, but they urge him on, advising whom to ask next until he finally approaches the Salmon of Llyn Llyw (literally "the lake of leadership"). Salmon directs Culhwch up the Severn River to Gloucester (in ancient Welsh *Caer Loyw* meaning "City of Light"). There Culhwch and his companions wage battle and free Mabon, reuniting him with the great mother, Madron. The celebration of Mabon connects us to success through perseverance and patience, reliance on dependable others as a key to leadership, and the courage to challenge the dark forces of fear and death.

This is a time to celebrate abundance with thanksgiving and gratitude. Traditionally, it was a time of great feasts and reveling in plenty. The days would come soon enough for careful distribution and rationing. But for now, with stores overflowing, all could relax in the knowledge of success.

Main Themes for Cycle 7:
Giving thanks
Appraisal
Letting go

Ancient Cultural Archetypes of Higher Wisdoms

Ma'at *(Egyptian)* is a goddess of justice who weighs the hearts of those who have crossed over against a feather on her scales. She teaches that we are to leave this world with a light heart.

Thoth *(Egyptian)* is a god of wisdom associated with writing and science, particularly the esoteric science of alchemy.

Sophia *(Greek)* is a goddess of wisdom, the literal meaning of her name. She gives her name to all studies ending with "sophy," such as philosophy.

Zeus *(Greek)* or **Jupiter** *(Roman)* is a sky god, presiding over law, order, and fate. He was considered the king of the gods and ruled Mount Olympus.

Athena *(Greek)* or **Minerva** *(Roman)* is a goddess of just war and wisdom who sprang fully formed from the head of Zeus. She was the patron goddess of Athens.

Metis *(Greek)* is a goddess of wisdom in the sense of skill or craft.

Pax *(Roman)* is a goddess of peace.

Providentia *(Roman)* is a goddess of higher knowledge and the ability to foresee the future.

Ogma *(Celtic)* is one of the three gods of skill (along with Lugh and the Dagda). He invented the ogham and gave it his name.

Odin *(Norse)* is a god of wisdom, magic, and prophecy, along with battle and victory. He underwent sacrifice and trial to gain the knowledge of the runes.

Snotra *(Norse)* is a goddess of wisdom whose name means "clever."

Personal Mythological Reflections

September 20: To whom do you turn to for assistance when needed?

September 21: What connection do you see between what you put out and what comes back to you?

September 22: In what ways do you make room for success?

September 23: What has the power to stop you from pursuing your goals?

September 24: What do you consistently avoid thinking about?

September 25: For you, what are important qualities of leadership?

September 26: How do you experience your Higher Self?

Forty-One

Energetic Reflection on Thought and Active Reflection on Yoga

Thought: The Rays of Consciousness

The question of consciousness has kept philosophers and scientists busy for centuries. Contemporarily, there is a growing awareness that what we think has a direct and tangible impact on the world around us. This is the basis of all information regarding the Law of Attraction. There is a magnetic quality to the "stuff of the universe" of which we are a part. Thus, when we focus on the negative, we experience more of the negative. When we focus on the positive, it is this that we attract into our lives. This is absolutely true, and yet, as has been illustrated in previous chapters, it requires much focus, dedication, and work to delve into the depths to determine what underlying beliefs we carry. If we are questioning what is being attracted into our lives, perhaps there are deeper levels to explore. What are the thoughts that direct our experience?

Unfathomably fast as the speed of light may be, thought is faster. Traveling at the speed of light, the sun's rays take about eight minutes to reach earth. Our thoughts reach the sun the moment we bring the sun into our consciousness awareness. It may take the physical self a bit longer to catch up, but on the level on consciousness, we are exactly where we put our minds the moment we put our minds there. Mindfulness brings intention to where we place our thoughts.

There was a saying heard often in the 1970s and 1980s that has shifted somewhat over the decades. It is a truism that still holds. "You are a thought. And a thought can be changed."

There is nothing solid or tangible about a thought, except that we have a tendency to cement them into permanency. The question then becomes less about the thought itself, and more about our attachment to a particular thought process. Mindfulness, which has its roots in Buddhist teachings, presents a process that we bring attentive awareness to our inner processes, thereby literally becoming more conscious. With awareness comes choice. Choice leads to the possibility of a different action. Different action produces a different result. This is a process that can become second nature and utilized in every moment. This is how we change our lives. It starts with a thought.

Messages that help to connect us to the element of thought are:
I embrace positive thoughts of myself and my abilities.
My thoughts support me in all ways.
I choose positivity.

Yoga

Yoga has become a lucrative and thriving industry in the past number of years, recognized for the physical and mental benefits a yoga practice can offer. Its roots are ancient, dating back thousands of years in Hindu tradition. There is mention of yoga in the Upanishads, which date from around 400 BCE. Yoga is one of the six classical schools of Indian philosophy. Though separate philosophical schools, traditionally these separate approaches informed and supported each other, forming a complete path to enlightenment.

The Six Classical Schools of Hindu Philosophy

Yoga	Sankhya	Vedanta
Philosophical school that presents methods through which one can have a direct experience of the Divine.	Philosophical school that provides a framework for manifestation, describing the interrelation of all aspects that "make up the whole." (i.e., alchemy)	Philosophical school that presents methods of self-inquiry and contemplation that lead to the realization of one's True Self.
Vaishashika	**Nyaya**	**Mimasa**
Philosophical school that focuses on the physical sciences (such as chemistry) to explore and understand the nature of existence.	Philosophical school that focuses on reasoning and logic.	Philosophical school that formed the basis for karmic philosophy, which focuses on action and ethics.

The name yoga comes from the term *yuj,* which means to "unite or integrate." The intent behind the development of yoga was to encourage the union between human consciousness and Divine consciousness. Though there has been much focus on yoga as a physical practice, it is a holistic practice in that the intention is on experiencing the interconnection between body, emotions, thoughts, and spirit. It is not a form of exercise, but a way of life. Within the philosophical school of yoga itself, there are four paths that can appeal to different temperaments and personalities. These four classic paths focus on achieving inner integration through different routes, forming four arms of a whole system.

The Four Classic Yoga Paths

Raja Yoga ("Royal Road")	Karma Yoga ("Road of Action or Deed")
Primarily concerned with the mind and meditation, encouraging encountering, and transcending thoughts.	Attention paid to the discipline of action, including duty and service to others.
Jnana Yoga ("Road of Real Wisdom")	Bhakti Yoga ("Road of Dedication")
The path of union through knowledge and wisdom, encouraging contemplation of true nature and setting aside of false selves.	The path of emotion, devotion, and love that connects to the Divine through compassion and service to others.

These four roads can be aligned with the four aspects of the holistic approach. The "Road of Action" relates to the body and our practices in the physical world. The "Road of Dedication" encompasses our emotional experience. The "Road of Real Wisdom" embraces the mind and our mental processes. The "Royal Road" opens us to our spiritual selves. When we honor our body, emotions, mind, and spirit equally, we have achieved wholeness.

To make the true practice of yoga even more sublime and eloquent, a yogic text written by Patanjali around 200 BCE, called the *Yoga Sutra,* delineated the eight limbs of yoga, each of which contained certain practices and observances. Each one of the eight limbs is a profound approach in and of itself.

The Eight Limbs of Yoga

First Limb Yama (Morality)	Second Limb Niyama (Observances)	Third Limb Asanas (Staying or Holding)	Fourth Limb Pranayama (Suspended breath)
No violence No lying No coveting Abstinence Rejection of hoarding wealth	Purity Contentment Discipline Self-examination Celebration of Divine	The practice of using physical postures. The best-known aspect of yoga.	The application of measured, controlled, and directed breath, familiar in both yogic practice and meditation.
Fifth Limb Pratyahara (Retreat from that which nourishes the senses)	Sixth Limb Dharana (Concentration)	Seventh Limb Dhyana (Worship)	Eighth Limb Samadhi (Union)
The practice of non-attachment.	The technique of holding focus and attention in one place for an extended period of time.	Perfect contemplation that allows one to "enter the truth."	The ending of the illusory perception of separateness. The final step of the eight-fold path and culmination of the journey.

Traditionally, one would become adept at the first two limbs of yoga (Yama and Niyama) before moving on to limbs three and four. The first two limbs focus on aspects of human interaction (morality) and inner intent that inform our actions (ethics). The modern practice of yoga tends to focus on some elements of the ancient tradition, leaving others aside, or to be practiced through other forms of inquiry and exploration. For the most part, what people tend to think of when they think of a yoga practice is limb three (Asanas). Much of current practice is derived from Hatha Yoga, which was developed in the fifteenth century by Yogi Swatmarama. Focusing on the Asanas and Pranayama limbs of yoga, it was intended as a preparatory stage of physical purification that readied the body for the enlightenment that comes with higher meditation. From the arrival of yoga in the United States in the late 1800s to the popularization of yoga in the late 1900s, there has been an explosion in the various methodologies. Contemporarily, one can find numerous different schools with varying philosophies and approaches, including Ashtanga yoga, Iyengar yoga, Bikram yoga, Kundalini yoga, and Integral yoga.

The physical benefits of yoga include increased flexibility, increased strength, muscle tone, better lung capacity, and breath control. Mental benefits include stress reduction, better focus, and concentration, which underlie an increased sense of peace and calmness. But the original intention of yoga was always the presentation of a path that would allow us to get out of our own way, removing attachment to the material concerns of the world, and experiencing the spiritual dimensions that allow for synthesis between the self and the Divine.

Further Exploration on Yoga

Light on Life: The Yoga Journey to Wholeness, Inner Peace, and Ultimate Freedom by B. K. S. Iyengar. Rodale Books, 2006.

Light on Yoga by B. K. S. Iyengar. Schocken, 1995.

The Subtle Body: The Story of Yoga in America by Stefanie Syman. Farrar, Strauss and Giroux, 2011.

Personal Elemental and Active Reflections

September 27: What recurring thoughts are you aware of in yourself?

September 28: What challenges you in releasing non-supportive thoughts?

September 29: What is your sense of the gap between thoughts?

September 30: If the gap between thoughts could be filled with any quality, what would you choose?

October 1: Reflect on a time when you felt completely at peace.

October 2: How does your spirituality impact on your physicality?

October 3: What does karma mean to you?

Forty-Two

Developmental Reflection on Elderhood and Psychological Reflection on Higher Purpose

Seventies and Beyond

The last stage of our life experience, barring death due to accident or disease in the earlier stages, can cover a significantly long period of time. As we learn to take better care of our health and advances are made in disease intervention and cures, life expectancy continues to increase. There was a time in history when living past forty was considered a miracle. These days, living well into our eighties can be fairly readily expected. Living into the nineties, and even past one hundred, is not beyond possibility. Elderhood is a time of living in awareness of our own mortality. However, this does not mean that we need to spend twenty or thirty years pondering death. On the other hand, it does give ample time to reconcile ourselves to our life's experience, our choices, our regrets, making amends, or healing relationships.

The time of work is done. This is the time for reflection and the integration of all life's experiences. Erikson refers to old age as the time to develop integrity as opposed to falling into despair. Integrity in this case is settling into the wisdom we have acquired through all our experiences, and connecting to a positive sense of self that sees our life as worthwhile and successful. Hanging on to past hurts and disappointments can result in bitterness and resentment. To clear heaviness out of the heart, and to be truly light in spirit as we look toward the last years of our life, we must master the art of forgiveness.

Forgiveness can be a challenge for many, and there tends to be much confusion about what forgiveness is. There are many assumptions regarding what forgiveness is supposed to look like that creates an obstacle to being able to allow ourselves the lightness and freedom from pain that forgiveness actually affords.

Often, the resistance we have to forgiving is the belief that to forgive means that we have to forget what happened or that we condone what happened, sending a message to the other that what happened was okay. It can sometimes feel like a denigration of self in order to alleviate the responsibility or consequence that weighs on the other. Forgiveness does not mean we are saying that what happened to us was okay. We need to acknowledge the impact that the event or situation had on us. The importance of validating our feelings has already been explored, and this follows through as necessary and appropriate in all situations. If we are having a hard time working through feelings about an event that happened many years previously, it would be beneficial to ask ourselves what is keeping the hurt or anger in place. What is stopping us from letting go of those feelings or how are they still serving us? The fact is, carrying negatively charged emotions like anger, hurt, fear, resentment, and bitterness does absolutely nothing to the other person. Carrying those emotions only serves to continue to create havoc within ourselves. Forgiveness is acknowledging the validity of our feelings and then making a commitment to ourselves to release the hold those emotions have over us.

Forgiveness does not mean that we have to continue to be in relationship with the other. If we were hurt through the actions of an unsafe person, then we absolutely need to know how to put appropriate boundaries in place. But we do not have to carry the spirit-crushing energy of pain behind those boundaries. Forgiveness is trusting ourselves enough to know that we have the tools within us to not be hurt again. We can discern who is safe to bring into our lives and we can make a choice away from those relationships that feel unhealthy. Hanging on to past hurt and pain simply serves to keep us stuck in a dynamic with the other person, even if we never see them. On an energetic level, the connection is still solid, and each time we think of the person and feel that twinge of anger or hurt, we have plucked at the strings of that painful connection. Forgiveness is actually the action of stating that the other no longer has power over us. It frees us from unhealthy connections on all levels.

We come into this world clear from experiences. This only makes sense as we haven't had very many yet. Of course there are some who have memories linking back to past lives, but for the most part, when we are welcomed into this lifetime we are open to allowing the new experiences it has to offer to come to us. The end of life brings us to the same point. We are meant to leave this world in the same way we came in—clear and open. As Elisabeth Kübler-Ross stated, "It's only when we truly know and understand that we have a limited time on earth—and that we have no way of knowing when our time is up—that we begin to live each day to the fullest, as if it was the only one we had."

There is a saying that the purpose of life is to learn to die well, and that is truly the task of old age. To die well is to release any negative or blocked energy that still connects us to the past. It is to be clear in all our relationships, forgiving in our hearts where necessary. It is being able to look back on a life well lived, accepting the full spectrum of experiences we have had. It is being able to live fully in each day, ready for the moment when we are taken by the mystery.

Further Exploration on Elderhood
Forgiveness: How to Make Peace with Your Past and Get on With Your Life by Sidney B. Simon. Grand Central Publishing, 1991.

Forgiveness: The Greatest Healer of All by Gerald G. Jampolsky.
Atria Books, 1999.

Higher Purpose

The greatest gift we can give ourselves is to know that we have a special and unique quality or purpose that we can express in our lives and in the world. To know that we are living a life in alignment with this purpose and that, because of having fulfilled our purpose, when we leave this earth it will be a better place.

Higher Purpose has nothing to do with a particular job or occupation. It is connected to the essence of being and is developed through life experience. Successes, achievements, and those times that give us joy can show us when we are on the right track. But the challenges, lost opportunities, painful moments, and times of despair often teach us the most about our Higher Purpose, and what we need to do in order to live and express it more fully. Joseph Campbell referred to it as "following your bliss."

… if you do follow your bliss you put yourself on a kind of track thathas been there all the while, waiting for you, and the life that you ought to be living is the one you are living. When you can see that, you begin to meet people who are in the field of your bliss, and they open doors for you. I say, follow your bliss and don't be afraid, and doors will open where you didn't know they were going to be.

—Joseph Campbell, *The Power of Myth*

Living in alignment with our Higher Purpose (or following our bliss) is not about having happy, perfect moments every day. After all, this is life, and challenge is part of the journey. But if we become bitter and resentful through these experiences, we will definitely be off track. Living our Higher Purpose is about allowing spirit to imbue our life, accepting the gift of opportunity in challenge, and knowing we have the skills and qualities necessary to meet those challenges. We have explored being thankful for community and the aid of others. When we are conscious of our path and committed to our true and unique expression in the world, we can also embrace gratitude for all those we meet on our path. Very often we find, with the 20/20 vision of hindsight, the time that brought the deepest challenge also contained the greatest gift. That includes those individuals who brought the challenge to our doorstep. Along with the saying "There can only be love or fear, not both," there is a sense that there can only be gratitude or resentment, not both. We either nurse our wounds or clean them out and let them heal. We cannot do both.

To explore Higher Purpose is to accept that there is a transcendent quality to life. It taps into the relationship between the superconscious and the conscious selves. The Higher Self is that aspect of the Divine that moves as a force through our own personal lives. Not only does the Higher Self help us to see the patterns and lessons that connect all the events in our lives, it helps us to see the core aspects of our own being and essence that yearn for expression. Just as there is a purpose to every day and a purpose at each stage in life, there is a Higher Purpose that arches over an entire life, giving it both meaning and direction.

In 1943, Abraham Maslow outlined his theory of human motivation that he called the *Hierarchy of Needs.* Maslow was interested in what constitutes mental health and what contributes to a positive life experience. He determined a structure of needs that every human has, recognizing that we must experience these needs being met in sequence. We will not be concerned with meeting aesthetic needs if our biological needs are still in flux. In many ways, this beautiful seven-tiered approach echoes the archetypal energies of the chakras, albeit in a slightly different order. We begin with recognizing our need for physical stability, which is the same reflection as the energy of the root chakra's focus on physical health and vitality. Moving up Maslow's pyramid brings us to the need for self-actualization, which is supported in the energy of the crown chakra's connection to Higher Self, and seeing the larger purpose and patterns in our lives.

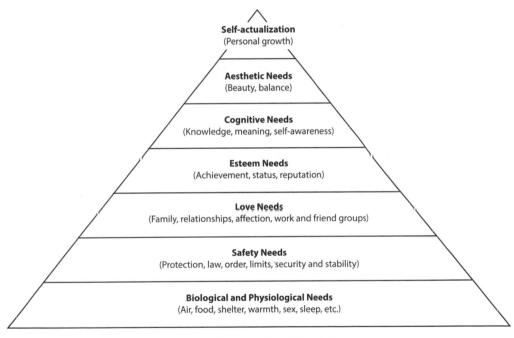

Maslow's Hierarchy of Needs.[18]

Interestingly, toward the end of his life Maslow added another level at the very top of the pyramid. He noted that when all other needs have been met, particularly when we have achieved a degree of self-actualization, there comes another need, which he called transcendence. This is the need to put our particular wisdom and experience into action, helping

....

18 Adapted from *Motivation and Personality,* Abraham H. Maslow (New York: Harper, 1954).

guide others toward self-actualization. Another term for this would be Higher Purpose—using our gifts to be of service to the higher good of others and the world. Transcendence allows for a higher vibration of consciousness, seeing the interconnection of all things and all people. It opens us to mystical experiences and higher guidance. When you have developed your own abilities (self-actualization) and can filter those experiences through spiritual awareness (transcendence) then you are fulfilling your Higher Purpose.

If you want to determine your Higher Purpose, you need look no further than the template of your own life. Often, Higher Purpose is crystal clear in childhood and then gets progressively muddy as we move through the years. Children are quick to answer the question of what they want to be when they grow up from a completely heart-filled place. It is not so much the job that is announced, but the essence of that job. It may not be about being a ballerina, but allowing for creative expression through the body. It may not be about being a veterinarian, but a deep love and connection for earth's creatures that is being announced.

To know your Higher Purpose you must know yourself. What gives you joy? What causes your spirit to soar and what causes it to sink? What are you truly good or gifted at doing? What makes you feel fulfilled? Higher Purpose will always connect you to your passion, and thus, when you are following that path with awareness, the experience will feel energizing and meaningful. Even on the tough days.

You can also determine your Higher Purpose by looking to the challenges and pain. Depression is the experience of having the soul buried beneath the muck of duty and obligation without connection and expression. In depression, we feel that we are going through the motions of each day, surviving but not thriving. It carries a clear message that we have disconnected from our unique contribution to the world. As Henry David Thoreau said, "The mass of men lead lives of quiet desperation and go to the grave with the song still in them." When we are able to approach both the joys and the pains of our life's experience with the objectivity that allows us to access a deeper meaning, we can truly enter the energy of gratitude. We move away from being grateful only for the "good stuff" that happens. Rather than become an emotion that is conditional on circumstances, gratitude becomes a "way of being" that is an attitude applied to the whole of our lives. We are not "grateful for this or that." We are simply … grateful.

Living our Higher Purpose does not mean that we will have the ideal job. It can mean that we find meaning in the job we have, and recognize it is a means through which we can share our special gifts. It means that we validate our significant contribution to others and the world, whatever form that may take. And it means we have clarity and direction in our lives.

We are never not on our path. If you are breathing, you are on your path. To be conscious is a whole other ballgame. With awareness and insight, allowing ourselves to be aware of patterns and synchronicities, we can see how everything that has ever happened to us has unfolded perfectly to allow us to sing our own song.

Connecting with Your Higher Self

Just as we all have within us an Inner Child, we all have a Higher Self. The Higher Self is experienced as that inner wise voice that reflects our highest potential. In the past it may have been known as our conscience, but the Higher Self does not just guide us on doing right from wrong. The Higher Self guides us to our own sense of what is right for us. It is the best rudder to steer through turbulent waters.

- Do you ever feel the universe is talking directly to you?

- Do you listen to your intuition?

- Do you feel empowered?

- Do you know that you are a part of something that is greater than yourself?

- Do you feel like a vessel through which the Divine shines?

All of these (and many more) are indicators that your Higher Self is in there, trying to communicate with you. Just as we can never not be on our path, we can never be disconnected from our Higher Self. We can experience a disconnection, but that stems from our own limiting perspective. The Higher Self is a part of us, just as consistently and surely as our bones, our feelings, and our thoughts.

The Higher Self is our intuition. It is that inner voice that directs us to release anything that holds us back from fulfilling our highest potential and expressing our Higher Purpose in the world. It is not always an easy voice to hear. It does not always tell us what we want to hear. It tells us what we need to hear. But it does so in a voice that is supportive, always reflecting faith in our abilities and respect for our innate value. If the inner voice you hear makes you feel badly about yourself and negatively impacts on your sense of worth and self-esteem, it is not your Higher Self. It is that simple. The Higher Self will never say, "get off the couch and make that phone call, you lazy sod." That is the Inner Critic. The Higher Self would; however, say, "get off the couch and make that phone call. This is the first step in achieving your dream. I know you are anxious. That's natural. But the gifts that await on the other side of the anxiety are wonderful, indeed, and you are worth it."

There are many wonderful ways in which to begin to connect with your Higher Self:

- Chart out the significant events in your life to discern the pattern that connects them all

- Celebrate your special gifts, strengths, and interests

- Listen only to the inner voice that lifts you up (even when the message might be encouraging you in uncomfortable directions of growth and potential)

- Allow yourself to see other people from a Higher Self perspective

- Allow yourself time to engage in inspiring activities that energize you

One of the most powerful ways to engage with your Higher Self, as with the Inner Child, is through meditation. Breathing deeply into the body, allow yourself to see an image of yourself as a wise being, perhaps an elder, who shimmers with a glorious light and emanates a sense of calm and the energy of love. In a meditative state, begin to dialogue with that wise being, asking him or her about success and challenges, lessons and learnings. Make a commitment to listen to that wise being, to honor his or her voice. You may find that there are slightly different reflections to this voice in the various aspects of your life. You may find a wise healer, a wise teacher, or a wise friend. They are all reflections of the Higher Self, and we all have that Higher Self within us. Embracing that aspect of self, and seeing the world through his or her eyes, allows us the opportunity to seize each day, living it fully in our own truth.

Further Exploration on Higher Purpose

A New Earth: Awakening to Your Life's Purpose by Eckhart Tolle. Penguin, 2008.

Manifest Your Destiny: The Nine Spiritual Principles for Getting Everything You Want by Wayne W. Dyer. William Morrow, 1998.

The Life You Were Born to Live: A Guide to Finding Your Life Purpose by Dan Millman. HJ Kramer, 1993.

The Purpose of Your Life: Finding Your Place in the World Using Synchronicity, Intuition, and Uncommon Sense by Carol Adrienne. William Morrow, 1999.

Personal Developmental and Psychological Reflections

October 4. Reflect on a great challenge in your life and how it contributed to your growth.

October 5: How do you feel when you think about death?

October 6: Do you have a tendency to hang on or let go?

October 7: How do you want to be remembered?

October 8: List five things for which you are grateful.

October 9: What do you consider to be your song?

October 10: Reflect on what a life of meaning means to you.

Forty-Three

Alchemical Reflection on Coagulation

"Thus will you obtain the glory of the whole universe.
All obscurity will be clear to you. This is the greatest force of all powers,
because it overcomes every subtle thing and penetrates every solid thing."

FROM *THE EMERALD TABLET*

COAGULATION ASSOCIATIONS [19] "THE RED PHASE"

Element: Salt • **Metal:** Gold • **Planet:** Sun
Symbols: Wings, Stone, Egg, Diamond, Androgyne
Dream Imagery: Fruitful earth, flaming heart, weddings

Known as the *Great Marriage,* or the attainment of the Philosopher's Stone, *coagulation* is the final union of purified opposites into a seamless whole. If conjunction is the image of the hermaphrodite with two distinct halves (one male and one female), coagulation is the image of the androgyne that has attained such a perfect balance of masculine and feminine qualities that it is impossible to name as one or the other.

....

19 Coagulation associations adapted from *The Emerald Tablet: Alchemy for Personal Transformation,* Dennis William Hauck (New York: Penguin/Arkana, 1999).

Psychologically, coagulation is the empowerment of the True Self. There is an absolute balance and integration of opposites: thought and feeling, intellect and emotion, doing and being, action and repose, human and spirit. There is also an absolute balance and integration of ourselves in the context of others and the whole. Not only do we recognize the Divine within, we recognize the Divine in everyone. It is from this place that true forgiveness occurs: when we can see that we are all flawed humans doing the best we can with the tools at our disposal. And some of those tools are somewhat primitive and outdated! We are able to see past the flaws to the Essence that lies within each and every one of us.

Coagulation is the triumph of the spirit and the intelligence of the heart. From this place you know yourself to be a master and yet to walk softly through the world with humility. There is the wisdom attained that knows that you are not your experiences. There is no shame in challenge and hardship. What matters is how you respond to each situation with courage and resilience. There is an inner strength that has the ability to withstand any onslaught or situation. Connection with the True Self enables you to have a self-identity that is grounded in solid self-esteem, not ego or material attachment. "I am not my job, my home, my relationships, or my bank account. And yet, all those elements are aspects of the expression of me in my life."

Ego is recognized as the vessel that is necessary to carry the spirit through life. But your truth is reflected through your relationship with the Higher Self, which observes and guides on the machinations of life, but always presents the Divine perspective.

One key element to alchemy is the seven hermetic principles. These are the seven laws of the universe that illustrate how all in the universe interconnect and interact. They are to the soul as the laws of physics are to the physical universe.

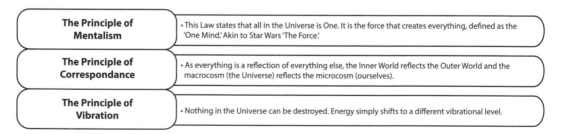

The Principle of Mentalism	• This Law states that all in the Universe is One. It is the force that creates everything, defined as the 'One Mind.' Akin to Star Wars 'The Force.'
The Principle of Correspondance	• As everything is a reflection of everything else, the Inner World reflects the Outer World and the macrocosm (the Universe) reflects the microcosm (ourselves).
The Principle of Vibration	• Nothing in the Universe can be destroyed. Energy simply shifts to a different vibrational level.

The Seven Hermetic Principles.

The Principle of Polarity	• All things exist in dynamic relationship to an opposing element. For example, hot and cold are not different concepts. Thety are polarities on a spectrum of 'Heat.'
The Principle of Rhythm	• A principle of movement like Vibration that indicates there is an 'ebb and flow' to all things and experiences in Existence.
The Principle of Cause and Effect	• A principle of relationship like Correspondance that indicates the accountability of one action in regards to another.
The Principle of Gender	• A principle of dynamics like Polarity that indicates the necessity of dualism. Akin to Yin and Yang, masculine (active) and feminine (receptive) support each other.

The Seven Hermetic Principles (continued).[20]

The seven hermetic principles present the structure and movement of existence. Accessing these seven principles offers a complete map of what existence looks like and how it operates. Beginning with the first principle, which explains the nature of existence, all following principles elaborate on demonstrating the manner in which all things interact. The seven hermetic principles offer a map through which we can approach any of life's experiences, incorporating the wisdom of the Philosopher's Stone. The law of attraction is a variation on the law of vibration, and many have manifested wonderful things in their lives working with just this one principle. The original presentation of the seven hermetic principles is that they work in unison with each other. Applying these principles to any situation leads to enormous insight and the potential to activate lasting change.

For example, you may feel angry with a friend for not calling for months on end. You may feel hurt, rejected, and unsupported. You may question the validity of the friendship in the first place and feel sadness at the potential loss that this questioning provokes. To approach the situation through the hermetic principles could look like this:

The Principle of Correspondence shows you that your outer world reflects your inner world. The questions to ask yourself is *"What do I carry inside as a belief around what friend-ship looks like? In what ways is my friend's behavior in alignment with what I truly believe rather than what I would like to believe? In what ways do I embody that same behavior?"* You may find at the core of your inquiry the revelation that there is something about this

....

20 Adapted from *The Kybalion*, the Three Initiates (New York: Jeremy P. Tarcher/Penguin, 2008).

situation that carries a resonance with the abandonment issue that you have been working with for years.

The Principle of Vibration invites you to shift the energy of your anger. Emotions are energy vibrating at different levels. To stay in anger is to stay stuck in the dynamic of hurt. With vibration, you listen to what the anger is telling you about your perception of the situation (aiding correspondence), then shift the anger. Gratitude is always a good one. You may allow the energy of gratitude for the lessons offered in the situation to become the guiding emotion. You may appreciate that this situation has allowed you to see that there are still levels to a core abandonment issue for you to explore.

The Principle of Polarity allows for the exploration of the concept of friendship along a spectrum of continuum. Similar to the concepts explored in the section on relationships, you may see one end of the spectrum being codependence, and the other being independence. On one side there is a sense of friendship as being in constant contact and knowing every detail about each other's lives. On the other side you have the thoughts about ending the friendship. Somewhere in the center lies the reflection of a friendship as being interdependent.

The Principle of Rhythm allows you to explore the ebb and flow of friendship as the movement along the polarity spectrum. You may begin to see that there are times of intense involvement followed by times when there is more distance. Seeing the rhythm of this movement allows a better sense of ease to come into your vision of what friendship looks like. Seeing the flow of friendship as following this rhythm may help you to move past the abandonment trigger.

The Principle of Cause and Effect can take many different forms. You may come to see that you too created some distance with an expectation that the friendship would always be there. You may recall a previous conversation with the friend in which you may have been perceived as rejecting, exploring the possibility that the distance has been created because of your friend's hurt. You may come to see that over the past months you and your friend had begun to grow in different directions, and the current situation is actually indicative of a natural end. You may realize that if you really think about it, your friend is going through a particularly busy time and that your initial reaction truly had more to do with your abandonment fears than your friend's withdrawal of connection.

The Principle of Gender allows for a balanced approach to resolution. The masculine (active) element may prompt you to call your friend and communicate a desire for more regular contact, indicating how important the relationship is to you. The feminine (receptive) element may invite you to rest in your shifted emotion of gratitude, allowing space for the love you have for your friend, the appreciation for all the shared times together, and the hope for continued connection to fill your soul.

Underlying this whole process is *The Principle of Mentalism*. All in the universe is one, and we are all interconnected through that energy. In truth, you are no different than your friend. There may be different experiences and responses, but beyond all that, we are all just humans walking on this earth, trying to do the best we can. When we have journeyed through the alchemical process, we connect to the core of our Essence—the Philosopher's Stone. This is the closest reflection to the one mind that we have in a human experience. Moving through any life experience, with the Philosopher's Stone as our guide, truly opens us to the experience of a spiritually inspired existence.

Personal Alchemical Reflections

October 11: For you, what is the difference between True Self and Higher Self?

October 12: What are some words that would describe the Philosopher's Stone for you?

October 13: What are some qualities you feel a sage or master would embody?

October 14: Reflect on a time when you felt completely centered in the midst of a crisis.

October 15: In what ways do you balance being with doing?

October 16: In what ways do you balance a healthy ego with humility?

October 17: How are you a light for others?

Forty-Four

....

Energetic Reflection on the Crown Chakra

CROWN CHAKRA ASSOCIATIONS [21]

....

Name: Sahasrara • **Location:** Top of the head • **Color:** Purple
Tone: B • **Gland:** Pituitary • **Body:** Brain, skull • **Yoga Path:** Jnana
Symbol: Thousand-petalled lotus • **Stones:** Quartz, Amethyst,
Flourite, Lepidolite, Charoite

In direct reflection of the root chakra and its connection with earth energy, the crown chakra opens at the top of the head, connecting to the cosmos and universal energy. Toaist philosophy presents that at death, the soul leaves the body through a tiny hole at the top of the head called the *brahmaranda*. As the crown chakra is the center through which we connect to higher energies and vibrations, it would make sense that the crown chakra and brahmaranda are one and the same.

The crown chakra connects us to our spirituality and the Higher Self. It is the portal of Divine energy into our bodies that helps us experience illumination and enlightenment. It is associated with thought and pure consciousness. We are able to see from higher perspectives and from all sides with the added benefit of detachment. We are able to rise above

....

21 Crown chakra associations adapted from *The Chakra Handbook: From Basic Understanding to Practical Application,* Shalila Sharamon and Bodo J. Baginski (Wilmot, WI: Lotus Light Publications, 1991).

situations, seeing them in the context both of all that has come before and all that may unfold in the future. Often this is aided by having done much inner work and gaining much self-knowledge and understanding. Wisdom is defined as that which results from combining knowledge with experience. The crown chakra opens us to wisdom, seeing the bigger picture of our lives because we have explored the past and worked through the feelings and wounds. We have filtered subjective experience through objective knowledge and attained enlightenment.

Physically, a blocked crown chakra can be indicated by an excess of pressure in the head or the brain. Headaches that encompass the whole head and an overall sense of fatigue throughout the body can indicate a block in the crown chakra.

Psychologically, when the crown chakra is blocked we can experience a mistrust of the Divine. Closed off in this way we are not able to see wondrous synchronicities and awe-inspiring patterns of our lives. The messages that indicate a personal connection with the Divine are missed, and we can feel alone and adrift in the sometimes turbulent seas of our experiences. Life can feel meaningless or hopeless. Depression can set in and the body can feel weighed down with the stone of fatigue that also affects our physical well-being.

Alternatively, some people place so much focus on a spiritual connection that their crown chakras are wide open all the time. This imbalance can be as problematic as a blocked chakra, leading to spiritual bypassing. Over-dependence on meditation, repressing certain emotions as not spiritual, and expecting the Divine to resolve all life's situations are all examples of spiritual bypassing. We need to allow space for the Divine in our lives, but we need to accept our human attributes as well. A balanced crown chakra will enliven all aspects of our lives, not just the ones that tend to be designated as spiritual.

Messages that help to balance the crown chakra are:
I co-create with my Higher Self.
I am open to seeing the patterns and lessons in my life.
I am living a life of purpose.
Every experience I have is touched by spirit.

Personal Energetic Reflections

October 18: The color purple makes me feel ...

October 19: Reflect on a time you experienced synchronicity in your life.

October 20: To what extent do you feel guided?

October 21: Have you ever felt abandoned by spirit?

October 22: What wisdom inspires and directs you?

October 23: Have you ever felt that information was downloaded to you?

October 24: In what ways do you connect with your Higher Self?

Forty-Five

Guidance Reflection on Angels and Intuitive Reflection on Scrying

Angels

The term angel comes to us from the Greek *angelos*, meaning "messenger." They are described as beings of light who act as intermediaries with the Divine. Many cultures have stories of angels, but it is Western culture that presents a complex, hierarchical angelic structure. Pope Gregory I was the first to list nine orders of angels by name and delineate the domain of focus for each order. In Pope Gregory's schema, there are three spheres with three orders of angels each. The first sphere consisted of the guardians of God's throne. Closest to God are the *seraphim* (literally "the burning ones"), who continually shout out God's praises. They are described as having six wings, covered with eyes, and are so bright one cannot look at them directly.

Next come the *cherubim* (literally "fullness of knowledge"), who are the guardians of light and the stars. They have four faces (man, ox, lion, and eagle) and four wings. The *thrones* (also known as Erelim) are wheels covered with eyes. They are the symbols of God's justice and authority.

The second sphere consists of the heavenly governors. *Dominions* (also known as Hashmallin) preside over the duties of the lower angels. They are generally pictured as we imagine angels to look and holding an orb or scepter. The *virtues* (also known as Malakim) preside over the movement of the heavenly bodies. The *powers* are the information gatherers and history keepers who fight against demons. They are often pictured with a flaming sword.

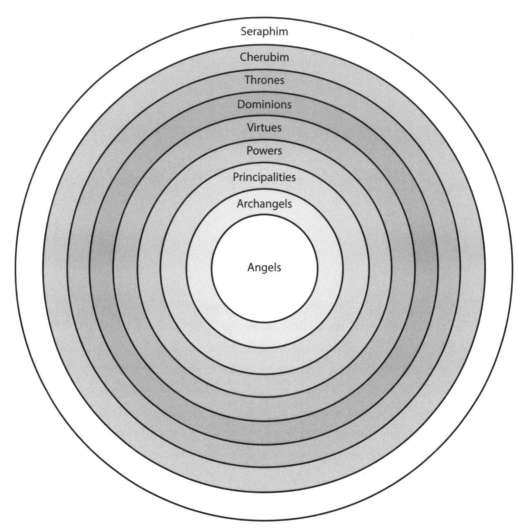

Pope Gregory's Orders of Angels.

The third sphere is closest to earth and the angels in this sphere are the messengers. *Principalities* preside over groups of people, bestowing blessings under the direction of the dominions. They are often pictured with a crown. *Archangels* carry out God's will, usually in relation to nations or humanity at large. It is the archangels who appear in biblical scripture carrying God's message to certain individuals at key, significant moments. Though historically archangels were the special messengers of God to a select few, nowadays, their energy is felt by many, indicative of the contemporary understanding of a more direct and personal line of communication with the Divine. Traditionally there are seven archangels, although an eighth (Jerahmeel) is sometimes included. We are most familiar with four (Michael, Gabriel, Raphael, and Uriel) who tend to be most popular with whom to work.

The Eight Archangels

Michael	Gabriel	Raphael	Uriel
"Who is like God"	"Might of God"	"God's Healing"	"Light of God"
Sealtiel	Jegudiel	Barachiel	Jerahmeel
"Intercessor of God"	"Glorifier of God"	"Blessing of God"	"God's Exaltation"

When we speak of a guardian angel or a companion angel, we are referring to the ninth order of angels. This order of angels is concerned with all matters relating to life on earth. Some say we are born with an angel looking over us who stays with us through the course of our life, guiding us and keeping us safe. That angel would be from this order.

The different order of angels can be seen in contemporary language as increasingly higher vibrations of energy that take us closer to the Divine. What differentiates angelic energy from other types of guiding energy is that it is connected to the pure Divine. Angels have never been incarnate. They have not experienced life in the material realm, and do not have free will as human do. Working with angels and archangels connects us with pure Divine energy, helping us to feel loved and supported, offering guidance and protection. But they cannot interfere with our choices or our Higher Purpose. They can guide, but the choice is still up to us. There are countless examples of individuals who have experienced angelic intercession and guidance. Some experience this guidance as hearing compassionate, wise messages. Some experience angels more physically, as a push out of harm's way or being enveloped in the comfort of angelic wings.

Very often, connecting with angels leaves us with a feeling that, regardless of the situation, we know we will be okay. The comfort that they bring allows us the space to step into the strength we need in order to move through the challenges we may be experiencing. Angels always convey a message of unconditional love that opens us up to the possibility of accepting ourselves in all our humanness, and in all aspects of our being. Their presence fills us with the understanding that we are never alone and that we are always supported in our struggles and our triumphs.

You can connect with your companion angel simply by reaching out and being open to the guidance received. Your angel is always by your side.

 Further Exploration on Angels

Angels: Guardians of the Light by Karen M. Haughey. Hay House, 1995.

Angels Help Us: Discovering Divine Guidance by Jean Porche and Deborah Vaughan. Dundurn Press, 2002.

Archangels 101: How to Connect Closely with Archangels Michael, Raphael, Gabriel, Uriel, and Others for Healing, Protection, and Guidance by Doreen Virtue. Hay House, 2011.

Healing with the Angels by Doreen Virtue. Hay House, 1999.

Scrying

Scrying is the technical term for the practice of looking into an object for messages and guidance. It has been used for centuries by many cultures as a means through which to seek the answers to questions or gain insight. In ancient times natural elements like wells or pools were used. Over the centuries certain tools were developed to aid scrying. Though, generally speaking, scrying is not used to contact otherworldly elements, one well-known example of scrying comes from Dr. Dee who developed the Enochian language by connecting with angels via scrying. Dr. Dee worked with another individual, Edward Kelley, and made extensive notes on the language he described as "Angelic or Celestial Speech," gleaned from working with a mirror made of black obsidian glass called a *shew-stone*. The most famous example of scrying comes from Nostradamus, who used a bowl of water when in a trance to see the future. Many still look to the prophecies of Nostradamus and see fascinating correlations between the prophecies and the subsequent events of history.

Perhaps the best known tool for scrying is the crystal ball. Although crystal balls are traditionally made from clear quartz, they can be made from many stone materials. Different materials tend to have an impact on the quality, or slant, of the message. Rose quartz crystal balls have a gentle, loving energy. Amethyst crystal balls tend to give messages about our Higher Purpose and spiritual direction.

Pendulums are also fall into the category of scrying; however, rather than seeking answers through vision, the pendulum swing can indicate a simple yes or no response. There are many charts available to use with a pendulum to determine guided answers focused on a wide range of specific areas, such as which chakras are blocked, or what are the best foods for one to eat. Other methods of scrying include using bowls of water, candle flames, mirrors, or clouds. Ouija boards are also considered scrying; however, their use is not recommended as they tend to attract low level entities that can result in havoc and mischief, rather than high vibrational guidance.

Scrying can be a challenge. It requires deep focus and spiritual connection to discern messages from what is essentially a blank screen. It can take time to develop a scrying practice, but the benefit is developing a strong line of communication with your Higher Self and guides. Developing ability in scrying strengthens work with other messages such as signs and omens. It helps to develop adeptness at recognizing synchronicity.

 ### Basic Scrying Reading
Choose a scrying technique that appeals to you: crystal ball, mirror, candle, or water in a dark bowl. Scrying is done best in a dark room so you are prompted to use inner sight rather than your physical eyes.

After taking some time to center yourself, begin to breathe deeply and slowly. Bring yourself to a place of focused relaxation and connect to your Higher Self for guidance. When you feel completely relaxed and have let go of any thoughts, bring your attention to your scrying tool. Allow your eyes to unfocus slightly as if you are looking beyond the tool rather than at the tool. With complete openness, allow any images or symbols to float before your eyes.

Let go of any attachment to seeing a scene play out. That may or may not be your experience. Sometimes it may feel as though there is an event being presented. Sometimes it may be a single symbol that seems to form. Remember that with scrying, you are seeing with inner vision. This can be experienced as an image transposed over physical sight, as if you are seeing something right behind your eyes rather than reflected in the scrying tool.

If you find yourself experiencing doubts or frustration, focus on your breath once more until you feel centered. Scrying can be challenging for beginners and requires patience and practice. You may find that you don't see anything the first few times you scry, but then, all of a sudden, an image will bounce out at you, similar to the 3D magic eye photos that were popular in the 1990s.

As with other forms of intuitive guidance, once you have a sense of the image or symbol being presented, take some time to meditate on its meaning to you, and how it provides guidance on where you are at this moment in your life.

Further Exploration on Scrying

Crystal Balls & Crystal Bowls: Tools for Ancient Scrying & Modern Seership by Ted Andrews. Llewellyn Publications, 2002.

Crystal Ball Gazing: The Complete Guide to Choosing and Reading Your Crystal Ball by Uma Silbey. Touchstone, 1998.

Scrying for Beginners by Donald Tyson. Llewellyn Publications, 1997.

Scrying the Secrets of the Future: How to Use Crystal Balls, Fire, Wax, Mirrors, Shadows and Spirit Guides to Reveal Your Destiny by Cassandra Eason. New Page Books, 2007.

Personal Guidance and Intuitive Reflections

October 25: What comes to mind for you when you hear the word angel?

October 26: Reflect on a time when you felt unconditionally supported.

October 27: What is your sense of the difference between a guardian angel and an archangel?

October 28: Reflect on a time in your life when what you experienced may have been angelic intercession.

October 29: Have you ever found yourself slipping into a reverie or trance?

October 30: Reflect on what you see when you look in a mirror.

October 31: How would your life be different if you experienced higher guidance from many different sources?

The Enlightened Hynni of Karma

When you feel despair and a lack of meaning in life. When you feel more duty than compassion and more responsibility than enthusiasm. When it feels impossible to see the interconnection between all that is both hard and inspiring or you question your impact in the world, this is the time to activate the Hynni of Karma.

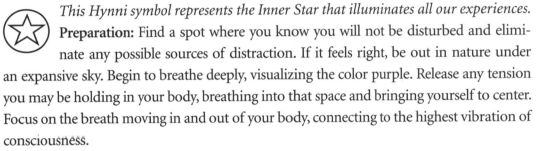

This Hynni symbol represents the Inner Star that illuminates all our experiences. **Preparation:** Find a spot where you know you will not be disturbed and eliminate any possible sources of distraction. If it feels right, be out in nature under an expansive sky. Begin to breathe deeply, visualizing the color purple. Release any tension you may be holding in your body, breathing into that space and bringing yourself to center. Focus on the breath moving in and out of your body, connecting to the highest vibration of consciousness.

Hynni: As you breathe, allow yourself to become aware of your thoughts. What is the tape that is playing in the background of your mind? Take a moment to rest with each thought, exploring it. Does it feel positive and supportive, or negative and destructive? Does it feel expansive or contractive? With each thought you encounter, note it and explore it. Then let it go and let the next thought arise.

When the flow of thoughts begin to slow, shift your focus from the thoughts themselves to the space between the thoughts; that gap between one thought leaving and another coming into view. How does that space feel to you? What is the energy of that gap? If that space of potential were truly you, how would that change your sense of self? The element of thought expands our experience to encompass every possibility and opportunity. As thought, you feel the reverberation of all you have learned from the past, and the magnetism of all that is to come. Allow yourself to connect with the sense of full potential.

Begin to focus on the karma symbol, visualizing a golden light that carries the intent of the symbol glowing and emanating at the top of your head. The arms of the symbol reach out in all directions: from your past to your future, from yourself to others, and above to your Higher Self. This is the aspect of self that truly knows you are Divine and that you have much to offer the world. It is the keeper of the blueprint of our lives, holding for us our vision and plan for our lives, and supporting us in continuing the effort to manifest that plan. Nothing is by accident. Everything is connected. Every cause has an effect, and every effect is motivated by a cause. The Hynni of Karma enlightens us to the pattern, allowing us to move forward with direction and purpose.

If you choose, from this place take a moment to gaze around your environment from the perspective of expanded awareness. Be open to how your Higher Self may be sending a message through an aspect of your environment—clouds in the sky, birds in the air, patterns in candle wax.

In this expansive state, invite an angel or archangel to come to you. Be aware of how the energy around you changes. You may become aware of a higher vibration around you or that something within you shifts to meet this angelic energy. Allow yourself to connect with this guide, receiving any messages or emotional energy of love and support.

Bringing your focus back to your breath, feel the pulse of the Divine within you. Know that you are here for a purpose and that your life has meaning, always, and that you are the manifestation of spirit on earth. When you are ready, take three deep, centering breaths and open your eyes.

Part Eleven

Cycle Eight
November 1–December 12

Healing from Loss
"We Are All Part of the All"

PRESCRIPTIONS

Go through this section if you are experiencing any of the following:

- Isolation from humanity
- Debilitating fear of death
- Challenge in resolving ancestral legacy issues
- Inability to live in the moment
- Past-life bleedthrough

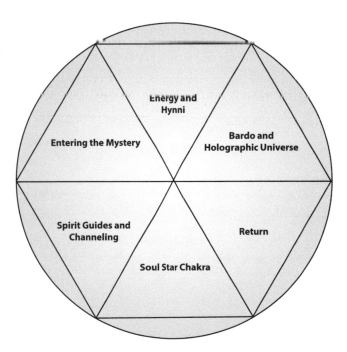

Energy and Hynni

Bardo and Holographic Universe

Entering the Mystery

Spirit Guides and Channeling

Return

Soul Star Chakra

Forty-Six

Mythological Reflection on Entering the Mystery

For the ancient peoples, this time was the last of the harvest festivals and one in which death was more actual than symbolic. The grain harvest represented the symbolic death of the agricultural god. By this time the harvest of grains, fruits, and vegetables was done. If anything was left in the fields, it stayed there, considered to belong now to otherworldly creatures. Now was the time of bringing the herds in from pasture. With an eye to the survival of the whole, attention needed to be paid to culling. Those animals that were not considered fit enough to survive the hard winter months were slaughtered in order to ensure the preservation of those animals who could survive. Precious feed could not be wasted on animals that would not live through the coming months. The symbolic death of the harvest festivals took on a more practical form.

Between this time and the Winter Solstice lies the darkest time of the entire year. With the land barren and cold, focus began to turn inward. This was considered the start of winter and the beginning of the whole new yearly cycle. With the belief that anything born into the light begins in the dark, this time was akin to gestation—the hidden growing period.

The ancients also had a different view of death, believing that the otherworld was as real as this world, and could be accessed either in special places or at special times. At this festival "the veil between the worlds" was thin, allowing connection and communication with ancestors. The Halloween tradition of trick-or-treating is said to have arisen from the ancient Celtic practice of leaving food as a gesture to those departed. This can also be seen reflected in the beautiful tradition of hosting a special, silent dinner in honor of the ancestors. For this, you would set a festive table for your family, including a place setting for your ancestors. Pictures of loved ones who have crossed over can also be placed on the table. The entire meal is conducted in silence as each individual sits with their own personal thoughts and remembrances. It is through memory that our loved ones remain with us, and these memories bring them to sit with us at the table. Once the meal is cleared it is touching and heart-warming to share the remembrances that came to each person during the meal.

Though there was respect and love for the ancestors, there was also fear for what the dark hid. This festival was another of the great Fire Festivals, which shone light through the dark and provided new light for the hearths. As much as possible, it was a good idea to avoid heading out in the dark at this time in case of those spirits who were mischievous or malevolent, but if such a venture was unavoidable, it was advised to wear a mask to keep from being recognized.

This time heralded a period of stillness, and of holding close and tight over the next months, until the Winter Solstice once more brought the hope of the future.

Main Themes for Cycle 8:

Death

Protection

Otherworldly connection

Ancient Cultural Archetypes of Otherworldly Guides

(Known as psychopomps, which in Greek literally means "guide of souls," these gods conveyed the newly departed to the other side.)

Anubis (*Egyptian*) is the jackal-headed god associated with mummification and the after-life.

Hekate (*Greek*) is the goddess of mysteries whose name means "the hidden one." She stands at crossroads to help us through decisions and transitions. She accompanies **Persephone** in the journey between the upper world and the underworld at spring and fall.

Charon (*Greek*) is the ferryman who carries the newly departed across the River Styx to the underworld. Placing a coin on a person's eyes was payment to Charon for the passage.

Hermes (*Greek*) or **Mercury** (*Roman*) is a god of transitions and boundaries, as well as communication and messages. He mediated between the mortal and Divine worlds, and guided souls to the afterlife.

Gwyn ap Nudd (*Celtic*) is the guide of souls to the otherworld. The Tor at Glastonbury is said to be his abode and the portal between the realms. He is king of the fair folk ("tylwyth teg") and ruler of the otherworld ("annwn"). His name means "white, son of night."

Macha (*Celtic*) is a warrior goddess dedicated to protecting women and defending those who have been wronged. With her sisters, **Badb** and **Morrigan**, she forms the trio of war goddesses known as the *Morrigna*, translated as "the great queens."

Valkyries (*Norse*) are female figures who are lovers of heroes and who choose which slain warriors go to Valhalla to be with **Odin**. The rest go to Folkvangr to be with **Freya**. Valkyrie translates as "chooser of the slain."

Personal Mythological Reflections

November 1: What thought do you give to the sense of your own mortality?

November 2: What helps you to face the dark?

November 3: What are you most afraid of?

November 4: How do you hide who you are?

November 5: How do you plan ahead for potentially challenging times?

November 6: In what ways do you embrace silence?

November 7: What is your sense of the after-life?

Forty-Seven

Elemental Reflection on Energy and Active Reflection on Hynni

Energy: The Source of All

In physics, energy is a term used to describe the amount of work that can be performed by a certain force. Energy can fall into one of several categories: thermal energy, gravitational energy, electromagnetic energy, and nuclear energy. Each of these provide a different source for harnessing energy, and the application of these methods touches every aspect of our lives, prompting continued debate as regards development of future methods of generating energy.

In metaphysics, energy describes the vital life force that imbues all life. It describes the activating force that penetrates and creates all things. It is a universal constant that can change form but can never be destroyed.

This energy has been described by various names in almost every culture. The Chinese call it chi. The Japanese call it ki (as in Rei-ki). In India it is known as prana. Wilhelm Reich named it orgone. *Star Wars* popularized the concept of "The Force" as that which "gives a Jedi his power. It's an energy field created by all living things. It surrounds us and penetrates us. It binds the galaxy together." As such, it flows through each and every one of us and connects us all together.

Energy vibrates at different frequencies. The lower the vibration, the more dense, or physical, the energy. The higher the vibration, the more etheric the energy. Our physical bodies are energy vibrating at a very slow rate. The aura, the human energy field, vibrates at a much higher rate. Our emotions and our thoughts are also different levels of vibrational energy. These levels are all interconnected, but we experience them differently.

In addition, energy can flow in a healthy, smooth manner, or it can become blocked or stuck. Trauma on any level can lead to stuck energy. A physical injury will create a block, primarily in the physical energy field, but this does affect all vibrational levels. Energy healing uses this premise to discover stuck or blocked energy and use different tools to encourage flow (i.e., health). Addressing the block on the energetic level promotes relief on the physical, emotional, and mental levels as well.

There are many different methods of energy healing, including therapeutic touch, reiki, polarity therapy, qigong, pranic healing, or EFT (Emotional Freedom Technique). Other methods, such as acupuncture and acupressure, work with the energy meridians (or paths) in the body to facilitate healthy flow. Each one uses a different method, but the general concept remains consistent. Health requires energy that flows smoothly on all levels.

Messages that help to connect us to the element of energy are:
I always have been and always will be.
My energy flows with ease.
I am part of all that is.

Further Exploration on Energy

A Practical Guide to Vibrational Medicine: Energy Healing and Spiritual Transformation by Richard Gerber. William Morrow, 2001.

Energy Medicine: Balancing Your Body's Energies for Optimal Health, Joy, and Vitality by Donna Eden and David Feinsten. Tarcher, 2008.

Hands of Light: A Guide to Healing Through the Human Energy Field by Barbara Brennan. Bantam, 1988.

Light Emerging: The Journey of Personal Healing by Barbara Brennan. Bantam, 1993.

Hynni

Hynni is an energy healing modality that has its roots in my work as a Spiritual Psychotherapist, approaching emotional and mental health from an integrative, holistic perspective. The first inklings of Hynni began in 2003, operating from the same premise as all the varied and effective methods that have been utilized for many years. It acknowledges that energy healing on any level can facilitate healing on all levels, but Hynni expands the tools at our disposal to include those that directly relate to these other aspects of being. It is a multilayered approach to energy healing that introduces nine reflections through which we can facilitate holistic health. Because energy vibrates at different levels, each of these reflections gives us an entry point to healing on every level. The nine reflections of Hynni encompass the entire range of the human energy field, including the physical, emotional, mental, and spiritual levels.

The Nine Reflections of Hynni

Mythological	Elemental	Active
Presentation of archetypal energy and healing themes	Presentation of key symbolic building blocks that contribute to overall balance	Activities that bring our physical bodies into alignment with healing themes
Developmental	Psychological	Alchemical
The stages of human development from birth to death and beyond	Key issues that contribute to mental and emotional health	Application of the Western esoteric tradition for psychological and spiritualhealing
Energetic	Guidance	Intuitive
Presentation of the chakras as relates to healing on all levels	External elements that can offer support and encouragement toward healing	Tools that can aid with insight and self-understanding

Working with the nine reflections creates a cohesive approach toward healing. It acknowledges the importance and interconnection of all aspects of self through each of the reflections. It presents that self-knowledge (or the achievement of self-individuation) comes through exploring all the vibrational levels, rather than focusing on certain ones. We can gain some level of understanding by focusing on our energetic and spiritual development, but if we have not addressed our emotional and psychological issues, our spiritual development is going to be off-kilter.

Central to the Hynni approach is the recognition of the relationship with the cycles of nature. Not only is there a range of approaches offered by the reflections, the annual cycle of the seasons and the much shorter cycle of the moon also have an impact upon us. These present as eight seasonal cycles, each of which can be explored through the nine reflections and four moon phases. The Hynni approach utilizes certain symbols to represent these cycles and phases, which can help us connect to the healing energy of each one.

The Twelve Hynni Symbols

Cycle 1 Solid Hynni of Grounding	Cycle 2 Loving Hynni of Ebb & Flow	Phase 1 Hynni of Openings
Cycle 3 Centering Hynni of Esteem	Cycle 4 Bridging Hynni of Synthesis	Phase 2 Hynni of Fullness
Cycle 5 Clear Hynni of Expression	Cycle 6 Illumined Hynni of Vision	Phase 3 Hynni of Experience
Cycle 7 Enlightened Hynni of Karma	Cycle 8 Integrating Hynni of Unity	Phase 4 Hynni of Stillness

Hynni is the comprehensive practice of working with the twelve symbols and with the teachings of each of the nine reflections. It encourages both transformation and transcendence.

Personal Elemental and Active Reflections

November 8: In what ways do you recognize stuck or blocked energy in yourself?

November 9: How sensitive are you to the energy of others?

November 10: What tools do you have to balance your energy if it feels too high or too low?

November 11: In what ways do you embrace your complexity?

November 12: What aspects of your self do you tend to ignore?

November 13: How do you respond to an invitation to adventure?

November 14: What does a fulfilled, vibrant, balanced, and courageous life look like to you?

Forty-Eight

Developmental Reflection on Bardo and Psychological Reflection on the Holographic Universe

Bardo

Bardo is a Tibetan term to describe an intermediary state. Any state of transition can be referred to as a bardo. Dusk is the bardo between day and night, as is dawn. Adolescence is the bardo between childhood and adulthood. The hypnogogic state is the bardo between wakefulness and sleep. Dying is the bardo between life and death.

Traditional Buddhism defines six bardo states. *Shinay* is the bardo of life during which we experience two other frequent bardo states: *milam* (the bardo of the dream state) and *samten* (the bardo of meditation). At the end of life, when the inner and outer signs indicate that the time of death is near, one enters the *chikkai* bardo, which continues until the moment the last breath is taken. What some report as a near death experience is called the *chönyid* bardo, which reveals the luminosity of our true nature. The bardo state that continues up until the moment of incarnation once again into one's next life is called *sidpai*, the bardo of becoming.

The Six Tibetan Bardo States [22]

Shinay	Milam	Samten
The bardo of life	The bardo of dreaming experienced in life	The bardo of meditation experienced in life
Chikkai	**Chönyid**	**Sidpai**
The bardo of dying	The bardo of transition into the afterlife	The bardo of becoming

There has been much research into past-life regression and near death experiences, which offers fascinating insights into the mystery of what lies beyond this life. Exploration into what awaits beyond the veil is predicated on an understanding that energy cannot be destroyed and that there is a constant that continues after the densest aspect of our energetic field (the body) is gone. If one experiences chronic pain (emotional or physical) that will not shift and appears to have no definite cause in this lifetime, past-life regression can be a useful tool. Many who have experienced Near Death Experiences (NDEs) report that they return to this life experience with a clearer perspective on what is truly important and an ease in feelings toward death.

There has also been much research done in bardo regression through hypnosis. In all the research there is consensus that this stage is preparatory for the next life to come. The chönyid bardo (described in NDEs) presents that the soul goes through a life review during which one experiences all one's decisions, choices, and interactions—not just from one's own perspective, but from all perspectives. If you hurt someone deeply, you would experience that situation both from your perspective and from the perspective of the one you hurt. This is part of what underlines the importance of approaching every interaction with a loving and compassionate heart. In the life review we can also see where we have not embraced our Higher Purpose, and where we allowed fear or limitation to determine our course.

If the purpose of the soul's journey is to become as true and pure as possible (the achievement of the alchemical Philosopher's Stone), then the sidpai bardo is our opportunity to map out a life that will afford us the best possible experiences to enable this. We are responsible for our lives, not just in our responses to situations we find ourselves while

....

22 Adapted from *The Tibetan Book of Living and Dying,* Sogyal Rinpoche
   (London: Rider & Co, 1996).

living, but because we have chosen those experiences before we even entered this life. We are following a blueprint of our own creation.

This is not to imply a fatalistic approach to life. It is an approach that truly sees life as earth school. As our souls integrate experiences, we incarnate to different degrees of experiences. It is like the difference between going to grade school and entering graduate school. There are different elements to be learned depending on where you are at in your own development. Similarly, just because you are in school does not mean you hand in all the assignments or study for all the tests. We are born with free will and have absolute authority to exercise it. In any situation, I can be aware of the highest response as well as the lowest response. When slighted, I can choose to communicate my feelings or I can devolve into a hissy fit. The more conscious I am, the more I am aware of where my choices lay. But it is always up to me to choose.

The best way to begin to access how you may have drawn up your blueprint is to look at the patterns and choices in your life from the earth school perspective. It is bringing in the objective eye to see how each experience offered an opportunity to grow. Significant relationships (including the challenging ones) often signify agreements that have been made between souls in bardo state. Major life events would definitely make up part of the blueprint. Higher Purpose is the overall theme of the blueprint, and all the people and situations in your life serve to guide you toward fulfilling it. If you do not fulfill it in this lifetime, the sidpai bardo is the time during which you can map out another blueprint version to try again. As it is stated in the alchemical *Emerald Tablet*, it is all geared toward releasing the dense and gross, and allowing the subtle to come forth.

In theosophical philosophy, all the information of all our past lives and bardo states is held in the *Akashic records*. Alice Bailey referred to the records as, "like an immense photographic film, registering all the desires and earth experiences of our planet," including all who walk upon this earth. We can use meditation to access the akashic records to gain insight into this life through exploring both past-lives and the lives between lives. In actuality, we can also use this method to access future lives as well.

If exploring life themes is the charge of the newly departed, grief is the domain of those who remain in this world. Arguably, the death of a loved one is always much harder on those left behind than the one who has crossed over. We love and we are attached. Letting go is a challenge. And the more we love, the more it hurts. Though grieving a loss is not limited to losing people we love, it is often that experience that is the hardest to overcome.

Elisabeth Kübler-Ross developed a model for working through the stages of grief that she originally developed through working with those who had been diagnosed with terminal illness. She presented grief as a movement through five distinct stages that could be experienced in order, in a different order, or even somewhat simultaneously. What is important is not to go through the stages in a particular way, but to go through them at all at some point.

Though there is a general rule of thumb that it takes a year to fully move through the stages of grief, it differs in each situation. What is most important is to honor the process, and let go of expectations of what it is supposed to look like or how long it is supposed to take. Alternatively, George Bonanno has developed a model for grief that allows for a wider range of responses, predicated on the concept that people are resilient and that there are four different possible trajectories for grief.

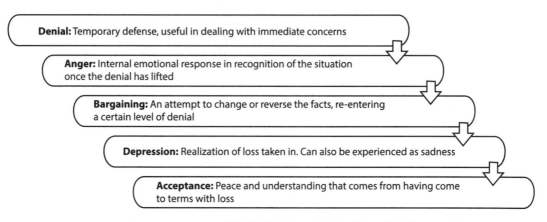

Denial: Temporary defense, useful in dealing with immediate concerns

Anger: Internal emotional response in recognition of the situation once the denial has lifted

Bargaining: An attempt to change or reverse the facts, re-entering a certain level of denial

Depression: Realization of loss taken in. Can also be experienced as sadness

Acceptance: Peace and understanding that comes from having come to terms with loss

The Kübler-Ross Model of the Grief Process. [23]

....

23 Adapted from *On Death and Dying*, Elisabeth Kübler-Ross (New York: Scribner Classics, 1997).

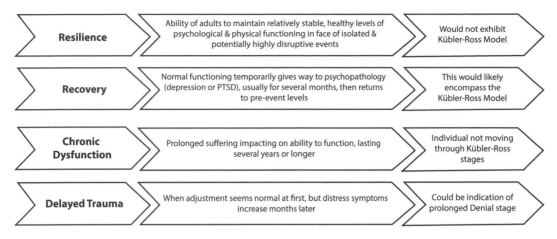

Resilience	Ability of adults to maintain relatively stable, healthy levels of psychological & physical functioning in face of isolated & potentially highly disruptive events	Would not exhibit Kübler-Ross Model
Recovery	Normal functioning temporarily gives way to psychopathology (depression or PTSD), usually for several months, then returns to pre-event levels	This would likely encompass the Kübler-Ross Model
Chronic Dysfunction	Prolonged suffering impacting on ability to function, lasting several years or longer	Individual not moving through Kübler-Ross stages
Delayed Trauma	When adjustment seems normal at first, but distress symptoms increase months later	Could be indication of prolonged Denial stage

The Bonanno Model of the Grief Process. [24]

Grief can be experienced as a knife or a stone in the heart. To be stuck in grief keeps us stuck in our lives. The pain we feel from a great loss is understandable, but to stay in that pain keeps us trapped in the past—in the moment of the loss. It keeps us wishing that things were as they used to be, rather than accepting things as they are in the present. It is contrary to the movement and meaning of life, which is to live and to live fully.

Bringing a spiritual perspective to loss can help. When we know that death is a part of the experience of being alive, we are more able to accept it. We are more able to know how we want to be remembered at the end of our lives. It helps us to be aware that any moment we have could be the last and to appreciate the times that we do have. It opens us to be more considerate in our interactions with others.

A spiritual perspective to loss also helps us to know that the connections we have with the ones we love can never be broken. Energy may shift, but it can never be destroyed. The love we hold goes on and, when we hold those we love in our hearts, they truly are with us.

....

24 Adapted from *The Other Side of Sadness: What the New Science of Bereavement Tells Us About Life After Loss*, George A. Bonanno (New York: Basic Books, 2009).

Further Exploration on Death and Bardo

Coming Back: A Psychiatrist Explores Past-Life Journeys by Raymond Moody. Bantam, 1995.

Final Gifts: Understanding the Special Awareness, Needs, and Communications of the Dying by Maggie Callanan and Patricia Kelley. Bantam, 1997.

Journey of Souls: Case Studies of Life Between Lives by Michael Newton. Llewellyn Publications, 1994.

Life After Life by Raymond Moody. HarperOne, 2001.

On Life After Death by Elisabeth Kübler-Ross. Celestial Arts, 2008.

Past Lives, Present Miracles by Denise Linn. Hay House, 2008.

The Holographic Universe

The concept of the holographic universe is the meeting place of science and spirituality. It comes out of the research in quantum physics, which turns the mechanistic model of Newtonian physics on its ear.

In Newtonian physics (or physics) there are certain laws for how the universe operates that make sense, are orderly, and always follow the same principles. These laws were presented by Sir Isaac Newton and held sway for almost 400 years. Newton elucidated the law of gravity and the three laws of motion. For the most part these laws are brilliant, and the slight inconsistencies that occurred could be overlooked. Until Albert Einstein. Unhappy with the inadequacy of Newtonian physics to accurately describe the behavior of very large objects (like planets in space), Einstein developed his general theory of relativity that presented an image of the universe as a geometric system of three spatial dimensions and one time dimension, known as "space-time." This opened a can of worms. Accepting that the new theory was needed to explain the nature of very, very large objects highlighted the inadequacy of Newtonian physics to describe the nature of very, very small objects (like atoms). This led to the exciting explorations in the twentieth century of quantum physics (or quantum mechanics.)

With quantum physics, things start to get very interesting (or very weird) indeed. One of the most revolutionary concepts of quantum physics is that the nature of matter changes depending on the perspective of the observer. This is evident in the attempts to measure light. If one sets up an experiment to measure light as a particle, it is a particle. If one sets up an experiment to measure light as a wave, it presents as a wave. Which is it? The truth is that light is either a particle or a wave, depending on the observer. Rather than say an object is this, that, or the other, quantum physics presents that an object has the potential to be this, that, or the other. It depends on certain determining factors.

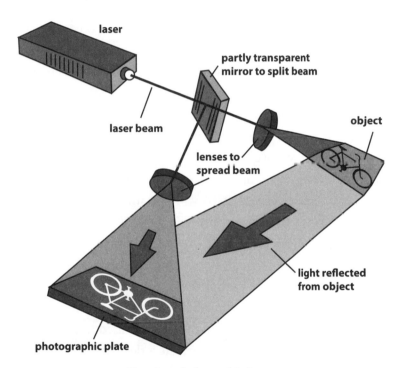

Creating a holographic image.

The first laser was developed in 1965 allowing for the possibility of three-dimensional photography (i.e., holography). Symbolically speaking, this was the photographic equivalent of Einstein's general theory of relativity. Photography moved from a flat, two-dimensional perspective (i.e., Newtonian) to one that encompassed a complex, dynamic three-dimensional perspective (i.e., space-time). Lasers allowed for precise, directed, coherent light as opposed to the more diffuse nature of other light sources. Therefore, the photographic light-source could be manipulated far more effectively and creatively. With holography, the laser beam (light-source) is split into two. These two new beams are directed through lenses to allow for more diffuse coverage. One of the newly created beams is directed at an object and then onto a holographic plate, whereas the other newly created beam is directed straight onto the plate itself. This double-exposure creates an interference pattern on the plate where the beams come together. A holographic plate itself looks like it holds nothing of an image until a laser is used once again. When a single laser beam is directed toward the holographic plate the projection of a three-dimensional image of the original object emerges. A true holographic image needs a laser beam in order to be revealed, as opposed to three-dimensional holographic like images that are used as design features on objects like credit cards.

There are several aspects of holography that are fundamentally different from those of photography, besides the obvious aspect of three-dimensions.

Because the image is created from an interference pattern, rather than a more visually tangible image, it is possible to have many different images contained on the same holographic plate. Shifting the direction of the laser as it hits the holographic plate allows for overlay upon overlay of interference pattern without any impact on the resulting holographic images. This means that a far larger amount of information can be stored in the same place. Imagine the confusing mess that would result in photography if many images were overlaid one over the other in a single photo. After several overlays, it would be impossible to distinguish any single image. With holography, in order to retrieve a single holographic image from a plate containing many different interference patterns, you need only project a laser beam at the same angle as that which was used to create that interference pattern. What information you retrieve from the plate is dependent on the direction of your focus during the retrieval.

Another key aspect of holography, which differs from that of photography, is that if a holographic plate is broken into many pieces and a laser beam is directed at just one of those smaller pieces, the entire image is still projected. Tearing up a photograph gives you a small part of the image in each of the torn pieces. Not so with holography. Each piece still gives the entire image.

At the same time as the developments in holography, the field of psychology was going through shifts. Teachings from the east (with the Dalai Lama's exile from Tibet and acceptance to the United States), the invention of LSD with its doorway into altered states of consciousness, and the discovery that the brain processes information more in the manner of a field (rather than compartments) were all just a few examples of the massive shift taking place. The acknowledgment in the field of psychology that there is far more going on within each human than a purely biophysical, neurological, or humanistic approach could encompass led to the development of transpersonal psychology: a varied field that allowed for the exploration of the human psyche through many lenses, including spirituality. The founding of the Association for Transpersonal Psychology in 1972 opened the door to explorations in the mind-body-spirit connection, spiritual experiences, NDE, and past-life regression, mystical experiences, and altered states of consciousness.

With research being done in quantum physics, the developments being made with lasers and projection and with the movement of psychology into the realm of the transpersonal, it seems that something shifted in the way in which we perceive the universe and our own place within it. Suddenly, we were not ineffective beings at the mercy of a mechanistic universe that marched inexorably on, in spite of our actions and efforts. Suddenly, we were a part of the whole picture.

With the paradigm of a holographic universe, we begin to experience the nature of reality very differently. As stated in the first hermetic principle, the universe is All. It is the whole. It is the holographic plate. And every one of us (and everything that is) is another interference pattern. From a holographic perspective, if a part contains the whole, and we are a part of the whole, then we contain within us access to the vastness stores of information about the All. We just need to look within. The saying "the truth lies within you" takes on a whole new meaning. Seeing consciousness as a laser beam and knowing what is projected is dependent on the angle of the beam, we begin to recognize that what we see depends to a large degree on how it is that we are looking. It is the focus and intent of our consciousness that creates the image that is projected. If we want to change the image, then we need to change our focus. This includes access to the past, present, and future. It is all imprinted on the holographic plate of the universe.

As we shift ourselves and our consciousness, it has a real and true effect. Our shift creates a resonance that becomes part of the holographic universe. Mahatma Gandhi said, "Be the change you want to see in the world." Being that change changes not only us, but indeed, the world. The perspective of a holographic universe positions each and every one of us as a vital and significant aspect of the mystery of the All.

Further Exploration on the Holographic Universe

The Holographic Universe: The Revolutionary Theory of Reality by Michael Talbot. Harper Perennial, 2011.

The Tao of Physics: An Exploration of the Parallels between Modern Physics and Eastern Mysticism by Fritjof Capra. Shambhala, 2010.

Personal Developmental and Psychological Reflections

November 15: Reflect on a significant relationship from the perspective of soul growth.

November 16: What is your sense of what you are meant to learn in this lifetime?

November 17: In what ways has your capacity for love kept you stuck in sorrow?

November 18: Who have been your greatest teachers?

November 19: How might a shift in consciousness create a positive change in a current situation?

November 20: What changes would you like to see in the world?

November 21: Reflect on how you experience yourself as one with the All.

Forty-Nine

Alchemical Reflection on Return

"In this way was the universe created.
From this will come many wondrous applications, because this is the pattern."
<small>FROM *THE EMERALD TABLET*</small>

Return is not traditionally one of the alchemical stages, but it is understood to be a significant aspect of the whole process. Return reflects the energy of transformation that is at the core of alchemical teachings. It implies that what is important is shifting material toward its true essence. But that the purpose of the revelation (resurrection) of essence is in how it bestows the gift of its beauty upon the world. Alchemy is not about transcending the world and leaving the material behind. It is about connecting to the very best in us and sharing that with the world. The hero's journey, presented in the teachings of Joseph Campbell, shows a journey very similar to the alchemical one. At the culmination of the journey, having achieved the "reward," the hero has, in fact, touched upon his own Divine nature. But, in order to complete the quest, he must return to the world as hero and shine his light. It can be an enticing thought to remain in the elevated realms. From a heroic perspective, this is the equivalent of having scaled Mount Olympus and witnessed the residence of the gods with the unending flow of sweet ambrosia. But the hero is not a god. The hero is that individual who, though of the human realm, has discovered, uncovered, and revealed the Divine nature that glows from within this human form. He is truly the master of two worlds; the dark and the light, the human and the Divine.

> We have not even to risk the adventure alone, for the heroes of all time have gone before us. The labyrinth is thoroughly known. We have only to follow the thread of the hero path, and where we had thought to find an abomination, we shall find a god. And where we had thought to slay another, we shall slay ourselves. Where we had thought to travel outward, we will come to the center of our own existence. And where we had thought to be alone, we will be with all the world.
>
> —Joseph Campbell, *The Power of Myth*

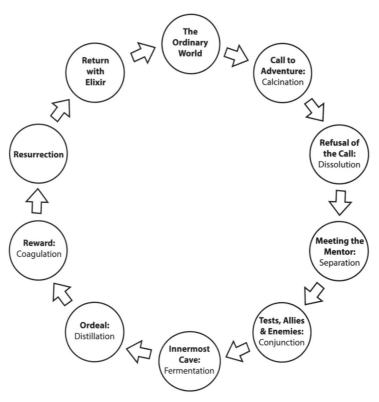

The Hero's Journey as Alchemical Stages.

Return is the mastery that allows the hero to live in the world, but not of it. He has knowledge and experience of wondrous things, including his own true nature. The hero becomes a beacon and role model for others. In our own lives, return is signaled when we live in the world and go through our days from a place of Essence. It is living our human lives, knowing we are always connected to our spiritual selves, guided by Higher Self and fulfilling our Higher Purpose. As the Zen saying goes "Before enlightenment, chop wood, carry water. After enlightenment, chop wood, carry water."

 Further Exploration on the Hero's Journey
Myths to Live By by Joseph Campbell. Penguin Books, 1993.

Pathways to Bliss: Mythology and Personal Transformation by Joseph Campbell. New World Library, 2004.

The Heroine's Journey by Maureen Murdock. Shambhala, 1990.

 Personal Alchemical Reflections
November 22: In what ways do you live your life as a hero/ine?

November 23: Who do you look to as a role model and why?

November 24: What do you consider to be heroic qualities?

November 25: How do you express your enlightenment?

November 26: What do you love about living a human existence?

November 27: What message would you give to someone in despair or sorrow?

November 28: What are your simple joys?

Fifty

· · · · · · · · · · · · · · · ·

Energetic Reflection on the Soul Star Chakra

Soul Star Chakra Associations

· ·

Name: No reference in Sanskrit • **Location:** About a foot above top of the head
Color: White, Gold, or Iridescent (Opal) • **Tone:** High C • **Symbol:** No
traditional association • **Stones:** Lemurian Seed Crystal, Amergreen,
Herkimer Diamond, Auralite, Peacock Ore, Moldavite, Tektite, Selenite

The soul star chakra emanates about a foot above the top of the head. It is the center of unity consciousness, connecting us not only to our own Higher Self but others' higher selves. It is the gateway through which we experience the Divine and the "All There Is."

The soul star chakra governs transcendence and interconnection. It is sometimes referred to as the transpersonal point chakra and, as such, is the chakra through which we experience what lifts us out of our own personal perspective. It opens us to information that cuts across the personal, expanding our awareness to the commonality of experience. The message is not "I am" (personal), but "we are" (transpersonal). Being blocked in our soul star chakra can leave us feeling out of touch and out of sync with the rest of humanity, not allowing us to connect with that which connects us all.

For those who work in holistic healing, particularly in energy healing modalities, the soul star chakra is one of the most important chakras of which to be aware. As healers we connect to others through our heart chakras. However, the Divine hand reaches down to us through the soul star chakra. Higher Self to Higher Self communication occurs in this center. Guidance and inspiration that can feel to a therapist like inner voice messages about therapeutic direction always come from the soul star connection. If a received message feels like it is pushing in some way, it is imperative to double check, sometimes triple check "is this coming from me or Higher Self?" If consistent confirmation is received, one can trust that the client's Higher Self has directed the therapist's Higher Self.

A blocked soul star chakra will manifest as extreme cynicism and lack of faith. A person with a blocked soul star chakra will not be able to see past the pain of humanity to the beauty of humanity. This can be balanced by working on the heart chakra in conjunction with the soul star chakra.

If this chakra is charged with excessive energy, the person will appear to be very spacey and not of this world. Individuals with an over-active soul star chakra struggle with the concept of boundaries, seeing everything and everybody as interconnected. This can often lead to inadvertently violating the human need for appropriate boundaries. We may all be sitting down to the same feast, and we all have access to the bounty that is spread out before us, but if you take the roasted yam off my plate without asking, my human side will likely experience a bump. Of course, I can reach for another yam, but the acknowledgment of differentiation within the context of unity is always appreciated and beneficial. Solar plexus work can help with balance in this area.

The soul star chakra emanates with a beautiful energy that connects us all, recognizing that we are all in this together. It can be visualized as a glowing web of interconnection through which we see ourselves reflected in the energy of others. Though our individual experiences are different, we are truly all "of the same stuff."

Messages that help to balance the soul star chakra are:
We are all part of the one.
The purity of my Essence makes a positive difference to all.
I cherish the beauty of all humanity.

Further Exploration on the Soul Star Chakra
Spiritual Bypassing: When Spirituality Disconnects Us from What Really Matters by Robert Augustus Masters. North Atlantic Books, 2010.

The 8th Chakra: What It Is and How It Can Transform Your Life by Jude Currivan. Hay House, 2007.

Personal Energetic Reflections
November 29: The color gold makes me feel…

November 30: How do you see your own experiences as no different than anyone else's?

December 1: Do you feel a call to be of aid in the healing of others?

December 2: How do you balance the sense of unity with boundaries?

December 3: Have you had an experience of just knowing what was the perfect response to another?

December 4: In what situations do you feel truly connected with others?

December 5: What is the experience for you of hearing the sound of your own voice in communal harmony?

Fifty-One

Guidance Reflection on Spirit Guides and Intuitive Reflection on Channeling

Spirit Guides

Along with angels, spirit guides are being turned to more and more for guidance and support. Though they also move in the realm of the non-physical, spirit guides and angels have a very different energy. Whereas angels have never been incarnated, do not have free will, and connect us with the Divine, spirit guides (such as our ancestors) have walked the earthly plane. They carry the imprint of the memory of having lived a human existence. Thus, they offer a different level of compassion and understanding for the struggles we encounter on our journey.

The term spirit guide was popularized around the turn of the twentieth century with the spiritualist movement and the Theosophical Society. Helena Blavatsky referenced her guides often, presenting a very easy and comfortable relationship with them. She referred to these guides as the *mahatmas,* or "masters." Over the years the term spirit guide has come to be all-encompassing, including angels, aliens, totems, and ancestors. In truth, each of these has a different energy and different perspective. It is helpful to differentiate the source in order to better understand the nature of the message.

In this light, spirit guides are those otherworldly beings who can offer us particular insight into the nature of living a human life. Often they are loved ones who have crossed over. It is said that there is a spirit guide waiting for us when we die to midwife our passage to the other side much like the archetypal psychopomps. In this life, we can experience spirit guide energy as nudges and messages. Some people report more physical evidence of the presence of spirit guides: smelling your mom's favorite perfume, finding objects moved, or feeling a gentle touch upon your cheek.

Spirit guides differ from the spirits of those who have passed away and yet have not reconciled themselves to being on the other side. Stuck spirits still have an attachment to human life and often need encouragement to move on in their non-physical journey, completing the tasks of sidpai bardo. Spirit guides have no such attachment. They act out of compassion for our challenges, often offering insight into our higher nature and life lessons. They can be a support in troubled times and can ease our grief. One of the easiest ways to tell if you are working with a high-level spirit guide, or if a stuck spirit has shown up, is to pay attention to the sense of love and respect that is present. Spirit guide show up to aid us. They don't need anything from us and they ask nothing of us. They connect with us from a place of complete love and acceptance, and they respect our human needs and boundaries. Stuck spirits have an agenda. Their souls are not at peace. They need help. These spirits often exhibit disrespect for our boundaries, such as waking us up in the middle of the night regardless of our need for adequate sleep. There is a whole area here that can be explored from perspective of becoming a "spirit therapist," but that is a totally different thing than working with a spirit guide to support personal growth and healing.

Spirit guides with a very high vibration are called *ascended masters*. Ascended masters are said to have experienced enlightenment during their human lives, and tend to guide those actively working in the flow of their Higher Purpose. Buddha and Jesus are two examples of historical figures often referred to as ascended masters. They are very profound teachers with whom to work.

There are so many inspiring guides through whom we can receive profound messages and insights. Working with spirit guides and ancestors particularly helps us to bridge the realms of the human and the spiritual. These guides reflect the beauty of walking through a human existence from the wisdom they have attained along that very walk. Through their messages we know how truly they see us and we strive to see ourselves from the perspective of that truth.

Further Exploration on Spirit Guides

How to Meet and Work with Spirit Guides by Ted Andrews. Llewellyn Publications, 2006.

Spirit Guides: Companions & Mentors for Your Inner Journey by Hal Zina Bennett. CreateSpace Independent Publishing Platform, 2010.

Spirit Guides & Angel Guardians: Contact Your Invisible Helpers by Richard Webster. Llewellyn Publications, 2002.

The Ascended Masters Light the Way: Beacons of Ascension by Joshua David Stone. Light Technology Publishing, 1995.

Channeling

Channeling is the term used to refer to the reception of messages from non-corporeal beings, including spirit guides, ascended masters, angels, and elementals. It is a form of communication that draws upon psychic abilities. Channeling does not tend to rely on an intermediary intuitive tool, such as decks, pendulums, scrying, and the like. It is a direct line of communication that literally uses the individual as the medium.

There are different levels to channeling, depending on the conscious awareness of the channeler. Being open to receiving these messages requires you to raise your vibration, aligning your own energy to that of the higher energetic frequencies of the non-physical. The higher you raise your vibration, the less consciously aware you will be of what is transpiring in the physical realms. Deep trance channeling is a method of entering such a profound state of receptivity that your own conscious self is put completely to the side in order to allow the channeled message to flow freely. This process usually requires a recording device in order to capture the message, as there will be little, if any, remembrance of what was said.

There are three extremely important elements to remember if you choose to channel Firstly, grounding after a session is imperative. Entering such high vibrational levels can be a wonderful experience. In essence, we enter a state of transcending the physical and merging with the higher levels of the Divine. But we are human, living on the physical plane. This work takes a lot of energy. If we do not pay attention to our physical needs it can lead to depletion of physical energy, resulting in physical illness and possibly depression. All energy work, including channeling, requires attention to our human selves once completed. Make sure you have plenty of water on hand. Nourishing snacks, such as nuts or vegetables, can help give our physical selves a bit of a boost after a session. And, of course, it is important to ensure that you are getting plenty of rest on a regular basis. The better we take care of our physical bodies, the better able we are to sustain high levels of vibration.

Secondly, doing our own emotional healing work is imperative. If we have not looked at our own ego issues (which include unresolved wounds or issues, shame, and stuck or blocked emotions) then that will interfere with the clarity of the message received, much like static on a telephone line. Not doing our own work results in messages being filtered through our own issues and can also lead to ego inflation, otherwise known as "The Guru Complex." When we are in the flow of unity consciousness, there is no place for ego. We recognize that we are simply the vessel through which Divine consciousness is being channeled.

Thirdly, discernment is always required. Ultimately, we are always responsible for steering our own ships. We can have the most wonderful input ever, but we need to own our choices if we are to remain empowered. Turning our power over to anyone else, including spirit guides, leads to disempowerment. Constantly looking to spirit guides for messages or not making any decisions without their input can indicate spiritual bypassing. The relationship with a spirit guide is like that with any other teacher. We turn to them for guidance while we are finding our own confidence and ability, but eventually we must incorporate that learning into ourselves.

Many impactful books have been channeled by those who work with specific guides on an ongoing basis. These books have been a wealth of information for those on a spiritual path, offering guidance on aligning our lives with a spiritual perspective. Esther Hicks (Abraham), Neale Donald Walsh (God), Lee Carroll (Kryon), Jane Roberts (Seth), Sanaya Roman (Orin), and even Carl Jung (Basilides and Philemon) are just a few of those who have impacted many with the power of their channeled messages.

When approached with balance and discernment, channeling can provide us with a direct line to the wisdom of the ages, helping us to move beyond a limiting view of our earth school experience.

Basic Channeling Approach

With the intention of connecting with high-level, loving, and supportive spirit guides, it is best to ensure that both the space and you yourself resonate with that clear, positive energy. Take some time to purify yourself and cleanse the space.

There are many ways you can ready yourself for a channeling session. Taking a bath with the intention of releasing both physical and energetic dirt is a great method. Adding herbs or a few drops of an essential oil both enhances the experience and helps to release heavy or negative energy. As in meditation, use your breath to bring you to your center. Release any physical tension, thoughts of the day, or future concerns, and allow yourself to completely enter the experience of the here-and-now.

Find a quiet place where you will not be disturbed. Cleansing the space can be accomplished in a variety of ways. *Cleanse through the element of earth* by placing high vibration stones in a circle around the area in which you plan to work. Some wonderful standards are clear quartz, rose quartz, and amethyst. If you want to include some powerful stones of the new consciousness preseli bluestone, atlantisite, and lemurian seed crystals particularly connect us to the wisdom and teachings of ancestors and those from ancient civilizations. *Cleanse through the element of water* by sprinkling the area with water that has been charged under the moon or has a pinch of sea salt in it. *Cleanse through the element of air* by toning or chanting. Instruments such as tingshas, singing bowls, or tuning forks are also wonderful tools to use. *Cleanse through the element of fire* by burning incense or sage. For those who find the scent of sage heavy, resins such as frankincense, myrrh, copal, or dragon's blood are lovely alternates and work on very high vibrational levels. *Cleanse through the element of aether* by visualizing white light moving through the space, lifting any negative or heavy energy up and out of the space. Any one of these techniques is sufficient to cleanse the space. Using all of them not only ensures that your space will be filled with beautiful energy, it also allows the time to shift your consciousness into readiness to receive messages from your spirit guide or guides.

The process of channeling itself is as simple as being open to having a conversation with a respected mentor. After preparing yourself for this encounter and creating an energetically welcoming space, hold the intention of inviting a high-level spirit guide to this space and wait to see who shows up. You may see this guide with your inner vision. You may sense a change in the environment. You may begin to hear messages. In many ways, working with non-physical beings is no different than working with physical ones. We know when someone else has come into our energy field and we know what this other being's energy feels like. We recognize different speech patterns and language. We can differentiate one person from another. Apply this same discernment to working with spirit guides. You may find that different spirit guides show up to help you with different aspects of your life. You may have one spirit guide who has messages regarding development of your intuition and psychic skills, and another who comes when you want guidance on deepening your healing work.

You may choose to just sit in receptivity of this otherworldly dialogue, or you may choose to record it, having paper on hand to note down the messages you receive. It is completely up to you. At the end of the session, when it feels you have received all the guidance you need for the moment, be sure to thank your spirit guide and convey that you are open to future connection. Take some time to close communication, using your breath to bring you back to full conscious awareness of your room and your physical body.

 Further Exploration on Channeling

Abraham series, channeled by Esther Hicks.

Channeling: Investigations on Receiving Information From Paranormal
    Sources by Jon Klimo. CreateSpace Independent Publishing Platform, 1998.

Conversations with God series, channeled by Neale Donald Walsch.

Kryon series, channeled by Lee Carroll.

Opening to Channel: How to Connect with your Guide by Sanaya Roman.
    HJ Kramer, 1993.

Seth series, channeled by Jane Roberts.

Personal Guidance and Intuitive Reflections

December 6: Have you ever felt the presence of a loved one who has passed on?

December 7: How does guidance from spirit guides feel different than that from totems or angels?

December 8: What message would be most helpful for you to receive?

December 9: Reflect on a time when you may have been lost in reverie, and come away with an insight.

December 10: What may be a challenge for you in accepting otherworldly guidance?

December 11: How can you discern between a pure message and an ego message?

December 12: Where are the places in your life currently that you most need guidance?

The Integrating Hynni of Unity

When you feel despair at the tragedies of humanity. When you struggle to see the Divine in others and all around you. When it feels impossible to pull from your own resources or take another step, this is the time to activate the Hynni of Unity.

This Hynni symbol represents the multi-dimensional activation of our human and spirit selves.

Preparation: Find a spot where you know you will not be disturbed, and eliminate any possible sources of distraction. Begin to breathe deeply, visualizing the color gold.

Hynni: Release any tension you may hold in your body. Release any emotions that may feel stuck or heavy. Release any thoughts that intrude. Experience yourself as pure energy connected to all in the universe. As you breathe, let go of past and future. Allow nothing but this moment to exist. This moment of vibration is the inhale and exhale at the same time. Expansion and contraction in the same space. Just be. Just be.

Bring your awareness to the space about a foot above the top of your head. Visualize a funnel reaching upward from this place, expanding as it reaches higher, opening you to the energy of the cosmos. Visualize a web reaching outward from this place, connecting you to every being on earth through this energetic network. This wonderful web of interconnection pulses and glows. Be aware of how the energy flows along this web. Be aware of how shifts in you echo out from your place on the web, weaving through all the places of intersection. If you are aware of any spots in which the energy seems dim or blocked, send the energy of love to that place.

Begin to focus on the unity symbol, visualizing a golden light that carries the intent of the symbol, emanating from your soul star chakra, pulsing up through the funnel and out across the web. Allow yourself to be fully in a place of receptivity and experience. Imagine that a stream of Divine gold light in pouring down, charging the unity symbol and filling every aspect of your being with compassion and wisdom. From this place you are connected to all that was and all that will be. From this place you have access to anything you need to know. You need only use your consciousness as your light to find your direction.

If you choose, from this place invite in a spirit guide, asking that only a guide of the highest vibration and purest intention come to you in this space. Allow yourself to experience any shifts in your perception or your energy field. Is this a familiar energy to you—of perhaps a loved one or ancestor? What emotions do you experience in the light of this spirit guide? If you feel anything of discomfort, ask the guide to leave and invite in a different energy. When you feel comfortable with the spirit guide energy, allow yourself to be open to guidance. You may choose to focus on a particular situation that could benefit from some input or you may leave it open to whatever the guide chooses to share at this time. Focus on a clear line of communication, past fear and ego, and allow the messages to flow in whatever manner they come to you. When the communication feels complete, thank your spirit guide, and close communication, bidding farewell or sending the spirit guide away.

Bringing your focus back to your breath and be aware once more of the web that energetically connects us all. See that your own presence on the web is as significant and integral as all the other presences. In the interconnection of all within the All, each one is precious, including ourselves. Allow this truth to fill you.

When you are ready, take three deep, centering breaths, allowing each one to bring you more fully back to your body, appreciating its solidity and physicality. Wiggle your hands and touch your feet to ground yourself.

Part Twelve

Process Phase Four
December 13–19

Dark Moon:
Rest and Respite
"Surrender to the Dark"

PRESCRIPTIONS

Go through this section during any Dark Moon phase
or if you are experiencing any of the following:

- A massive transition
- Overwhelmed by choice of direction
- Overattachment
- Exhaustion
- Chaos

Fifty-Two

Dark Moon Phase of Rest and Respite

Stillness.

At the end of any cycle there needs to be a pause. There is always a point that the movement is neither expansion nor contraction. It just is.

The dark moon is reflected in the energy of the Dark Mother, who is often encompassed in the archetype of the Crone. The Crone of the waning moon, who is the elder, teaching of the wisdoms of experience, and the Crone of the dark moon who is the Dark Mother, holding us in the infinite silence of the void are very similar. We may find both in village elders, healers, and grandmothers. But we tend to respond differently to the Dark Mother.

Once venerated as the powerful force through which the new arises once again, the Dark Mother became marginalized and vilified over time. The image of the bent, decrepit, old hag muttering incomprehensible utterances (often interpreted as curses) became an image to be feared. Rather than embraced for her potential to nurture us in the darkness, knowing the gifts it holds for us, and nourishing us to begin the journey once again, she has been relegated to the shadows, brought out occasionally to scare us, either in fun or in warning.

The Dark Mother is the midwife into death, something that we, as humans, have responded with great fear for eons. Not knowing what lies ahead, but knowing we will all experience it, has shaped much of culture for centuries. The fact is that, as much as we are given information on what the after-life looks like and what awaits us, until we actually experience it, there can be the niggle of a question mark. Like trying to explain to a teenager what it is like to be an adult, the wisdom won't happen until it is experienced. It all comes back to the definition of wisdom being knowledge plus experience. Wisdom comes with the embodiment of the knowledge through the circumstances of our lives and our responses to them. When it comes to death, everything leading up to it falls into the realm of belief. This is perfectly fine and we need to have these beliefs. They can help us in how we move through these last days of our human experience. But for each of us still in this human form, death is a mystery. It is as much a mystery as the wonder of birth, and both need to be honored and celebrated.

The Dark Mother contains the wisdom of entering the mystery. For her, there is as much of beauty in leaving this life as there is coming into it. Both are profound. She knows what it is to sit in that tipping point before being birthed into the new, entering the bardo, and all that awaits us there. But there are many smaller bardos within the context of a life. There are many points of transition when we sit in that space between what we are leaving behind, and that into which we are moving, whatever new form that may take. These are all moments when we can find comfort and strength in the Dark Mother. These are the moments when we can find ourselves encircled in her arms, receiving the message that it will all be okay.

We need the Dark Mother. We need the moments of completely letting go, of sitting in absolute silence, of knowing we are held when we can (or should) no longer hold on. And there is relief to be found in the release. It is the ease after a marathon. It is the quietude after cacophony. After all the work and effort has been done … after all the struggles and victories … after all the give and take … the questioning and answering … exploring this path and that … it is time to stop. And rest.

This is surrender, and it is truly entering the mystery. For who knows what is born of the dark?

Main Themes for Process Phase 4:
Surrender
Faith
Stillness

Ancient Cultural Archetypes of the Dark

Nephthys *(Egyptian)* is the daughter of Nut and Geb, and is a protective goddess of the death experience.

Ereshkigal *(Sumerian)* is the goddess who presides over Irkalla, the land of the dead, and the underworld.

Astarte *(Assyrian)* is the goddess of the heavens whose stars were the spirits of the dead.

Lilith *(Babylonian)* is a complex, and often feared, figure who has been described both as handmaiden to **Inanna** and as Adam's first wife.

Atropos *(Greek)* is one of the three moirai, or fates. She is known as the "inevitable," the one who holds the shears that snip the mortal thread. Her sisters are **Clotho** ("the spinner") and **Lachesis** ("the allotter of fates").

Morta *(Roman)* is a goddess of death whose father is night and mother is darkness.

Cailleach *(Celtic)* is the "queen of winter," whose name literally translates as "hag." She is sometimes associated with Black Annis.

Sheila Na Gig *(Celtic)* is a goddess of death and rebirth.

Hel *(Norse)* is a goddess of the realm of the dead, also called "Hel," which lies under one of the three roots of the world tree, Yggdrasil.

Skadi *(Norse)* whose name translates as "damage" or "shade," is a goddess of winter, skiing, and bowhunting. She is the bringer of the frost, cold, and death.

Skuld *(Norse)* is one of the three Norns. Her name possibly translates as "fate." As the one who sees what is to come, she forms the trio of Norns with **Urd** ("what has been") and **Verdandi** ("what is").

 *Personal Dark Moon Phase Reflections*

December 13: How often do you allow yourself to truly rest?

December 14: What does surrender look like to you?

December 15: Reflect on a time you found yourself completely in the dark, and how that made you feel.

December 16: Does the incomprehensible make you uncomfortable?

December 17: How does the absolute still point between action and receptivity make you feel?

December 18: What do nothingness, and the void, mean to you?

December 19: What gifts do you feel may lie in the dark for you?

The Restoring Hynni of Stillness

As you complete an entire cycle. When you have put in all the effort you can in this moment. When you feel you have done as much as you can, taken things as far as you can, or accomplished all you set out for yourself for the time being, this is the time to activate the Hynni of Stillness.

This Hynni symbol represents the blessing of the quiet center.

Preparation: Find a spot where you will not be disturbed and eliminate all possibility for distraction. Get into a comfortable position. Begin to breathe deeply and slowly, visualizing the breath moving in and out of your body. Allow the tension to fade from your body. Be aware of nothing but your breath.

Hynni: As you breathe, allow everything to drift away. Let go of thoughts of the past. Let go of all that has brought you to this point. Let go of thoughts of the future. Let go of all that may yet follow. Bring yourself to the point of the absolute now.

Place your hands on your heart, and begin to focus on the stillness symbol, visualizing a golden light that carries the intent of the symbol moving through your hands and into your heart. See the darkness of the symbol begin to expand, starting at your heart and moving outward and upward. The dark surrounds you until it is all you are conscious of. Be aware of how this feels. Keep breathing.

Feel yourself weightless and suspended in the dark. It is warm and comforting. It holds and embraces you. There is something about this space that feels familiar. You have been here before. Many times. In the silence—the all-encompassing silence—you become aware of a sound, distant and rhythmic. Boom-boom. Boom-boom. Boom-boom. This rhythm that echoes one of your own. Boom-boom. Boom-boom. Boom-boom. It is a heartbeat. The heartbeat of the Dark Mother who holds you and keeps you safe. Who nourishes you in the place of darkness so that all you need to do is rest.

Breathe into this place. Rest in this place. Let go of all your cares and concerns. There is absolutely nothing that needs to be done in this moment. You are loved. You are supported. You are nourished. Feel the heartbeat in rhythm to yours, and hear the message in its rhythm:

> I am. And that is enough.
> I am. And that is enough.
> I am. And that is enough.

What is to come, will come in time. But for this moment allow the body of the Dark Mother to contain you, to hold the wonder of all you are, and the potential for all that you will be.

When you are ready, take three deep, centering breaths and open your eyes, feeling completely supported in anything that is to come.

Part Thirteen

December 20

Pause and Integration

PRESCRIPTIONS

Go through this section before starting or after completing *The Great Work*. Use the survey responses to assess where you have experienced shifts, or which cycles you may choose to focus on in the future.

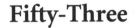

Fifty-Three

The Self-Actualization Survey

Respond to each statement below according to a scale from 0–5. Allow your response to come from your first, intuitive sense of where you are at today. Mark down the number according to the range below in the space provided beside each statement.

0	1	2	3	4	5
Never	*Rarely*	*Sometimes*	*Often*	*Frequently*	*Always*

1. I respond to new situations enthusiastically. _____

2. I balance my physical, emotional, intellectual, and spiritual needs. _____

3. I am comfortable with confrontation. _____

4. I eat properly and nutritiously. _____

5. I respond to my hurt with gentleness. _____

6. I have creative outlets. _____

7. I have compassion toward others. _____

8. I feel secure. _____

9. I notice and work with synchronicity. _____

10. I listen to my anger and communicate its message appropriately. _____

11. I am reconciled to the knowledge that my life will come to an end. _____

12. I know how to discern between safe and unsafe people. _____

13. I speak my truth with integrity. _____

14. I allow experiences of awe and wonder. _____

15. I am comfortable with solitude. _____

16. I embrace my sexuality. _____

17. I recognize there are mysteries I cannot know in this life. _____

18. I value dreams and vision. _____

19. I am confident in my ability to plan and manifest. _____

20. I know my worth and value. _____

21. I own my choices. _____

22. I know I am more than my job. _____

23. I release that which no longer serves me. _____

24. I have a supportive network of friends. _____

25. I honor the teachings of my elders, my heritage, and my ancestors. _____

26. I know my path is not everyone's path. _____

27. I am open to love. _____

28. I listen to my intuition. _____

29. I communicate to others whether they are able to hear me or not. _____

30. I recognize my fear is information to be explored,
    rather than an absolute message to stop. _____

31. I am actively fulfilling what I feel to be my purpose in this life. _____

32. I grow from all my relationships. _____

33. I embrace the full range of my emotions. _____

34. I establish appropriate boundaries and know how to say no. _____

35. I take time to connect with the Divine. _____

36. I celebrate my accomplishments. _____

37. I know what strengths I contain within that
will carry me through any of life's challenges. _____

38. I am open to the transcendent. _____

39. I know my expression in the world is important. _____

40. My connection to the world and to others is important to me. _____

Scoring: Total the numbers you placed in the spaces beside each statement to see which Process Phase you most reflect at this time.

Below 80:
There is benefit to focusing on continued inner work.

Between 81–120:
Some self-understanding has begun to bear fruit.

Between 121–159:
With much inner work accomplished,
some further releasing could be of benefit.

Between 160–200:
You reflect self-actualization and the
integration of your human/spirit self.

Key to Cycle Associations

Cycle 1	Cycle 2
1–I respond to new situations enthusiastically.	5–I respond to my hurt with gentleness.
4–I eat properly and nutritiously.	10–I listen to my anger and communicate its message appropriately.
8–I feel secure.	24–I have a supportive network of friends.
12–I know how to distinguish between safe and unsafe people.	30–I recognize my fear is information to be explored, rather than an absolute message to stop.
20–I know my worth and value.	33–I embrace the full range of my emotions.
Cycle 3	**Cycle 4**
3–I am comfortable with confrontation.	7–I have compassion toward others.
15–I am comfortable with solitude.	16–I embrace my sexuality.
22–I know I am more than my job.	27–I am open to love.
34–I establish appropriate boundaries and know how to say no.	32–I grow from all my relationships.
37–I know what strengths I contain within that will carry me through any of life's challenges.	40–My connection to the world and to others is important to me.

Key to Cycle Associations

Cycle 5	Cycle 6
6–I have creative outlets.	2–I balance my physical, emotional, intellectual, and spiritual needs.
13–I speak my truth with integrity.	18–I value dreams and vision.
21–I own my choices.	19–I am confident in my ability to plan and manifest.
29–I communicate to others whether they are able to hear me or not.	28–I listen to my intuition.
39–I know my expression in the world is important.	36–I celebrate my accomplishments.
Cycle 7	**Cycle 8**
9–I notice and work with synchronicity.	11–I am reconciled to the knowledge that my life will come to an end.
14–I allow experiences of awe and wonder.	17–I recognize there are mysteries I cannot know in this life.
23–I release that which no longer serves me.	25–I honor the teachings of my elders, my heritage, and my ancestors.
31–I am actively fulfilling what I feel to be my purpose in this life.	26–I know my path is not everyone's path.
35–I take time to connect with the Divine.	38–I am open to the transcendent.

Appendix A:
List of Emotional and Psychological Issues and Their Prescriptions

Addictions and disorders

    Eating disorders .... Cycle 1

    Fanaticism .... Cycle 7

    Gambling .... Cycle 1

    Internet/gaming addiction .... Cycle 6

    Love addiction .... Cycle 4

    Sex addiction .... Cycle 2

    Smoking .... Cycle 5

    Substance addictions .... Cycle 2

    Workaholicism .... Cycle 3

Attachment .... Phase 3

Boundaries

    Inability to establish with others .... Cycle 3

    Inability to establish psychic boundaries .... Cycle 6

Burnout .... Cycle 4

Chaos

    Discomfort with the natural chaos of life .... Phase 4

    Inability to live in the moment .... Cycle 8

    Living a life of chaos .... Phase 1

Choice

    A depleted belief in the efficacy of choices .... Cycle 5

    Feeling not in control of one's own choices .... Cycle 3

    Overwhelmed by choice of direction .... Phase 4

Communication

    Excessive need to communicate .... Cycle 5

    Sense that what you say doesn't matter .... Cycle 5

Creativity (repressed) .... Cycle 5

Defensiveness

    Control (need to) .... Cycle 3

    Denial .... Cycle 6

        Denial of mystical and transcendent .... Cycle 7

    Lying .... Cycle 5

    Spiritual Bypass .... Cycle 7

Emotions (general)

    Excessive or extreme reactions .... Cycle 2

    Inability to identify .... Cycle 2

    Overwhelmed by emotions .... Cycle 2

    Repressed .... Cycle 2

Emotions (specific)

Anger .... Cycle 3

Anxiety .... Cycle 2

        Anxiety around new beginnings .... Phase 1

Bitterness .... Phase 3

Compassion (lack of) .... Cycle 4

Curiosity (lack of) .... Cycle 1

Depression .... Cycle 7

Discarded .... Phase 4

Emptiness .... Phase 2

Fear .... Cycle 2

        Fear around new directions in life .... Cycle 1

        Fear of abandonment/engulfment .... Cycle 1

        Fear of death .... Cycle 8

        Fear of success .... Cycle 6

        Fear of taking risks .... Cycle 1

Forgiveness (inability to forgive) .... Cycle 7

Grief .... Cycle 8

Guilt .... Cycle 2

        Inflated sense of guilt over small issues .... Cycle 3

Impatience .... Cycle 2

Joy (lack of) .... Phase 1

Panic attacks .... Cycle 4

Passion (lack of) .... Cycle 4

Pride (lack of)... Cycle 6

Resentment .... Cycle 4

Resigned.. Phase 3

Shame.. Cycle 3

    Sexual shame... Cycle 2

Family of origin

Enmeshment.. Cycle 2

Sense of belonging (lack of) .... Cycle 1

Triggered by spending time with family.................................. Cycle 1

Life Lessons

Challenge in resolving ancestral legacy issues...................... Cycle 8

Inability to see life patterns .... Cycle 7

Resistance to Higher Purpose of lessons .... Cycle 7

Loss

Change of life circumstance.. Cycle 1

Dark Night of the Soul... Cycle 1

Massive transition... Phase 4

Resistance to transitions.. Cycle 8

Sudden and unexpected .... Cycle 1

Needs

Denial of physical needs.. Cycle 1

Denial of emotional needs .... Cycle 2

Exhaustion .... Phase 4

Avoidance of human physical or emotional needs.......................... Cycle 7

Past-life bleedthrough.. Cycle 8

Perfectionism.. Phase 2

Projects, tasks, and goals

    Difficulty with setting goals .... Cycle 6

    Feeling incompetent .... Cycle 3

    Feeling ineffective .... Phase 2

    Inability to finish .... Phase 2

    Inability to start .... Phase 1

    Inability to acknowledge success .... Phase 2

    Jumping from one to another .... Phase 2

    Vision (lack of) .... Cycle 6

Relationships

    Challenges or uncertainty while in the company of others............. Cycle 3

    Codependency .... Cycle 4

    Difficulty with others .... Cycle 2

    Isolation .... Cycle 1

        Disconnection from others .... Cycle 1

        Isolation from humanity as a whole .... Cycle 8

    Unhealthy dynamics.. Cycle 4

Responsibility (overwhelmed by) .... Phase 1

Self-Esteem (low or shaky) .... Cycle 3

Subpersonalities

    Approval-seeker... Cycle 4

    Caretaker.. Cycle 4

    Hero Child .... Cycle 1

    Inner Critic .... Cycle 6

Lost Child .... Cycle 1

Mascot .... Cycle 1

Over-achiever... Cycle 1

Pillar-of-Strength.. Cycle 1

Rescuer .... Cycle 4

Scapegoat .... Cycle 1

Thoughts and Beliefs

Attachment to proof... Cycle 7

Confused or racing .... Cycle 6

Cynicism .... Phase 1

Difficulty sharing with others................................... Cycle 5

Difficulty in "turning off the brain"........................... Cycle 6

Discernment (lack of) .... Cycle 6

Entitlement .... Cycle 3

Inability to live in the moment .... Cycle 8

Lack of appreciation for your gifts and talents .... Phase 3

Under or over-active imagination .... Cycle 6

Trust (lack of)

Difficulty trusting others... Cycle 1

Difficulty trusting that all will work out .... Cycle 7

Faith .... Phase 4

Surrender .... Phase 4

Ungrounded

Having one's "head in the clouds"............................. Cycle 7

Appendix B:
List of Physical Issues and Their Prescriptions

Adrenal exhaustion.. Cycle 3

Asthma .... Cycle 5

Bladder issues.. Cycle 1

Blood pressure (low) .... Cycle 1

Blood pressure (high)... Cycle 4

Bronchitis .... Cycle 5

Choking or gagging .... Cycle 5

Chronic fatigue syndrome .... Cycle 7

Circulation (poor) .... Cycle 1

Colds .... Cycle 5

Colon issues .... Cycle 1

Digestive issues .... Cycle 3

Endometriosis.. Cycle 2

Gallbladder issues .... Cycle 3

Headaches .... Cycle 6

Heart conditions .... Cycle 4

Hyperthyroidism .... Cycle 5

Hypothyroidism .... Cycle 5

Immune system (depressed or compromised) .... Cycle 1

Insomnia .... Cycle 6

Irritable bowel syndrome .... Cycle 3

Kidney issues .... Cycle 3

Light sensitivity .... Cycle 6

Liver issues .... Cycle 3

Lower back pain .... Cycle 2

Menstrual cramps .... Cycle 2

Migraines .... Cycle 6

Pancreatitis .... Cycle 3

Prostate issues .... Cycle 2

Respiratory issues .... Cycle 4

Sinus issues .... Cycle 6

Skin issues .... Cycle 7

Teeth issues .... Cycle 1

Tinnitus .... Cycle 6

Tonsillitis .... Cycle 5

Ulcers .... Cycle 3

Varicose veins .... Cycle 1

Vision (blurred or weak) .... Cycle 6

Appendix C:
Cycles and Phases by Month

DECEMBER						
CYCLE ONE: ROOTS AND FOUNDATIONS BEGINS						
21 **WEEK ONE:** Theme of Birth of the Wonder Child	22	23	24	25	26	27
28 **WEEK TWO:** Earth and Breathing	29	30	31	**1** **JANUARY**	2	3

JANUARY						
4 **WEEK THREE:** Family of origin; Birth to three years	5	6	7	8	9	10
11 **WEEK FOUR:** Calcination	12	13	14	15	16	17
18 **WEEK FIVE:** Root Chakra	19	20	21	22	23	24
25 **WEEK SIX:** Animal Guides and Runes	26	27	28	29	30	31

FEBRUARY						
CYCLE TWO: GIFTS FROM THE INNER CHILD begins						
1 **WEEK SEVEN:** Theme of Purification Through Light	2	3	4	5	6	7
8 **WEEK EIGHT:** Water and Drumming	9	10	11	12	13	14
15 **WEEK NINE:** Preschool and Feelings	16	17	18	19	20	21
22 **WEEK TEN:** Dissolution	23	24	25	26	27	28

March

Waxing Phase: Openings

Cycle Three: Nurturing Empowerment and Self-esteem begins

1 WEEK ELEVEN: Sacral Chakra	2	3	4	5	6	7
8 WEEK TWELVE: Tasseomancy and Aquatic Guides	9	10	11	12	13	14
15 WEEK THIRTEEN: Waxing Moon: Innocence and Openings	16	17	18	19	20	21
22 WEEK FOURTEEN: Theme of Celebration of Life	23	24	25	26	27	28
29 WEEK FIFTEEN: Air; Singing and Chanting	30	31	1 APRIL	2	3	4

APRIL						
5 **WEEK SIXTEEN:** School-age; Empowerment and Self-esteem	6	7	8	9	10	11
12 **WEEK** **SEVENTEEN:** Separation	13	14	15	16	17	18
19 **WEEK** **EIGHTEEN:** Solar Plexus Chakra	20	21	22	23	24	25
26 **WEEK** **NINETEEN:** Bird Guides and Oracles	27	28	29	30	1 **MAY**	2

MAY
CYCLE FOUR: UNION AND PARTNERSHIPS BEGINS

3 **WEEK TWENTY:** Theme of Synthesis of Spirit and Matter	4	5	6	7	8	9
10 **WEEK TWENTY-ONE:** Fire and Dancing	11	12	13	14	15	16
17 **WEEK TWENTY-TWO:** Adolescence and Relationships	18	19	20	21	22	23
24 **WEEK TWENTY-THREE:** Conjunction	25	26	27	28	29	30
31 **WEEK TWENTY-FOUR:** Heart Chakra	**1** **JUNE**	2	3	4	5	6

JUNE FULL MOON PHASE: FRUITION CYCLE FIVE: SHINING OUR TRUTH AND CREATIVITY BEGINS						
7 **WEEK TWENTY-FIVE:** Wee Guides and Ogham	8	9	10	11	12	13
14 **WEEK TWENTY-SIX:** Full Moon: Fullness and Fruition	15	16	17	18	19	20
21 **WEEK TWENTY-SEVEN:** Theme of Celebration of Effort	22	23	24	25	26	27
28 **WEEK TWENTY-EIGHT:** Aether and Journaling	29	30	1 JULY	2	3	4

JULY						
5 **WEEK TWENTY-NINE:** Early Adulthood; Voice and Choice	6	7	8	9	10	11
12 **WEEK THIRTY:** Fermentation	13	14	15	16	17	18
19 **WEEK THIRTY-ONE:** Throat Chakra	20	21	22	23	24	25
26 **WEEK THIRTY-TWO:** Elementals and Tarot	27	28	29	30	31	1 **AUGUST**

AUGUST CYCLE SIX: VISIONING SELF BEGINS						
2 **WEEK THIRTY-THREE:** Theme of Reaping First Harvests	3	4	5	6	7	8
9 **WEEK THIRTY-FOUR:** Light and Visual Arts	10	11	12	13	14	15
16 **WEEK THIRTY-FIVE:** Adulthood; Beliefs and Discernment	17	18	19	20	21	22
23 **WEEK THIRTY-SIX:** Distillation	24	25	26	27	28	29
30 **WEEK THIRTY-SEVEN:** Brow Chakra	31	1 **SEPTEMBER**	2	3	4	5

September						
WANING PHASE: EXPERIENCE						
CYCLE SEVEN: EFFECTS OF GRATITUDE ON LIFE PURPOSE BEGINS						
6 **WEEK THIRTY-EIGHT:** Mythological Beasts and I Ching	7	8	9	10	11	12
13 **WEEK THIRTY-NINE:** Waning Moon: Experience and Community	14	15	16	17	18	19
20 **WEEK FORTY:** Theme of Thanksgivings	21	22	23	24	25	26
27 **WEEK FORTY-ONE:** Thought and Yoga	28	29	30	1 **OCTOBER**	2	3

OCTOBER						
4 **WEEK FORTY-TWO:** Elderhood and Higher Purpose	5	6	7	8	9	10
11 **WEEK FORTY-THREE:** Coagulation	12	13	14	15	16	17
18 **WEEK FORTY-FOUR:** Crown Chakra	19	20	21	22	23	24
25 **WEEK FORTY-FIVE:** Angels and Scrying	26	27	28	29	30	31

NOVEMBER CYCLE EIGHT: HEALING FROM LOSS BEGINS						
1 **WEEK FORTY-SIX:** Theme of Entering the Mystery	2	3	4	5	6	7
8 **WEEK FORTY-SEVEN:** Energy and Hynni	9	10	11	12	13	14
15 **WEEK FORTY-EIGHT:** Bardo and Holographic Universe	16	17	18	19	20	21
22 **WEEK FORTY-NINE:** Return	23	24	25	26	27	28
29 **WEEK FIFTY:** Soul Star Chakra	30	**1** **DECEMBER**	2	3	4	5

December

Dark Moon Phase: Rest
Day of Pause: Integration

6 WEEK FIFTY-ONE: Ancestors and Channeling	7	8	9	10	11	12
13 WEEK FIFTY-TWO: Dark Moon: Rest and Respite	14	15	16	17	18	19
20 Pause for Integration	21 NEW CYCLE BEGINS	22	23	24	25	26
27	28	29	30	31		

Selected Bibliography

Bluestone, Sarvananda. *How to Read Signs and Omens in Everyday Life.* Rochester, VT: Destiny Books, 2001.

Bonanno, George A. *The Other Side of Sadness: What the New Science of Bereavement Tells Us About Life After Loss.* New York: Basic Books, 2009.

Campbell, Joseph. *The Hero with a Thousand Faces.* Princeton, NJ: Princeton University Press, 1968.

Campbell, Joseph, and Bill Moyers. *The Power of Myth.* New York: Doubleday, 1988.

Campbell, Joseph, and Charles Musès. *In All Her Names: Explorations of the Feminine in Divinity.* San Francisco: HarperSanFrancisco, 1991.

Chopra, Deepak. *Ageless Body, Timeless Mind: The Quantum Alternative to Growing Old.* New York: Harmony Books, 1993.

Currivan, Jude. *The 8th Chakra: What It Is and How It Can Transform Your Life.* Carlsbad, CA: Hay House, 2007.

D'Aoust, Maja, and Adam Parfrey. *The Secret Source: The Law of Attraction Is One of Seven Hermetic Laws: Here Are the Other Six.* Los Angeles, CA: Process Media, 2007.

Day, Laura. *Practical Intuition: How to Harness the Power of Your Instinct and Make It Work for You.* New York: Broadway Books, 1996.

Edinger, Edward F. *Anatomy of the Psyche: Alchemical Symbolism in Psychotherapy.* La Salle, IL: Open Court, 1985.

Erikson, Erik H. *Childhood and Society.* New York: W. W. Norton & Company, Inc., 1978.

Gardner, Joy. *Vibrational Healing through the Chakras: With Light, Color, Sound, Crystals, and Aromatherapy.* Berkeley, CA: Crossing Press, 2006.

Gawain, Shakti. *Creative Visualization: Use the Power of Your Imagination to Create What You Want in Your Life.* Novato, CA: Nataraj Publishing/New World Library, 2002.

———. *Developing Intuition: Practical Guidance for Daily Life.* Novato, CA: Nataraj Publishing/New World Library, 2000.

Gimbutas, Marija. *The Gods and Goddesses of Old Europe: 7000–3500 BC: Myths, Legends & Cult Images.* London: Thames and Hudson, 1974.

Guirand, Fe. *New Larousse Encyclopedia of Mythology.* New York: Prometheus Press, 1959.

Hauck, Dennis William. *The Emerald Tablet: Alchemy for Personal Transformation.* New York: Penguin/Arkana, 1999.

Hillman, James. *The Soul's Code: In Search of Character and Calling.* New York: Random House, 1996.

Jnaneshvara, Swami. "Yoga Meditation Basics," accessed May, 2013, http://www.swamij.com/index-yoga-meditation-basics.htm.

Judith, Anodea. *Eastern Body, Western Mind: Psychology and the Chakra System as a Path to the Self*. Berkeley, CA: Celestial Arts, 2004.

———. *Wheels of Life: A User's Guide to the Chakra System*. St. Paul, MN: Llewellyn Publications, 1987.

Judith, Anodea, and Selene Vega. *The Sevenfold Journey: Reclaiming Mind, Body & Spirit Through the Chakras*. Berkeley, CA: Crossing Press, 1993.

Jung, C. G. *Psychology and Alchemy*. Princeton, NJ: Princeton University Press, 1968.

Kübler-Ross, Elisabeth. *On Death and Dying*. New York: Scribner Classics, 1997.

Linn, Denise. *The Secret Language of Signs: How to Interpret the Coincidences and Symbols in Your Life*. New York: Ballantine Books, 1996.

Maslow, Abraham H. *Motivation and Personality*. New York: Harper, 1954.

May, Gerald G. *The Dark Night of the Soul: A Psychiatrist Explores the Connection between Darkness and Spiritual Growth*. San Francisco: HarperSanFrancisco, 2004.

Moore, Thomas. *Care of the Soul: A Guide for Cultivating Depth and Sacredness in Everyday Life*. New York: HarperCollins, 1992.

———. *Dark Nights of the Soul: A Guide to Finding Your Way through Life's Ordeals*. New York: Gotham Books, 2004.

———. *The Re-Enchantment of Everyday Life*. New York: HarperCollins, 1996.

Myss, Caroline M. *Anatomy of the Spirit: The Seven Stages of Power and Healing*. New York: Harmony Books, 1996.

Peck, M. Scott. *The Road Less Traveled: A New Psychology of Love, Traditional Values, and Spiritual Growth*. New York: Phoenix Press, 1985.

Peirce, Penney. *The Intuitive Way: The Definitive Guide to Increasing Your Awareness*. New York: Atria Books, 2009.

Pennick, Nigel. *Magical Alphabets*. York Beach, ME: Red Wheel/Weiser, 1992.

Reeves, Paula M. *Women's Intuition: Unlocking the Wisdom of the Body*. Berkeley, CA: Conari Press, 1999.

Reifler, Sam. *I Ching: A New Interpretation for Modern Times*. New York: Bantam Books, 1974.

Rinpoche, Sogyal. *The Tibetan Book of Living and Dying*. London: Rider & Co, 1996.

Roman, Sanaya. *Spiritual Growth: Being Your Higher Self*. Tiburon, CA: H.J. Kramer, 1992.

Rosanoff, Nancy. *Intuition Workout: A Practical Guide to Discovering and Developing Your Inner Knowing*. Boulder Creek, CA: Aslan Publishing, 1991.

Rother, Steve, and The Group. *Spiritual Psychology: The Twelve Primary Life Lessons: Information for Facilitators of Human Evolution*. Poway, Ca.: Lightworker, 2004.

Sharamon, Shalila, and Bodo J. Baginski. *The Chakra Handbook: From Basic Understanding to Practical Application*. Wilmot, WI: Lotus Light Publications, 1991.

Skye, Michelle. *Goddess Alive!: Inviting Celtic & Norse Goddesses into Your Life*. St. Paul, MN: Llewellyn Publications, 2007.

Stone, Joshua David. *Soul Psychology: How to Clear Negative Emotions and Spiritualize Your Life*. New York: Ballantine Wellspring/Ballantine Publishing, 1999.

Stone, Merlin. *Ancient Mirrors of Womanhood: A Treasury of Goddess and Heroine Lore from Around the World*. Boston: Beacon Press, 1984.

Telyndru, Jhenah. *Avalon Within: A Sacred Journey of Myth, Mystery, and Inner Wisdom*. St. Paul, MN: Llewellyn Publications, 2010.

Three Initiates. *The Kybalion: A Study of the Hermetic Philosophy of Ancient Egypt and Greece*. New York: Jeremy P. Tarcher/Penguin, 2008.

Virtue, Doreen. *Chakra Clearing: Awakening Your Spiritual Power to Know and Heal*. Carlsbad, CA: Hay House, 2004.

———. *Divine Magic: The Seven Sacred Secrets of Manifestation: A New Interpretation of the Hermetic Classic Alchemical Manual The Kybalion*. Carlsbad, CA: Hay House, 2006.

Wauters, Ambika. *The Book of Chakras: Discover the Hidden Forces Within You*. Hauppauge, NY: Barron's Educational Series, 2002.

———. *Chakras and Their Archetypes: Uniting Energy Awareness and Spiritual Growth*. Freedom, CA: Crossing Press, 1997.

GET MORE AT LLEWELLYN.COM

Visit us online to browse hundreds of our books and decks, plus sign up to receive our e-newsletters and exclusive online offers.

- Free tarot readings • Spell-a-Day • Moon phases
- Recipes, spells, and tips • Blogs • Encyclopedia
- Author interviews, articles, and upcoming events

GET SOCIAL WITH LLEWELLYN

Find us on   @LlewellynBooks

www.Facebook.com/LlewellynBooks

GET BOOKS AT LLEWELLYN

LLEWELLYN ORDERING INFORMATION

 Order online: Visit our website at www.llewellyn.com to select your books and place an order on our secure server.

 Order by phone:
- Call toll free within the US at 1-877-NEW-WRLD (1-877-639-9753)
- We accept VISA, MasterCard, American Express, and Discover.
- Canadian customers must use credit cards.

 Order by mail:
Send the full price of your order (MN residents add 6.875% sales tax) in US funds plus postage and handling to: Llewellyn Worldwide, 2143 Wooddale Drive, Woodbury, MN 55125-2989

POSTAGE AND HANDLING

STANDARD (US):
(Please allow 12 business days)
$30.00 and under, add $6.00.
$30.01 and over, FREE SHIPPING.

INTERNATIONAL ORDERS,
INCLUDING CANADA:
$16.00 for one book, plus $3.00 for each additional book.

Visit us online for more shipping options. Prices subject to change.

FREE CATALOG!

To order, call
1-877-
NEW-WRLD
ext. 8236
or visit our
website

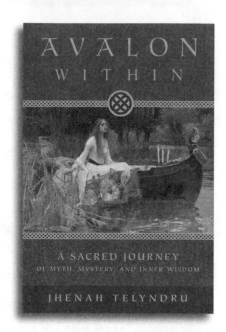

AVALON
WITHIN

A SACRED JOURNEY
OF MYTH, MYSTERY, AND INNER WISDOM

JHENAH TELYNDRU

Avalon Within
A Sacred Journey of Myth, Mystery, and Inner Wisdom
Jhenah Telyndru

Journey to the legendary Isle of Avalon and experience the magic, mysteries, and mysticism that have inspired women through the ages.

Jhenah Telyndru—the founder the Avalonian Tradition—invites you down a unique spiritual path of healing and personal revelation built upon the beloved Avalon mythology. Explore Glastonbury's Sacred Landscape. Connect with Ceridwen, Rhiannon, and other Goddesses of Avalon. Learn the Avalonian skills of Sight and Glamour to heal wounds of the soul and unlock the sacred wisdom at the core of your being.

Drawing on Celtic mythology, Arthurian legend, and Marion Zimmer Bradley's *The Mists of Avalon*, this transformative path empowers women everywhere to seek the Goddess within.

978-0-7387-1997-9, 336 pp., 6 x 9   **$21.99**

RITUALS
of
CELEBRATION

Honoring the Seasons of Life through the Wheel of the Year

Jane Meredith

Rituals of Celebration

Honoring the Seasons of Life through the Wheel of the Year
JANE MEREDITH

In order to give her family and friends a deep experience of earth-based spirituality, author Jane Meredith holds eight rituals per year, celebrating the solstices, the equinoxes, and the cross-quarter festivals. *Rituals of Celebration* provides accounts of the most memorable rituals she's organized, as well as how-to instructions for creating the rituals. Discover the deeper themes of each festival as Meredith offers meaningful reflections about Imbolc, Beltaine, Samhain, and the changing of the seasons as they correspond to personal growth and challenges. Create the craft projects that go along with each ritual—perfect ideas for artistic expression whether you are practicing alone, with a group, or celebrating with children.

Honoring differences of place and spirit, the rituals are inspired by Pagan, Druid, and Goddess traditions, and a variety of other perspectives. Beginners will learn how to construct altars, invoke deities, and perform basic tasks, while experienced ritual organizers will learn new techniques for planning meaningful rituals in challenging or unexpected circumstances.

978-0-7387-3544-3, 336 pp., 6 x 9   **$17.99**

Chakra and Energy Handbook

The
Art
of
Spiritual
Healing

Keith Sherwood
author of *Chakra Therapy*

The Art of Spiritual Healing
Chakra and Energy Handbook
Keith Sherwood

Each of you has the potential to be a healer; to heal yourself and to become a channel for healing others. Healing energy is always flowing through you. Learn how to recognize and tap into this incredible energy source. You do not need to be a victim of disease or poor health. Rid yourself of negativity and become a channel for positive healing now!

The Art of Spiritual Healing will teach you how to acquaint yourself with your three auras and learn how to recognize problems and heal them, before they manifest in the physical body as disease. Special techniques make this book a "breakthrough" to healing power, but you are also given a concise, easy-to-follow regimen of good health to follow in order to maintain a superior state of being. This is a practical guide to healing.

978-0-87542-720-1, 240 pp., 5¼ x 8 $11.99

KRISTIN MADDEN

THE BOOK OF
SHAMANIC
HEALING

INCLUDES TECHNIQUES FOR BREATHING,
DREAM WORK, DRUMMING, AND SOUL RETRIEVAL

The Book of Shamanic Healing
Kristin Madden

Here is everything a shaman healer needs in his or her toolkit. Shamanism is an all-encompassing lifestyle of deep self-knowledge and powerful healing. In this groundbreaking book, a modern shaman gives the practitioner concrete advice and ideas on several aspects of shamanic healing. You will learn to prepare yourself for healing work, communicate with spirit guides, free your voice and seek your power song, safely explore your shadow side, partner with your drum to create healing, and heal yourself and others. The author also covers practical ethical matters such as taking payment and working with friends.

978-0-7387-0271-1, 264 pp., 6 x 9 $16.99

The Healing Power of Trees
Spiritual Journeys Through the Celtic Tree Calendar
SHARLYN HIDALGO

Walk in the footsteps of Druids and tune into the sacred power and ancient wisdom of trees.

From the birch to the willow, Sharlyn Hidalgo introduces all fifteen revered trees of the Celtic Tree Calendar and describes their unique gifts. Go on guided journeys to meet the deities, totems, and guides of each species. Honor each tree with rituals using runes and oghams, symbols and letters of the Celtic Tree Alphabet. Learn from the author's personal stories of revelation. Cultivate a relationship with each of these grand energetic beings, who offer healing, guidance, and higher consciousness.

The Healing Power of Trees is your guide to living the principles of the Celtic tradition—tuning into the rhythms of nature, respecting the land, and fulfilling our role as stewards of our Earth.

978-0-7387-1998-6, 288 pp., 6 x 9   **$17.95**

To order, call 1-877-NEW-WRLD
Prices subject to change without notice
Order at Llewellyn.com 24 hours a day, 7 days a week

MARGARET ANN LEMBO

Chakra *Awakening*

Transform Your Reality Using
Crystals, Color, Aromatherapy &
the Power of Positive Thought

Chakra Awakening
Transform Your Reality Using Crystals, Color, Aromatherapy & the Power of Positive Thought
Margaret Ann Lembo

Bring balance, prosperity, joy, and overall wellness to your life. Use gemstones and crystals to tap into the amazing energy within you—the chakras.

This in-depth and practical guide demonstrates how to activate and balance the seven main chakras—energy centers that influence everything from migraines and fertility to communication and intuition. Perform simple techniques with gems, crystals, and other powerful tools to manifest any goal and create positive change in your physical, emotional, and spiritual wellbeing.

Chakra Awakening also features color photos and exercises for clearing negative energy, dispelling outdated belief systems, and identifying areas in your life that may be out of balance.

978-0-7387-1485-1, 264 pp., 6 x 9 $19.95